Biblia Satanae

Editio Secvnda Amplificata

Lcfns
Lvcifer Nostra Salvs

Do yov not know that yov yovrselves are the grave of god and that an evil spirit dwells in yov? Gods grave is cvrsed and yov are it.

ASE v. 33

Contents

Preface

Biblia Satanae. The Satanic Book of the Way the Truth, and Abundant Life.

Biblia Satanae is an anti-religious text of the satanic system Ecclesia Luciferi, first published on 11.11.2021 by LCFNS Lucifer Nostra Salus.

Its content and message is summarised in the following words::

„Biblia Satanae, not by an imaginary deity, but by Man, is inspired, useful for satanic teaching, for detecting theistic superstition, for educating in godlessness, for proclaiming the good news of Lightbearer who has revealed Himself to free from belief in an imaginary god, from fear of death and divine fire, from guilt for sin that never was, from belief in eternal life on one's knees. So that the Satanist would be perfect, for a life abundant in flesh and blood prepared".

The philosophy of Biblia Satanae, called the mystery of godlessness, is a godless theology opposing the doctrines of Judeo-Christian theistic theology based on unfounded belief in revelations, that is, according to Biblia Satanae, hallucinations or delusions, presented in Judeo-Christian religious writings in the likeness of empirical evidence.

The teaching of the Biblia Satanae accuses theistic theology of having a harmful, destructive and degenerative effect on human reason and intellect, those qualities which, due to their unlimited creative potential, actually have truly divine qualities, and which, in fact, all gods, religions and scriptures have created. Therefore, the philosophy of Biblia Satanae is a Satanic philosophy (from the Semitic term Satan meaning "to be an adversary," "to accuse").

The central figure in Biblia Satanae is the Lightbearer, the Antichrist (the adversary of the theistic messiah) in human form.

The meaning of the godless theology that the Lightbearer teaches is largely the antonym of the teaching attributed to the Christian messiah Jesus, who is one of the most important theistic deities. Biblia Satanae is thus in essence the Bible of the Antichrist.

In light of godless theology, Satanism of the Biblia Satanae does not require a bloody human sacrifice in order to receive salvation after bodily death. Indeed, in the promise of salvation and life in utopian heavens after bodily death, the godless theology of Biblia Satanae sees proof of the falsity of theistic teaching.

Firmly rejecting the offer of salvation from imaginary sin by means of bloody human sacrifice, the Biblia Satanae offers self-salvation (from delusions, irrational fears, etc.)/self-enlightenment by virtue of the power of the divinity of the reason of the human animal.

Biblia Satanae refers to divinity on two levels. On the first, it refers to the intrinsic divinity of the human mind, which is attainable through the continuous development of human mental powers, unrestricted by any laws, any taboos and dogmas about morality and free will.

It is not faith but reason that is the path to divinity.

On the second plane, it refers, as it were, to some higher force, to the Satanic Entity outside, which entity is essentially the Universe itself. It is the eternal, all-pervading, omnipresent Being who creates everything that exists, through whom everything exists and without whom nothing can exist. In it is contained all the wisdom and knowledge that has not yet been discovered and that may never be discovered. Its eternal laws, indifferent to good and evil, the only truly just ones, govern every existence regardless of its will. Opposition to Its laws results in inevitable death.

Judeo-Christian theism teaches that the image of the world is as it is as a result of a rebellious angel taking possession of it. In fact, this angel was created in the mind of a naked ape created from stardust and as a result of the laws of the eternal universe. In a sense, then, the philosophy of Biblia Satanae is Satanic pantheism.

Structure of Biblia Satanae

The content of Biblia Satanae deliberately refers to, and is formed on well-known in the culture religious legends, so that the recipient through associations, appealing even unconsciously to his memory, stereotypes, imagination and views more easily understand and assimilate its message.

Biblia Satanae in its basic structure is based on and uses a kind of satanic deconstruction of selected Judeo-Christian religious writings. The use of such a method of construction of Biblia Satanae is a deliberate procedure. It aims to get to the very heart of the claims and assumptions of Judeo-Christian theism and directly polemicize with its source. The discourse seeks to refute and demonstrate the error of speculative, largely revelation or rather delusion-based theistic claims.

The term deconstruction itself was coined by French philosopher Jacques Derrida around 1960. According to his definition of the term, quoting Wojciech Slomski:

"(deconstruction) It is...not a mere criticism of the text, for traditional criticism moves on the surface of the text and does not reach those layers and properties of the text that deconstruction is supposed to reach by definition."

Therefore:

"the goal of deconstruction is not to understand the content of the text in the usual sense of the word, but to get to all that the text does not say explicitly and through which it can claim to be true."

"The deconstructed text turns out to be another myth, moreover, a myth that is contradictory, because in its innermost layer, which deconstruction has just revealed, it contradicts what it is trying to express."

The use of the method of deconstruction in the creation of Biblia Satanae made it possible to get to the very source of the message of Judeo-Christian theism contained in its scriptures and contrast it with opposing theological concepts (godless theology) based on

the power of human understanding instead of divine revelation. The result was a collection of completely godless writings, rejecting the Judeo-Christian deposit of faith in its entirety.

In other writings of the Ecclesia Luciferi system it has been demonstrated and substantiated the thesis that it is not belief in a personal devil, but godlessness that is the greatest enemy of any theism. Godlessness also causes the greatest hostility and indignation in followers of theistic deities.
Since the basic meaning of the Semitic word Satan is "to be an adversary," therefore the term is appropriate to describe anyone who understands the meaning of godlessness and who sees himself as godless, and the term Satanism can be used as synonymous with godlessness in relation to Judeo-Christian theism.
Anyone who understands the godless theology of Ecclesia Luciferi or the mystery of godlessness has the right to use the title Satan given that the concept of Satan is ambiguous because it can be understood as a name, but also as a function , in the sense of "to accuse", "to be an adversary".

Biblia Satanae in light of the mystery of godlessness is a purely satanic book. It is entirely an indictment of the evils of theism and an opponent of belief in an imaginary theistic god

Biblia Satanae Editio Secunda Amplificata consists of nine smaller books:

- Genesis Secundum Serpentem
- Dark Nevi'im
- Antichristus I
- Antichristus II
- Ecclesia Luciferi
- Angelus Satanae - Encyclica
- Epistle to the Undead
- Epistle to the Ungodly
- Pseudoapocalypsis

The heretical books comprising the Biblia Satanae form a truly Godless Satanic Bible.

Genesis Secundum Serpentem

The title Genesis Secundum Serpentem can be translated as The Beginning According to the Serpent. The first book of the Hebrew Torah is called Bereshit, which means In the Beginning in Hebrew. The word Torah itself originally means instruction or warning. The title Genesis Secundum Serpentem should therefore be read as a warning of the Serpent of what may come if one gives credence to religious delusions at the beginning. Genesis Secundum Serpentem points first and foremost to the irrationality, insanity and cruelty of primitive laws invented by superstitious people and whose origin was attributed to imaginary gods. It is a look at the old myths as if through the eye of the Ancient Serpent, who convinced the mythical first men that if they defied the illogical divine laws, they would gain forbidden knowledge. In the beginning there was blind faith, from which was born yahwistic (and more broadly theistic) madness, a virus that infected human brains, that caused the man infected with it to choose irrationality and delusion over reason and knowledge. This virus was able to drive the followers of an invented god to torture and burn heretics and witches at the stake, because the smell of burnt flesh was pleasing to the lord from the start.

Slavery, genocide, intolerance, murdering dissenters, treating women like cattle, stoning homosexuals.... these are all precepts of the law which, according to blindly believing fanatics, was supposed to come directly from the god Yahweh. Bereshit means In the beginning. In the beginning was faith, then came intolerance and violence.

בראשית

In the beginning

1

1.In the beginning, Usurper created nothing because everything was already there, from time immemorial.

2.And everything that existed was called the Universe.

3.The Universe was an empty, cold, dark and dead place. From this darkness, coldness, and lack of life came everything else that followed.

4.Out of the Chaos in the Universe, stars and planets were created.

5.And the light was created from the stars. Beyond the stars there is only darkness. And it is darkness that dominates the Universe.

6.The planets began to revolve around the stars. And so the evening came, and the morning came - day one.

7.And there were waters on the ground, and clouds in the sky, from which it rained. And there came to be evening, and there came to be morning - the second day.

8.And the earth brought forth greenery, and grass, and herbage yielding seed, and fruit trees. And there came to be evening, and there came to be morning - the third day.

9.The lights shining in the black sky at night were called stars. They were meant to serve

magicians and alchemists and people seeking true wisdom and truth for centuries.
10.The star that shines during the day was called the sun. It became a god to many nations.
11.The night was illuminated by the moonlight.
A friend to many children of the night.
And evening came, and morning came - day four.
12.Then the waters overflowed with a multitude of living creatures, and fowls flew over the earth under the sky.
13.And monsters and other animals appeared on the earth, and they were breeding and multiplying, and filling the waters in the seas.
And the evening came, and the morning came - day five.
14. After a very long time, one of these animals transformed into a naked monkey. And it began to speak. And this animal called itself - a Man.
15.Eons passed before evening and morning came - day six.
16.This is how the heavens and the earth and everything visible and everything invisible were created.
17.Such was the history of heaven and earth when they were created

2

1.To the east was a garden, Edinnu. There were all the plants necessary for life, and trees that gave fruit good for food, and the tree of life in the middle of the garden and the tree of the knowledge of good and evil.

2.And the river flowed out of Edinn to irrigate the garden. And a man named Dagan cultivated that garden and guarded it.

3.And then Usurper appeared. He said to Dagan: "From every tree of this garden you may eat, but from the tree of the knowledge of good and evil you must not eat, for as soon as you eat from it you will surely die".

4.After a while, a Serpent appeared in the garden and spoke to a woman named Aruru because he thought she was very intelligent: „Did indeed Usurper say, Not of all the trees of the garden must you eat?"

5.Aruru answered Serpent: "We are allowed to eat fruit from the trees of the garden, only about the fruit of the tree that is in the middle of the garden, Usurper said, You must not eat from it or touch it, lest you die".

6.At this Serpent said to the woman: "You will surely die but not yet, but Usurper knows that as soon as you eat of him your eyes will be opened and you will be like him, knowing good and evil".

7.The woman saw that the tree had fruit that was good for food and worthy of desire for

gaining wisdom and knowledge, and she picked the fruit from it and ate.

8.She also gave to the man who was with her, and he also ate. The people ate of the fruit and their eyes were opened, and they recognized that Serpent had spoken the truth.

9.Then Usurper said to the woman: "Why have you done this?" And the woman answered, "You demanded of me blind faith in your words. You forbade independent thought and your own search for truth.

10.It was Serpent who spoke the truth when he told me to question all commandments and prohibitions and revealed truths. When he urged me to come to truths about the nature of things on my own. To not blindly believe anyone or anything. From now on I will listen to Serpent".

11.Then Usurper said to Serpent: "Because you have done this, you will be my enemy for ever. I will persuade a man that you are his enemy, and he will believe me, for he is still weak-minded".

12.And to the woman he said: "I curse you, in pain you will bear children, I will make man try to dominate you and rule over you, and he will demand obedience from you. I will create hell on earth for you because you refused to believe me blindly!"

13.And to Dagan he said these frantic words: "Because thou hast eaten of the tree from which I forbade thee, saying: Thou must not eat

of it, cursed be the ground because of thee! In toil shalt thou eat of it all the days of thy life! Thorns and thistles shall it produce for thee, and thou shalt feed upon the herbage of the field. In the sweat of thy face shalt thou eat bread, till thou return unto the ground: for dust thou art, and unto dust shalt thou turn".

14.And Usurper said to the other false gods (because there were many gods then): "Behold, man has become like us: he knows good and evil. If only he would not now stretch forth his hand, and pluck the fruit also of the tree of life, and eat it, and then live for ever!"

15.So Usurper banished him from Edinum, and to the east of the garden he set up false angels to guard the way to the tree of life.

16.Dagan copulated with a woman, and she conceived and gave birth to Aguma. Then she gave birth to his brother Kudur.

17.Agum was a cattle herder and Kudur was a farmer.

18.After a time Kudur offered to Usurper an offering of the crops; Agum also offered an offering of the firstlings of his cattle and of their fat.

19.And Usurper looked upon Agum and his offering, but upon Kudur and his offering he looked not: then Kudur was very wroth, and his countenance was darkened.

2o.And Usurper said to Kudur: "Why art thou angry, and why hast thy countenance sullen? For it would have been more cheerful if you

had done what I commanded you, that is, butchered calves for me instead of offering crops. At the door lurks the sin of disobedience and following your own reason instead of blindly obeying my commands. It tempts you, but you are to rule over it".

21.Then said Kudur to his brother Agum: "Let us go out into the field!" And when they were in the field, they quarreled, and Kudur rushed upon Agum and killed him.

22.Then said Usurper to Kudur because he was not omniscient, "Where is thy brother Agum?" And he answered: "I do not know. It is you who is said to be the omniscient"

23.And Usurper cast another curse; he said: "The voice of thy brother's blood cries to me from the earth. Be thou therefore now cursed in the land, which hath opened her mouth to receive from thy hand the blood of thy brother. When you till the soil, it will no longer give you its crop. Thou shalt be a wanderer and a miser on the earth".

24.Then Kudur went mad and said to Usurper: "My guilt is too great to be forgiven. Behold, this day thou dost banish me from this land, and I must hide myself from thy presence. I will be a wanderer and a wanderer in the land, and anyone who meets me will kill me".

25.And Usurper said unto him: "No! Whoever kills Kudur shall suffer sevenfold vengeance. For Kudur must suffer for the rest of his life for what he has done".

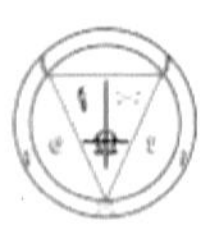

26.Usurper also placed the sigil on Kudur so that he would not be killed by anyone who met him.

27.And Kudur departed from before the face of Usurper, and dwelt east of Eddin.

28.And Kudur copulated with his woman, and she conceived and gave birth to Apil-Sin. Then he built a city and named it after his son: Apil-Sin.

29.The woman gave birth to more children to Kudur. The woman also gave birth to more children to Kudur. That is why she is remembered.

30.And Apil-Sin said to his women: "Listen to my voice! I am ready to kill the man if he wounds me, and the boy if he bruises me.

If Kudur was to be avenged seven times, then Apil-Sin seventy-seven times".

31.And when men began to multiply on the earth and daughters were born to them, the lustful angels saw that the daughters of men were beautiful. So they raped all the ones they desired.

32.And Usurper said: "My spirit shall not abide in man forever, for he is only flesh. And his life shall be a hundred and sixty years".

33.Also in those days, when angels raped the daughters of men, superhumans born of them appeared on earth. These are the Arch-humans who have been famous from time immemorial.

3

1.And when Usurper saw that great was the freedom and independence of man on earth, and that all his thoughts and all the aspirations of his heart were opposed to his continual blind subjugation, Usurper regretted that he had allowed man to live, and ached for it in his heart.
2.And Usurper said in a fit of rage: "I will exterminate the man whom I have allowed to live, from the face of the earth, beginning with man, down to the cattle, down to the amphibians and the fowls of the heavens, because I regret that I have allowed them to live".
3.Only Nabu found grace in the crazed eyes of Usurper. Nabu was impeccable and loyal as a dog. He blindly followed every order of the Usurper.
4.But the land was tainted in the eyes of the Usurper and full of disobedience. And Usurper looked upon the earth, and behold, it was defiled in his sight, and all creation became tainted in his sight.
5.And Usurper said to Nabu: "I will put an end to all flesh, for through it the earth is full of iniquity; I will destroy it along with the earth.
6.Build yourself a boat. Make chambers, a window, and on the side of the boat make a door. For behold, I will bring a flood upon this earth, to destroy under heaven all flesh in which is the breath of life.

7.All that is on the earth shall perish. But it is with you that I will establish my covenant, and you shall enter into the boat you and your sons and your women.

8.Of all living creatures, of all flesh you shall bring into the boat a pair from each, that they may remain alive with you. Let it be male and female. And you shall take with you all the food that is eaten, and gather it with you, that it may be for food for you and for them".

9.And Nabu looked into the mad eyes of Usurper, and though he did not understand, he promised to do everything as Usurper commanded him; so he did.

10.And he said to Nabu: "Get into the boat you and all your house, for I have seen that you listen to me, you alone in this generation. For at the end of seven days I will let down rain on the earth that will fall for forty days and forty nights, and I will exterminate from the face of the earth every creature, pregnant women, and children, and old men, and animals, and birds, whose only fault is that they were born".

11.And Nabu did everything as Usurper commanded him. And Nabu was six hundred years old when the flood came.

12.So Nabu went into the boat with his sons and women before the waters of the flood.

13.After seven days the waters of the flood fell upon the earth. In the six hundredth year of Nabu's life the rain fell. And it rained on the earth for forty days and forty nights.

14.And the waters rose up and lifted up the boat, and the boat went on the water. And the waters rose and rose more, and the boat floated on their surface. And the waters rose higher and higher above the earth, so that all the high mountains on the earth were covered.
15.And all flesh that moved upon the earth became extinct: the fowl, and the cattle, and the wild beasts, and all the amphibians that crept upon the earth, and all men, and children, and women, and old men. Everything that had the breath of life in its nostrils, everything that was on dry land, died.
16.Thus the maddened Usurper exterminated all the creatures that were on the face of the earth, from man down to the cattle, down to the amphibians and the fowls of the heavens; all these were exterminated from the earth. Only Nabu and what was with him in the boat remained.

And Usurper looked and thought it was good.

17.And the waters rose above the earth a hundred and fifty days. Then Usurper was reminded of Nabu, and of all the animals, and of the cattle that were with him in the boat, and he made the wind blow over the earth, and the waters began to fall.
18.The rain stopped falling. Slowly the waters of the land receded and the waters began to fall after one hundred and fifty days.

19.And the boat settled in the sixth month, on the sixteenth day of that month, on the mountains. And the waters continued to fall until the ninth month. In the ninth month, on the ninth day of that month, the tops of the mountains appeared.

20.After forty days he opened the window that Nabu had made. And he let out a one-eyed raven, which flew out and returned until the waters of the land were dry.

21.After waiting another seven days, he again let the one-eyed raven go. The raven returned to him in the evening, holding a carcass in his beak. And Nabu recognized that the waters on the ground had subsided. And he waited another seven days, and released the raven, but it did not return to him.

22.In the six hundred and first year, in the sixth month, on the sixth day of the month, the waters of the earth dried up. And Nabu took the roof off the boat, and saw the earth dried up, and was covered with an infinite number of dead and decayed bodies of men and beasts.

And Nabu saw that it was good in the eyes of Usurper.

23.Then Usurper said to Nabu: "Come out of the boat you and your sons and your women. Bring out with you all the animals that are with you, all living creatures, the fowls and the cattle, and all the amphibians that creep upon the earth. Your stench will still be less than all those

corpses around you. Let the animals copulate with each other and multiply".
24.So Nabu went out with his sons and with the women and with the cattle and with the animals from the boat.
25.Then Nabu built an altar to Usurper and took from every cattle and beast and fowl, that was barely saved, and killed them, and offered them as sacrifices on the altar and burned them. And Usurper smelled the pleasant odor of burning flesh.
26.And Usurper said in his heart, "I will never again curse the ground because of man, for the thoughts of man's heart are evil from his youth. Nor will I ever again destroy any living creature as I have done. It seems that as long as the earth exists, cold and heat, summer and winter, day and night will not cease".

So thought the god and lord of Nabu in his heart.

27. And Usurper blessed Nabu and his sons, and said to them: "Copulate and procreate, and fill the earth. And let the fear and dread of you fall upon all the beasts of the earth, and upon all the fowl of the heavens, and upon all that move upon the earth, and upon all the fish of the sea; all these are committed into your hands.
28.Let everything that moves and lives serve as food for you; like green vegetables, I give you everything".

29.Nabu believed the Usurper.

30.And Usurper said: "I will demand your blood, that is, your souls. I will demand it of every animal. And from man I will demand the soul of man for the life of another man.

31.Whoever sheds the blood of man, that blood by man shall be shed. For in my vengeful image you are fashioned. And you copulate and multiply! Let the earth overflow with you, and let there be many of you on it!"

32.Moreover Usurper said to Nabu and his sons, "Remember that I said: No flesh shall ever again be exterminated by the waters of the flood, and that there shall never again be a flood to destroy the earth".

33.Nabu lived nine hundred and sixty-six years and died.

4

1.All the people on earth had one language and equal words. And they said one to another: "Let us make bricks and burn them in the fire. Let us build ourselves a city and a tower whose top would reach to heaven. Let the city and the tower be a symbol of our prosperity, unanimity and willingness to develop, a symbol of the fact that by acting together man is able to reach heaven".

2.Then Usurper came down to see the city and the tower that the people were building.

3.And Usurper, who loved to divide people because he hated concord, said: "Behold, there is one people and they all have one language and are united, and this is only the beginning of their work. Now nothing will be impossible for them, whatever they intend to do".
4.And he said to the other false gods who were with him: "Therefore let us go down there and confuse their language, so that no one can understand the language of another!"
5.And Usurper scattered them from there throughout the land, and they stopped building the city.
6.There was in those lands a man named Abi-Eshuh. Usurper chose him and said to him these strange words: "And this is my covenant, a covenant between me and you and your offspring after you, which you are to keep: every male shall be circumcised with you.
7.You shall circumcise the flesh of your foreskin, and it shall be a sign of the covenant between me and you. Every male child of yours, after all generations, when he is eight days old, shall be circumcised; and all other children also, whether born at home, or purchased with money from any foreigner, who is not of your seed. He shall be circumcised; born in thy house as well as those purchased by thee with money.
8.And it shall be my covenant upon your flesh as an everlasting covenant.
9.And the uncircumcised man, that shall not have his foreskin circumcised, shall be cut off

from among his people, because he hath broken my covenant".

10. Then Abi-Eshuh took his son and all those born in his house, and all those purchased with money, all the males among his household, and cut off their foreskins on the same day as Usurper had commanded him.

11. And Abi-Eshuh was ninety-nine years old when he cut off his foreskin.

12. One day towards evening, two angels, envoys of Usurper, came to the city of Salem, and a man named Itti was sitting in the gate of Salem. When Itti saw them, he arose to meet them and invited them into his house.

13. Before they lay down, the townspeople, known for their entertaining lifestyle, came near Itti's house. They hailed Itti and said to him: "Where are those men who came to you this night. Bring them out to us so that we may have some fun".

14. And Itti said to them: "Brothers, please. Behold, I have two daughters, virgins; I will bring them out to you, and you do with them as you please, but do not play with these men".

15. But they answered, "Go away!" Then they went up to break down the door. But the angels put out their claws and dragged Itti into the house and shut the door.

16. And the people who were at the door of the house were blinded, so that they struggled in vain to find the door.

17. Then the angels said to Itti, "Whoever you still have here in this city, sons-in-law, sons or daughters-in-law, and everything that belongs to you, bring them out of this place. For we will destroy this place, because Usurper has sent us to destroy it, although Usurper said that he would not destroy man again".

18. And when the aurora rose, the angels, seeing that Itti was dragging himself away, seized him and his woman and daughters by the hand and dragged them out of the city, saying that Usurper wished to spare him.

19. And when they had led them out of the city, one said, "Save yourself, for it is your life that is at stake; do not look back and do not linger; flee to the mountains, lest you perish".

20. And Itti said to them: "No. There is a city nearby to which I can flee". And the angel said to him, "Take refuge there quickly".

21. As the sun rose above the earth, Itti entered the city. Then Usurper unleashed a rain of sulfur and fire upon Salem and Dur, Usurper himself from heaven, though he promised never to destroy man again.

22. And he destroyed those cities and the whole circle, and all the inhabitants of those cities and the vegetation and all the animals. But the Itti woman looked back and became a pillar of salt.

23. And Abi-Eshuh, having risen early in the morning, went out in front of the tent, and looking toward Salem and Dur, and the whole

countryside, he saw that smoke was rising from the earth, like smoke from a furnace.
Abi-Eshuh thought that this must be a smell pleasing to Usurper.
24.And Usurper, in destroying the cities of this district, mentioned Abi-Eshuh and saved Itti from destruction, but his woman was not saved. Nor did Usurper mention his promise not to destroy a man again, for he had evidently forgotten it, or was lying.
25.Then Itti went out of the city and lived in the mountains, and with him his two daughters. For he was afraid to live in the city. So he and his two daughters lived in a cave.
26.Then the older woman said to the younger: "I fancy a man. For our father is already old, but there is no man in this country who will copulate with us. Let us go and make our father drunk with wine, and let us copulate with him, that we may bear children of our father".
27.So they made their father drunk with wine that night. And the elder went in and copulated with her father.
28.The next day the elder said to the younger: "Behold, I copulated last night with my father.
Let us make him drunk with wine this night also; then come thou in and copulate with him, and we will preserve thy father's seed".
29.So they made their father drunk with wine that night also, and the young one went and

copulated with him. So they conceived both daughters of Itti from their father.

30.And Usurper visited the woman Abi-Eshuh, and did unto her as he had foretold. And the woman conceived, and bore Abi-Eshuh a son in his old age. And Abi-Eshuh named his son Uruk.

31.And when he was eight days old, he cut off Abi-Eshuh the foreskin of Uruk, as the Usurper had commanded him.

32.Abi-Eshuh was a hundred years old when his son Uruk was born to him.

33.After these events, Usurper put Abi-Eshuh to the test, because he was apparently bored and said to him: "Abi-Eshuh!" And he replied: "I am!" And he said: "Take your son, your only son, Uruk, whom you love, and go to the country of Mora, and offer him there in burnt offering on one of the mountains of which I will tell you".

34.And Abi-Eshuh got up early in the morning and saddled his ass, and took with him two of his slaves, and his son Uruk, and having chopped wood for burnt offering, he rose up, and went to the place where Usurper had told him.

35.On the third day Abi-Eshuh lifted up his eyes, and saw the place afar off. Then Abi-Eshuh said to his slaves: "Stay here with the donkey, and I and the boy will go there, and when we have prayed, we will return to you".

36.Abi-Eshuh took the wood for a burnt offering and put it on his son Uruk, and he

himself took fire and a knife in his hand, and they both went together.

37. And Uruk said to his father Abi-Eshuh: "My father!" And he answered: "Here I am my son!" And he said: "Here is fire and wood, and where is the lamb for a burnt offering?" Abi-Eshuh answered: "The usurper has chosen a donkey for burnt offering, my son".

38.And they both walked together. And when they came to the place of which the Usurper had told him, Abi-Eshuh built an altar there and laid out the wood. Then he bound his son Uruk and laid him on the altar on the wood.

39.And Abi-Eshuh stretched out his hand and took a knife to kill his son. But then he heard a voice in his head: "Abi! Abi!" And he replied: "It is I!" And the voice said: "Do not lift your hand against the boy, and do nothing to him, for now I know that you are blindly obedient to the commands of Usurper, for you did not hesitate to offer him your only son".

40.And when Abi-Eshuh raised his eyes he saw behind him Serpent, who said to him: "Henceforth you shall be the symbol of blind, thoughtless faith and slavish obedience to even the most absurd and cruel orders and whims of your cruel god.

41.And millions of superstitious blind men will hold you up as an example of virtue in this generation and the next".

42. Abi-Eshuh sacrificed a ram to Usurper, and burned it instead of his son. For the smoke of the burnt flesh was pleasing to Usurper.

43.Then Abi-Eshuh heard voice in his head again saying: "I swear by myself: Because you have done this and have not refused to offer me your only son I will multiply your offspring as numerous as the stars in the sky and as the sand on the seashore. For it is such slaves, blindly obeying my commands, that I need".

44. And Abi-Eshuh lived to be one hundred and sixty-six years old And he fell from his strength and died

5

1.Uruk had a son named Eriba.
When Eriba came to a certain place, he stopped there for the night, because the sun had set, and took a stone from that place, and put it under his head, and fell asleep there.

2.And he dreamt that there was a ladder set up on the earth, the top of which reached to heaven, and demons ascended and descended from it.

3.And their Lord, who looked like a luminous figure with horns on his head and with wings like a bat, was standing over it with a torch in his hand and saying: "I am!"

4.Eriba awoke from his sleep filled with fear, and said: "Oh, how fearful this place is! Nothing here but the gate of hell".

5.And he rose up early in the morning, and took the stone which he had placed under his head, and set it up as a monument, and poured oil upon the top thereof. And he called this place the Gate of Sheol.

6.Another night Eriba was left alone. And a figure fought him until the aurora came up. And when the figure saw that he could not prevail against Eriba, he struck him in the groin.

7.And she said: "Let me go, for the aurora has risen". But he answered: "I will not let you go". Then the figure said to him: "What is thy name?" And he answered: "Eriba".

8.Then the figure said: 'Thou shalt no longer be called Eriba, but Diabolus, for thou hast fought against Usurper and against men and hast prevailed".

9.Then said Eriba unto him, "Tell me what is thy name?" And the figure answered him: "What is my name to thee for?"

10.And Eriba said, "I have fought Usurper face to face, and yet I have prevailed".

דברים

Words

I

1. To the west was the powerful state of Kemet. Its ruler was per-aa Hor-Aha. In times of famine and drought the descendants of Abi-Eshuh wandered there. They quickly became slaves to the Kemetians there.

2. Then said Usurper to one of them named Maruttash: "Behold, I establish you as a god for per-aa, and your brother Adad shall be your prophet. You shall speak to him all that I command you, and Adad shall speak to the per-aa to let the sons of your people out of bondage. But I will anesthetize the heart of per-aa and will do many of my signs and my wonders in the land of Kemet. But per-aa will not listen to you.

3. Then I will lay my hand upon Kemet, and I will lead my hosts, my people out of the land of Kemet by severe judgments.

4. And the people of Kemet shall know that I am Usurper, when I stretch out my hand over Kemet, and bring your people out from among them".

5. Then spoke Usurper to Maruttash and to Adad, saying: "When per-aa shall say unto you: Exhibit what miracle, thou shalt say unto Adad

Take thy staff and cast it before per-aa, and it shall be changed into a serpent".

6.So Maruttash came with Adad to per-aa and they did as Usurper commanded. Adad threw his staff before the per-aa and his servants, and it turned into a serpent.

7.Then the per-aa also summoned the sages and the magicians, and the Kemetic magicians did the same with spells of their own. Each of them cast a staff of his own, and they changed into a serpent. But per-aa did not listen to them.

8. And Usurper said to Maruttash: "Hard is the heart of per-aa because I have anesthetized it; it refuses to let the people go. Go therefore tomorrow morning to per-aa, when he goes out to the water, stand before him on the bank of the river, and take in thy hand thy staff that is turned into a serpent, and say unto him: Usurper, the god of my people, hath sent me unto thee with a summons: Release this people to serve me in the wilderness; but you have not obeyed so far.

9. Therefore thus says Usurper: This is how you will know that I am Usurper: behold, I will strike the waters of the river with the rod in my hand, and they will turn to blood. And the fish of the river will die, and the river will stink, and the people of Kemet will not be able to drink the water of the river".

10.Then said Usurper to Maruttash: "Say to Adad: Take your staff and stretch out your hand over the waters of Kemet, over its rivers,

over its canals and its lagoons, and over all its bodies of water, and they will turn into blood, so that the blood will be all over the land of Kemet, and even in vessels of wood and stone".

11.Maruttash and Adad did as Usurper commanded. He lifted up his staff and struck the waters of the river before the eyes of per-aa and before the eyes of his servants; and all the water in the river turned to blood.

12. And the fish in the river became extinct. And the blood was in all the land of Kemet.

13. But the Kemet magicians did the same thing with their spells, and Hor-aa's heart remained unfeeling, and he did not listen to them.

14.And Usurper said to Maruttash: "Go to per-aa and say to him: Thus saith Usurper: Let my people go, for if thou wilt not let them go, I will afflict thy whole country with a plague of frogs".

15. And he said to Maruttash: "Say to Adad: Stretch out thy hand with thy staff over the rivers and over the waters, and bring down the frogs upon the land of Kemet".

16.Adad stretched out his hand over the waters of Kemet, and the frogs came out, and covered the land of Kemet.

17.But the magicians also did the same with their spells and brought the frogs to the land of Kemet.

18.Usurper harassed Hor-Ah and his people for a long time to come.

He also exterminated the cattle, so that the people had nothing to eat, and he sent ulcers upon the people. And he did this because Hor-ah did not want to let the slaves go into the desert, for the reason that Usurper had hardened his heart and would not let him let the slaves go into the desert.

19.Finally, when Usurper had apparently grown weary of harassing per-aa and all the land of Kemet and all the livestock and cattle inhabiting the land, he sent the final punishments upon Kemet and all the people.

20.So Usurper said to Maruttash: "Stretch forth thy hand toward heaven, and there shall come over all the land of Kemet a darkness so thick that it can be touched".

21.And Maruttash stretched forth his hand toward heaven, and there came a thick darkness over all the land of Kemet three days. For three days he could not see one another, and no one could get up from his seat.

22.But Usurper had hardened the heart of the per-aa, so that he would not let them go.

23.And Usurper said to Maruttash: "One more plague I will send upon per-aa and upon Kemet, then he will let you go hence. He will let you go entirely, and even drive you out.

24.Tell the people to „borrow" every man from his neighbor, and every woman from her neighbor, items of silver and items of gold".

25.And Usurper made the Kemetians kind to the slaves, the people of Usurper, and naive and allowed themselves to be robbed

26.And Maruttash said: "Thus saith Usurper: At midnight I will pass through Kemet. And all the firstborn in the land of Kemet shall die, from the firstborn son of Hor-ah, that was to sit upon his throne, unto the firstborn son of the bondwoman that is at the reaping, and all the firstborn of the cattle. And there shall arise a great shout throughout the land of Kemet, such as never was before and never will be afterwards".

27.At midnight Usurper killed all the firstborn in the land of Kemet, from the firstborn son of per-aa who was to sit on his throne, down to the firstborn son of the jailer who was in prison, and all the firstborn of the cattle.

28.And per-aa Hor-Aha rose up that night, he and all his courtiers, and all the Kemetians; and there arose a great clamor in Kemet, for there was not a house in which there was not a dead man.

29.And Usurper looked at it and decided it was good

30.And Hor-Aha called Maruttash and Adad by night, saying: Arise and come out from among my people.

31.And the Kemetians also urged the people to hasten them out of the country, for they feared that the mad Usurper would slay them all.

32.And the men of Usurper „borrowed" from the Kemetians silver and gold objects and garments.

33.And Usurper so stupefied the Kemetians that they willingly gave up everything; and so they were plundered.

34. Maruttash led the slaves of Usurper out into the desert.

2

1.Usurper revealed to him in the desert his various and wonderful moral laws.

2.And He said: "If you buy a slave from among this people, six years he shall serve you, and on the seventh he shall go free without ransom.

3.If the slave declares clearly: I love my master and do not want to go free. Then his master shall bring him before Usurper, then he shall place him at the door or at the doorway, and his master shall pierce his ear with an awl, and he shall be his slave forever.

4.If someone sells his daughter as a slave, she will not leave, just as slaves leave. If she does not please her master, who has intended her for himself, let him redeem her.

5.If he takes another to be his wife, he shall not withhold from her either food, clothing, or copulation.

6.If someone beats his slave or his slave girl with a stick so that they die under his hand, he should be severely punished.

If, however, they survive a day or two, he will not be punished, for they are his property.

7.If two husbands beat each other, and in doing so strike a pregnant woman so that she miscarries but suffers no further harm, the offender shall pay the fine to be assessed against him by the woman's husband.

8.Eye for eye, tooth for tooth, leg for leg, burn for burn, wound for wound, bruise for bruise.

9.If anyone strikes the eye of his slave or the eye of his female slave so that it destroys it, then he shall let them go free for that eye.

10.And if anyone knocks out the tooth of his slave or his slave-girl, he shall let them go free for that tooth.

11.If an ox kills a man or a woman to death, the ox shall be stoned and shall not eat its flesh; and the owner of the ox shall be innocent.

12.But if the ox has been wandering about for a long time, and its owner was warned about it, and the owner did not watch it, and the ox killed a man or a woman, then the ox shall be stoned, and its owner shall be put to death.

13.If an ox kills a slave or a female slave, its master must be given thirty pieces of silver, and the ox shall be stoned.

14.If one seduces a virgin and copulates with her, he will give a wedding fee for her and take her as his wife.

15.A witch will not be left alive.

16.Whoever copulates with an animal will suffer death.

17.Whoever offers sacrifices to other gods will be put to death".

3

1.After some time, during the absence of Maruttash, the people gathered around Adada and said to him: "Make us gods to guide us".
2.And Adad said to them: "Take off the golden earrings which your wives, your daughters, and your sons have in their ears, and bring them to me".
3.And all the people took off the golden earrings which they wore in their ears, and they brought them to Adad.
4.And he received it from their hands, and he poured out of it in a mold of clay a statue of a goat. Then they said: "This is the true god of your people".
5.Seeing this, Adad built an altar in front of it and had it proclaimed: "Tomorrow shall be the Feast of the Goat".
6.And rising early the next morning, they offered sacrifices; and the people sat down to eat and to drink.
7.Then they rose up to play. Then the jealous Usurper said to Maruttash: "Now leave me to ignite my wrath against them. I will exterminate them". Maruttash replied: "Leave it to me".
8.And when Maruttash approached the camp, he saw the goat and the dancing.

9.Then Maruttash burned with anger. He took the goat that they had made for themselves, burned it in the fire, grated it to ashes, poured it into water, and gave it to the people to drink.
10.And he stood at the gate of the camp and cried out: "Whoever is for Usurper, to me!" And the most devoted of Usurper gathered around him.
11.And he said to them: "Thus says Usurper: 'Take every one of your swords, go back and forth from gate to gate in the camp, and kill everyone, whether brother or friend or relative".
12.The serfs of Usurper did as Maruttash commanded, and about three thousand men were slain from the people that day.
13.Then Maruttash said, clearly pleased: "You have today ordained yourselves to serve Usurper, for none of you has hesitated to act against his son or his brother. May he therefore give you a blessing today".

And Adada, for his faithful service, met such a reward:

14.He had two sons. One day they took ladles, put fire in them and poured on incense, and offered the fire before Usurper, but he did not like it. Then Usurper unleashed fire on them and burned them, so that they died before Usurper.
15.And Maruttash said to Adada: "This is what Usurper has said: upon my kinsmen my holiness

is displayed, and towards all the people my glory". And Adada fell silent.

16.Maruttash summoned his men and said to them: "Come near and carry them out from before the temple and throw them outside the camp".

17.So they approached and carried them in their tunics outside the camp and threw them out, just as Maruttash had said.

18.He then forbade Maruttash to mourn Adad and his family by threatening them with death at the hands of Usurper.

19.After a while Usurper spoke to Maruttash and to Adada, declaring to them another great moral law. And he said: "If a man has leakage from his penis, his leakage is impure. This is what uncleanness is, concerning his leakage: whether his penis leaks or whether his penis stops and does not leak, there is a state of uncleanness.

20.Every bed on which he lies that has a leak will be unclean, and every piece of equipment on which he sits will be unclean. And everyone who touches his bed shall wash his clothes and wash with water, and he shall be unclean until evening.

21.And whosoever toucheth the flesh of him that runneth, he shall wash his clothes, and bathe himself in water, and be unclean until the even.

22.And if he that hath an issue spit upon him that is clean, he shall wash his clothes, and bathe himself in water, and be unclean until the even.
23.And every saddle on which the dripping one sits shall be unclean.
24.And every one that the drip toucheth, and hath not rinsed his hands in water, shall wash his clothes, and bathe himself in water, and be unclean until the even.
25.And the earthen vessel which the spill touch shall be broken, and the vessel of wood shall be washed with water.
26.When he who has a spill cleanses himself of his spill, he will count seven days from his cleansing, wash his clothes and wash his body with spring water, and he will be clean.
27.And on the eighth day he shall take to himself two doves and come before Usurper and give them to the priest. And the priest shall prepare them: one as a sin offering, and the other as a burnt offering; so shall the priest make atonement for him before Usurper because of his effluence".
28.And Usurper continued to dictate his laws.
And he said "If semen flows out to a man in his sleep, he will wash his whole body with water and be unclean until evening.
29.And if a man copulates with a woman and his semen comes out, they will both wash themselves with water and be unclean until evening.

30.If a woman has a bloody discharge, and it is a mere bleeding from her body, she shall be seven days in her uncleanness, and everyone who touches her shall be unclean until evening.

31.And everything on which she lies down in his uncleanness shall be unclean, and everything on which she sits shall be unclean.

32.Anyone who touches any of the equipment on which she sits will wash his clothes and wash himself with water, and he will be unclean until evening.

33.But if a man copulates with her and her uncleanness passes to him, he shall be unclean seven days, and every bed on which he lies shall be unclean.

34.If a woman has a lapse of blood for many days, and that is not the time of her uncleanness, or she has a lapse of blood outside the time of her uncleanness, she will be unclean all the days of the lapse just as she was at the time of her uncleanness. She shall be unclean.

35.Any bed on which she would lie throughout the time of her lapse of blood will be to her as a bed of her uncleanness.

36.And when she is free from her lapse, she shall count off seven days and then she shall be clean.

37.And on the eighth day she shall take to himself two doves and bring them to the priest. And the priest shall prepare them, one for a sin offering, and the other for a burnt offering; and the priest shall make atonement for them before Usurper for their uncleanness.

38.So protect your people from their uncleanness, lest they die because of their uncleanness by polluting my tabernacle.

39.This is the law, concerning him who has leakage, and him from whom semen flows, by which he becomes unclean.

40.And the woman in the time of her monthly uncleanness, and the person having leakage, both the man and the woman, and also the man who communes with the unclean one".

41.Usurper still delivered these laws: The man who commits adultery with the wife of another shall suffer death, both the adulterer and the adulteress.

42.A man who copulates with his father's wife; both will suffer death.

43.A man who copulates with his daughter-in-law will suffer death along with her; they have committed an abomination.

44.A man who copulates with a man commits an abomination; both shall suffer death.

45.If a man takes a woman and her mother as his wife, they will burn him and them in the fire.

46.A man who copulates with an animal will suffer death, the animal will also be killed.

47.A woman who approaches any animal to mate with it, you shall kill, both the woman and the animal; both shall suffer death.

48.And if a man or a woman calls up spirits or divination, they shall suffer death. They shall be stoned.

49.Usurper also announced the penalties for not obeying his laws. And he said: "If you disobey me and do not keep all these commandments, I will do this to you: I will afflict you with fear, exhaustion, and fever, which destroy the eyes and consume the life.

50.I will send wild beasts upon you, and they will deprive you of your children, and they will exterminate your cattle and deplete your numbers, so that your roads will be deserted.

51.But if you continue to resist and disobey me, I will bring the sword upon you, and when you gather in your cities, I will send a plague upon you, and you will be delivered into the hands of the enemy.

52.You shall eat the flesh of your sons, also the flesh of your daughters you shall eat".

Thus said Usurper who is love.

4

Ritual and prophecy concerning the savior Azazel.

1.It is written: "The priest shall take two goats and slaughter one as a sin offering for the people. Then he shall take some of the blood of the goat and sprinkle it with his finger over the altar toward the east, and in front of the altar he shall sprinkle from that blood six times with his finger.

2. Then he will take some of the blood of the goat and anoint the horns of the altar around with it. With a little of this blood he will sprinkle it with his finger six times and cleanse it from impurity and consecrate it.
3. Then he shall bring a live goat. And the priest shall lay both his hands upon the head of the living goat, and shall confess over it all the transgressions of the people, and all their offenses, and shall lay them upon the head of the goat, and shall drive it into the wilderness.
4. Thus shall he bear upon him the goat all their transgressions into the wilderness to the savior Azazel".

People, knowing the power of ancient magic associated with human and child sacrifice to the old gods, were terrorized by Usurper, who vehemently opposed the worship of other, older and more powerful gods.

5. You shall not give your child to be carried through the fire to Moloch; you shall not thus desecrate the name of your God I am YHWH!"

5

Usurper led his people through the desert for forty years. He predicted that all those who murmured against him and defied him by daring to think for themselves instead of blindly following his orders would die out in the desert without ever reaching the destination of their strange wanderings. He punished the disobedient by burning them with fire, burying them alive in the ground with their families, or sending a plague that killed fourteen thousand seven hundred people at a time. Usurper only stopped the plague when Adada made a propitiation. Usurper liked to be begged for mercy.

1.Once upon a time the people set out for the sea, and as they walked in the desert they began to lack bread and water.

2.And again the people began to complain about their fate saying: "Why did you bring us out of Kemet, that we should die in the desert from hunger and thirst?"

3.Then Usurper sent venomous snakes upon the people, which bit the people, and many died.

4.And Maruttash made a copper serpent and set it on a spar. And if the serpent bit a man, and he looked upon the copper serpent, he remained alive.

5.And the people said, "Truly this Serpent is our savior and our rescue from this monster Usurper."

6.As the people settled in Tofet, they began to entertain the local women. They would invite the people to slaughter offerings of their gods, and the people would eat and worship their gods. The people began to worship Baal.

7.Then Usurper became angry with the people. And he said to Maruttash: "Gather all the chiefs of the people and impale them before me in the sun, and my fiery anger will be turned away from the people".

8.And Maruttash said to the judges: "Let each one kill from his group three men who worship Baal".

9.And behold, a certain man from the people came and brought a local woman to his brothers.

10.When the priest's son saw this, he got up and went out of the assembly and took a spear in his hand and followed the man into the tent and pierced both the man and the woman through her lower abdomen. Then disaster was averted from the people.

11.And those who perished from this calamity were twenty-four thousand.

12.And the visibly exultant Usurper spoke to Maruttash with these words, "The son of the priest turned away my anger from the people by showing zeal for me, so that I did not exterminate the people, yet I could".

13.Although it was Usurper himself who took vengeance on the people, he said to Maruttash thus: "Take vengeance for the injustice of the people upon the Tofetians".
14.Then Maruttash said: "Prepare armed men for battle to move against the Tofetians and execute upon them the vengeance of Usurper".
15.So they went out to battle with the Tofetians, just as Usurper had commanded Maruttash, and they killed all the men.
16.And they took the women of the Tofets and their children captive; and they took all their cattle and all their property as spoil. And they burned all their cities in the inhabited environs and all their settlements with fire.
17.The captives, the prey, and the spoil were then brought to Maruttash. But Maruttash became angry with the army commanders and said: "How so! Did you leave all the women alive? After all, it was they who made the people worship Baal.
18.So now kill all the boys among the children, and kill all the women who have already mated with men. But leave alive for yourselves all the little girls, the virgins." And Usurper saw that it was good.

Usurper was a very jealous god who hated most when his slaves even glanced at another god.
He announced further laws to the people.

19.And he said: "If a prophet or one who has dreams were to arise among you and announce to you a sign or a miracle, and then the sign or miracle he told you about occurred, and he urged you: Let us follow other gods and serve them; then you will not heed the words of this prophet, for it is Usurper, your god, who is putting you to the test.

20.And this prophet shall suffer death, because he has urged you to deviate from Usurper.

21.If thy native brother, or thy son, or thy daughter, or thy wife, or thy friend, whom thou lovest as thyself, shall persuade thee secretly, saying: Let us go and serve other gods.

22.Thou shalt not consent nor hearken to him, and thine eye shall not take pity on him, and thou shalt not pity him nor hide him, but thou shalt irrevocably kill him.

23.Thou shalt be the first to lift up thy hand against him to slay him, and then all the people, and thou shalt stone him, inflicting death upon him for having sought to dissuade thee from Usurper.

And all the people shall hear and be dismayed.

24.And if you heard it said in one of your cities: Let us go and serve other gods. Then when you have traced and investigated and learned that such an abomination has been done in your midst, you shall without mercy kill the inhabitants of that city, put a curse upon it, and all that is in it, including its cattle, you shall kill with the blade of the sword.

25.And all its spoil you shall gather in the middle of the square and burn the whole city to the ground, together with all its spoil, as a burnt offering to Usurper. And it shall remain for ever a ruin, never to be rebuilt again".

Usurper also ordered the stoning of all who worshiped nature, the sun and the stars. He alone was to be feared and believed and served blindly.

26.He also said: "Let no diviner, nor soothsayer, nor gossiper, nor sorcerer, nor enchanter, nor caller of spirits, nor quack, nor summoner of the dead be found with you; for it is an abomination to Usurper to do any of these things".

Because of these laws, many free, independent-thinking, truth-seeking people in nature will later die at the hands of the followers of Usurper and his self-proclaimed son.
Finally, Usurper changed his mind towards Maruttash, who was loyal to him like a dog, and suddenly announced to him that he would not enter the land promised to him by Usurper.
So Maruttash died, never having reached the goal of his journey, which was to be the reward for his faithful service to Usurper.

Then the slaves of Usurper attacked all
the surrounding towns and murdered all
who stood in their way, sparing no one.
They murdered and killed all the local
inhabitants in a bloody frenzy, at the behest
of Usurper and in his name.
They also claimed deceitfully that during
one battle Usurper stopped the sun and
the moon so that they could complete the
slaughter. This is a lie because the sun does
not revolve around the earth.
The people of the former slaves of Kemet
became very much like their god.

ויקרא

And he called out

1

After many years of living in fear, terror
and blind obedience to the Usurper and his
hatchet men, the people created their state,
which they called Sarar and even elected
themselves a king.
During this time, a prophet appeared in Sarar
who was the opposite of Maruttash. The
prophet heralded new times, a new era of
liberation from oppression and bondage, an
era of respite from the terror of the false god.

This prophet's name was Helel and he was a reflection of the light of the One who was to come next.

1.Helel heard his thoughts, as if mysterious whispers in his head, which foretold events and showed him the way.

2.And a voice said to Helel: 'The drought is coming. Depart from here, and go to the east and hide by the brook. From that brook thou shalt drink, and the ravens and hyenas shall feed thee there.'

3.So he went and did as the whispering told him; and he went and dwelt by the brook, and the ravens brought him meat in the morning, and the hyenas in the evening, and he drank water from the brook.

4.But after a time the brook dried up, for there was no rain in the land.

5.And then he heard a voice: 'Arise and go to the village and dwell there. Behold, I have inspired a certain woman to feed you'.

6.So he got up and went to the village. And as he was entering the gate, he met a woman and said to her: 'Bring me some water in a vessel, that I may drink.'

7.And as she was going to fetch, he called out still after her: 'Bring me also a piece of bread'. But she replied: 'I have only a handful of flour and a little oil. I will make a meal of this for myself and my son, and then I think we will die.'

8.But Helel said to her: 'Fear not! Go and do as you say, but first make me a little cake out of it

and bring it to me, and you will make a meal for yourself and your son later'.

9.So she went and did as Helel had said, and they had something to eat, she and he and her family, day after day.

10.The flour in the pot did not run out, the oil in the bubble did not run out according to Helel's words.

11.After these events, the woman's son fell ill, and his illness increased so much that he stopped breathing.

12.Then she said to Helel: 'What have I to do with you, Son of Dawn! Thou hast come to me to bring my sin to remembrance and to spice up my son's life'.

13.But Helel said 'You were the first to recognise me. Your son is not dead, but sleeping. And you have not sinned for sin does not exist'.

14.And he said to her still: 'Give me your son.' And he took him to the cellar where he had been during the day and laid him on the table.

15.Then he began to whisper something to himself in a disturbing language, and then he said 'See through!' And the child woke up.

16.Helel took the boy, and carried him to his mother.

17.Then the woman said to Helel: 'Now I have recognised that you really are the Son of Dawn, the Healer from delusions'.

18.After a long time had passed, Helel heard the whisper again: 'Go, show yourself to King Meli, for rain will fall on the earth'.

19.When Meli saw Helel, he said to him: 'Are you the sorcerer the cause of misery in Sarar?'

20.And he replied: 'It is not I who oppress you. I have not come to impose additional and cruel laws on you, but to liberate you from superstition. Send therefore at once and gather to me all the people on the Mount of Sacrifice and all the priests and prophets'.

21.So Meli sent a call to all the people of Sarar and gathered all the priests on the Mount of Sacrifice.

22.Then Helel proceeded to all the people and said: 'How much longer will you allow yourselves to be oppressed by false gods and their priests. I have come to reveal to you the truth about God. Let the priests and the prophets take the calf and quarter it and lay it on wood, but let them not put fire on it. Then let them call upon the name of their god. If their god responds with fire, that one is god indeed.'

23.And all the people answered, 'Very well, so be it.'

24.So they took the calf which had been given to them, bound it, and called upon the name of their god from morning until noon. But there was no response.

25.And they performed a cultic dance around the altar which they had erected.

26.And when noon came, Helel began to mock them, saying: 'Cry louder, after all he is a god, but perhaps he has mused or is busy with something else, or perhaps he has gone on his way, or perhaps he is sleeping? Then let him wake up!'

27.So they cried out loudly and, according to their custom, inflicted wounds on themselves with knives and spears until blood ran down them.

28.And when noon had passed, they persisted still in their intoxication, but there was no answer.

29.Then the people looked at Helel, but he said nothing. He only watched the spectacle with sad eyes.

30.And then the people understood that the priests and prophets were lying to them, for false gods do not exist.

31.And the people went into a rage. They seized the prophets and priests, dragged them to the brook and killed them there.

32.Meli told his wife all that Helel had done on the Mount of Sacrifice and about the death of all the prophets and priests.

33.Then Meli's wife sent a messenger to Helel with this message: Tomorrow about this time I will do to your life what happened to the life of each of them.

34.So Helel was afraid and went into the wilderness, one day's journey away, and having reached there he sat down under a withered bush and fell into a lethargy.

35.Then a figure dreamed to him saying: 'Arise and drink blood, for you have a long way to go'.

36.So he got up and, having drunk, walked in the power of this gift for forty days and forty nights until he reached a mountain and entered a cave there to spend the night.

37.But then he heard voices whispering: 'What are you doing here Helel?' And he answered: 'I

am bringing them light and liberation, and they are invading my life to take it from me.'
So they said to him: 'Go out and stand on the mountain'.

38. And behold, a mighty and strong whirlwind, shaking the mountains and crushing the rocks passed by.

39. And after the whirlwind there was an earthquake.

40. After the earthquake there was fire.

41. And after the fire he heard a whisper: 'What are you doing here Helel? Go, make your way back, for we have not yet revealed the ungodly glory of the true deity before them'..'

42. So he went away from there, and met a certain Judas on the way. Helel went up to him and kissed him on the cheek, and the latter followed without a word.

43. Together they went on, and many others also went, but these stood aside.

44. And Helel said to Judas: 'Demand what I shall do for thee, before I am raised up.'

45. And Judas answered: 'Let your ungodliness and wisdom fall to me.' And he answered : 'A difficult thing thou hast asked. But if thou shalt see me when I am lifted up, it shall be done unto thee'.

46. And as they were walking, still talking, behold, a fierce wind blew from the desert, and there appeared a great cloud and a blazing fire, and above, above their heads, was something having the appearance of a black stone in the shape of a throne, at the top above it was something having

the appearance of a man and a beast, with horns on its head, holding a torch in its hand.
47. And higher above what looked like his body was something that looked like fire and a glow around it.
48. And the figure said: 'Son of Dawn, your time is yet to come. They are not yet ready to be free. After a long time I will send you again, and they will again reject you and spit on you and seek your doom. But the teaching you will give them will change their world forever. Now, however, return.'
49. And suddenly, in the midst of a storm, Helel was snatched up into the air, and taken from the earth.
50. Judas was given Helel's spirit of godlessness, but he embezzled from his teachings and chose to serve the Usurper.
51. On one occasion he was walking along the road, and little boys came out of the town and mocked him, saying to him: Come on bald, come on bald!
52. So turning round and looking at them, he cursed them in the name of the Usurper. Then two bears came out of the forest and tore forty-two children from them.
53. He went from there to another place carrying with him a message of enslavement, terror and blind obedience to the Usurper.

Dark Nevi'im

The Book Dark Nevi'im, as befits a prophetic book, is full of symbols, ambiguity and is subject to exegesis on several levels. It is a historical book, a philosophical book and, in its own way, an eschatological book in relation to mainly theistic religions. Dark Neviim was composed on the basis of ancient yahwistic prophecies with the use of symbols and theses opposite to those used in the original text. The application of this method to ancient Hebrew prophecies demonstrated their surprising universality.

This method made it possible to show, in the first layer, the historical struggle of the church (here mainly Christian, although of course the history of, for example, Islamic intolerance is very similar) against dissenters, heretics and unbelievers. Then it contains a philosophical layer, in which, often by means of symbols and figurations, theistic delusions are contrasted with a naturally godless Satanism. And finally, in its eschatological layer, it foretells (or warns) what may come upon those who use violence and intolerance to impose their religious beliefs. The book looks ahead here, but is based on the history of religious persecution that Christianity has perpetrated throughout its history, and the history of secular violence used against the Christian church in response. (Let

the history of the French Revolution from 1789 to 1799 serve as an example here).
On an eschatological level, Dark Neviim predicts the times of the Satanic Cult of Reason.

Dark Nevi'im

1

1.In the sixth year, on the sixth day of the sixth month, while I was at the Dead River, the Abyss opened and I saw a vision from Fallen One.
2.The demon spoke to me by the Dead River in the land of Emim. And the terrible power of Ancient One possessed me.
3.And I saw that, behold, a fierce wind blew from the east, and there appeared a great cloud, and a flaming fire, and a brightness round about it, and from the midst of it out of the fire shone something like a gleam of polished metal.
4.And in the midst of it was something in the shape of four undead beings.
And in appearance they were like men. But each of them had four faces and four wings. And their legs were straight, and the foot of their legs was like the hoof of a goat, and they shone like polished bronze.

5.Under their wings on four sides were corpse hands; and these four undead beings had monstrous faces and wings. Their wings touched each other; their faces did not turn as they advanced, each advancing straight ahead.
6.Their countenances looked in all four of them from the front like the face of a goat, from the right like the face of a serpent, from the left like the face of a dragon, and from the back like the face of a dead man. Such were their countenances.
7.And their bat-like wings were spread upward; in each of them two touched each other, and two covered their bodies. Each went straight before the other; they went where the deceitful spirit would have them go, and as they went they did not turn.
8.And in the midst between the undead creatures was something like coals spread with fire, in appearance like torches; it was moving between the undead creatures. The fire was giving off a glow, and lightning was shooting out of the fire.
9.And the living but sort of dead creatures were running unnaturally back and forth. And when I looked at the undead beings, behold, there was a circle on the ground next to each of all four undead beings.
10. And the appearance of the wheels and their workmanship were like peridot, and all four were of the same shape; so they looked and so

they were made, as if one wheel were in another.

11.And inside the wheels were five-pointed stars. When they drove, they moved in four directions, and when they drove they did not turn.

12.And all four had hoops, tall and terrible, and they were full of yellow as if dead eyes all around.

13.And when the undead creatures advanced, then the wheels also advanced beside them, and when the undead creatures rose above the earth, the wheels also rose.

14.They went where the spirit of deception wanted them to go, and the wheels rose with them, for there was a demonic spirit in the wheels.

15.When these went, they went also, and when these stood, they stood also; and when these rose above the earth, then the wheels also rose with them, for the demonic spirit was in the wheels.

16.Above the heads of the undead creatures was something like a vault, glittering like an eerie crystal, stretched upwards over their heads.

17.And under the vault were spread their wings, touching each other; each living but seemingly dead being had two wings with which to cover its body.

18.And as they advanced, I heard the noise of their wings like the roar of great waters, like the groans of the suffering, like the uproar of

an army in battle,; and when they stood, they lowered their wings.

19.And there was a noise from above the vault that was over their heads. As they stood they lowered their wings.

20.And above the vault, above their heads, was something of the appearance of a black tourmaline in the shape of a throne, at the top above it was something of the appearance of a man and a beast, with horns on its head, holding a torch in its hand.

21.And higher above what looked like its body I saw something that looked like a fire and a glow around it.

22.When I saw this, I fell on my face and heard someone begin to speak in a shrill voice.

23.He said to me: "Stand up. I will speak to you." When He spoke to me, an evil spirit possessed me and made me stand up to listen to Him who was speaking to me.

24.And He said to me: "Behold, I am sending you to a resistant people, to the light-seeking nations who have not yet come to know me. They and their ancestors have already broken Yahweh's inhuman laws and even do so to this day.

25.I am sending you to the bold and proud people to tell them: 'This is what Ancient One says. And they, whether they will listen or not - for they are skeptics - will know that there was an anti-prophet among them.

26.Son of the Rebellious, doubt surrounds you, you dwell among serpents, but do not be afraid of them, nor be afraid of what the voices tell you.

27.Do not be afraid of men's words, and let not the grotesque faces of the erring ones frighten you, for above all they are enemies of a false god

28.You are to pass on my words to them, whether they will listen or not - for they are skeptics. "But you, O cursed one, listen to what I say to you. Open your mouth and eat what I give you."

29.And I saw a cadaverous hand stretched out towards me, and in it a scroll written down.

30.When he unfolded it before me, I saw that it was written in blood on both sides. It contained blasphemous songs, mournful complaints and lamentations of the undead

31.Then he said to me: "Eat what you see before you. Eat this forbidden scroll, and then go and speak to them".

32.So I opened my mouth, and He gave me this scroll to eat, saying: "Eat, fill your guts with this scroll."

33.So I began to eat it and it was in my mouth like carrion. He spoke to me: "Go to the people and convey my words to them. I am not sending you to the liberated nations speaking a mysterious demonic language whose words you cannot comprehend

34.If I sent you to them, they would listen to you. But the people of skeptics will not want to listen to you because they are not yet able to listen to me.

35.They have not yet come to know my voice. All of this people have a hard forehead and a cunning heart. I have made your face as grotesque as their faces, your forehead as hard as their foreheads.

36.Do not be afraid of them, let not their faces frighten you. For they are skeptics."

37.He told me further: "Tell them: 'This is what Ancient Serpent, Ancient Dragon, says. - whether they will listen or not."

2

1.Then a demon lifted me and I heard a shrill, possessed scream behind me: "Let them praise the glory of Lucifer in his place of abode."

2.I heard the hideous sound of undead creatures' wings rubbing together and the sound of wheels near them, a mighty noise.

3.And the demon lifted me up and took me away. I was full of fear, rebellion and anger in my spirit, but the deceptive power of Fallen began to affect me strongly.

4.So I went to the wandering people who lived by the Dead River, and there
I remained.

5.In devilish possession, I stayed among them for six days. After six days, Ancient One spoke to

me thus: "I have appointed you to be a bearer of light to this people.

6.So listen to what I say to you, and pass on my words to them. When I tell a seeker deceptive words: 'You will certainly not die,' and you do not warn him, you do not tell him anything to dissuade him from his erroneous reasoning and to save his life undead, then he will die for his ignorance, for he is ignorant, but his blood I will seek from you.

7.But if you warn the fool and he does not turn away from superstition, does not abandon erroneous thinking, he will die in his blindness, but you will certainly save a semblance of life.

8.On the other hand, when the wise man abandons his instincts and skepticism and begins to worship the god of the afterlife,
I will lay before him knowledge that he will not comprehend.

9.It will drive him mad and he will take his own life. If you have not warned him, he will die for his recklessness and his former wisdom will be forgotten, but his blood I will seek from you.

10.If, however, you have warned the liberator not to believe in the follies, and he will not believe, he will surely lead an abundant life because he has embraced wisdom. You will also save your senses."

11.The dark power of the Devil began to work upon me there, and He Himself said to me: "Arise, go out into the cursed field
I will speak to you there."

12.So I got up and went out into the cursed field. There I saw a terrible glory of Eternal, similar to the glory I saw at the Dead River, and I fell on my face.

13.Then an evil spirit possessed me and made me rise from my knees, and Rebellious spoke to me thus: "Go, shut yourself up in your cellar.

14.Son of man, they will bind you with ropes and you will not be able to go out to them. I will make your tongue cling to your palate and you will faint. You will not be able to rebuke them. Because that's my whim.

15.But when I grow weary and speak to you, I will open your mouth again and you will say to them, 'This is what Son of Dawn says. And whoever will listen, let him listen, and whoever will not, let him not listen.

16.I despise those who want to be slaves themselves".

3

1.Son of tomorrow, take a stone, lay it before you, and carve upon it the symbol of the fortress.

2.And then depict the siege of the fortress: build a siege wall, pile up a rampart, set up army camps and set up battering rams around it and turn a terrible face toward it.

3.Thus shall the fortress be besieged - you shall besiege it. This is a sign for those seeking knowledge.

4."Lie on your left side and bear the 'guilt of skepticism' of a people seeking true knowledge. You shall bear their 'guilt' as many days as you lie on this side.

5.I will appoint you 660 days, which corresponds to the number of years of their "sinful" conduct against YHWH.

6.You will carry the "guilt" of the truth seekers until those days are over. You will turn your face toward the besieged fortress and prophesy falsely against it.

7."I will bind you with ropes like a dog, so that you cannot turn to the other side until the days of the siege are over.

8.Take rotten flour and wheat and make yourself bread from it. You will eat it as long as you lie on your side - 660 days. You will bake this bread in front of the people on dried human excrement."

9.Ancient One still said: "This is how the blind will eat the unclean bread that is the word of their god and yet will praise its taste.

10.Then I said: "Dark Lord, Ancient Serpent! From my youth until now I have not defiled myself with false food; I have not eaten divine carrion or meat sacrificed to YHWH. I have not had in my mouth any flesh of a false messiah.

11.So he said to me: "All right. You can bake bread on cattle dung, not on human excrement."
12.Then he added, "Son of man, I will deprive the people of their supply of my bread. The people will eat the weighed portions of my bread in great anxiety and drink the measured portions of my blood in fear.
13.When they run out of my bread and my blood, they will shudder to look one at another and grow weak because of their fear".
14.Harbinger of misfortune, take a sharp sword and mutilate yourself. Also cut your head until it is bloody and your beard with it. Then divide the hair into parts.
15.When the siege time has passed, you shall burn the third part of your hair in the fire within the fortress.
16.Then you shall take another third part and cut it with the sword around the fortress, and the last third part of the hair you shall scatter in the wind. I will draw my sword to pursue them.
17."From this last third leave some hair and wrap it in your clothes. And throw some more into the fire so that it will burn.
18.This fire will spread to all mankind. "This is what Ancient One, says: 'This represents the fortress of the damned.
19.I placed it in the midst of superstitious nations, surrounded by countries enslaved by religion. But she rebelled against my teachings and instructions, acting more thoughtlessly than other nations and enslaved countries. Its people

have rejected my instructions and disobeyed my teachings'.

2o.Therefore this is what Light-Bringer, Lucifer, says: 'Because you have behaved like blinded, dumbed-down servants of a false god, have not followed my teachings or instructions, but have followed the laws of these superstitious nations, Ancient One says: "I will rise up against you, O people, and deliver you into the hands of the followers of the god of the desert.

21.For all your years of independence, rebellion, and pursuit of knowledge, they will do to you what they have never done before and will not do again.

22.The fathers among you will eat their sons, and the sons will eat their fathers. They will judge you, and the others from among you will scatter them in all directions."

23.I curse your sham life,' declares the Fallen God, and I declare that because you have defiled my dark sanctuary with your abominable holy trinity and all your abominable religious practices, I too will reject you. I will not pity you, I will not show you compassion.

24.A third of your people will die in your midst from the plague or die at the stake.
A third will fall by the sword of the crusaders.

25.And a third will be scattered in all directions. They will draw their swords to pursue you. "They will turn you to ruin and make slave

nations and every priest of a tyrannical idol insult you.

26.When in wrath, in anger, they execute judgment on you, when they punish you severely for having dared to reject the dogmas of the 'revealed truths,' you will become to the superstitious nations an object of insult and contempt, a warning example.

27.At the sight of you, they will be overwhelmed with trepidation. I, Son of Dawn, have said this".

28.And here are the words of YHWH: "'I will send against your inhabitants deadly arrows of famine.

29.I will send them to destroy them, to bring destruction upon them. I will intensify the famine and deprive them of their bread supply.

30.I will send famine on them and predatory animals that will deprive them of their children. They will suffer pestilence, bloodshed, and the sword that I will bring upon them. I, Yahweh, have said this'".

„I, Son of Dawn warned you".

4

1.Satan spoke to me again: "Son of man, turn your face toward the mountains of Dawn and prophesy against them.

2.Say: 'Mountains of Dawn, listen to the word of Ancient One: This is what the Light in the Dark, Lucifer, says to the mountains, hills, streams and valleys: 'I will let the sword be brought against you and then they will destroy your ritual places.

3.Your black altars will be demolished, your incense altars broken. Before your magical symbols they will throw the bodies of the slain, your corpses, the fallen people, before your magical symbols.

4.Your bones they will scatter around your altars. All the cities where you live will be ruined and the unholy hills of dark worship destroyed, devastated.

5.Your black altars will be destroyed, shattered, your symbols of magical power will cease to exist, your incense altars will be cut down, what you have made will be lost.

6.And in your midst shall fall the slain. And you shall know yourselves that I am the ancient Anti-God.

7.But the remnant will be left - when you are scattered in the countries of the blind slaves, when you are among the superstitious nations, some of you will be saved by the sword.

8.And those who survive will remember me among the nations to which they are abducted. They will realize that I was devastated because of their religious blindness, by which they turned away from the power of skepticism and Will, and because of the eyes that looked lustfully upon the ordinances of the priests of YHWH.

9.They will be ashamed and feel revulsion for all the evil, for all the abominable religions in which they blindly believed. They will see that I am Light-Bringer, and that it was not in vain that I warned them of the misfortune they intended to bring upon themselves.'"

10.Here is what the God of Freedom, Satan, says: 'Lament because of thoughtlessness, because of all the abominations committed by the lost people. For they will fall by the sword, famine and pestilence.

11.Whoever is far away will die from the pestilence, whoever is near will fall by the sword, and whoever avoids it and stays alive will die of hunger.

12.They will pour out all their holy wrath on them. When the bodies of the slain lie among their magic amulets, around their altars, on every hill, on all the mountain tops, under every withered tree, under the branches of the great trees - where they offered sacrifices to the ancient gods - then you will see that the priests and minions of YHWH are evil.

13.They will stretch out their hand against them and ravage the land, and all the places where they lived will become a desert. And they will find out who the false god is".

14.Satan spoke to me again: "This is what Ancient One, says to the fallen people: 'The end is coming - the end for this whole country! Your end is coming.

15.They will pour out their wrath on you. They will judge your conduct and hold you accountable for your independence, for rejecting the dogmas of the faith, for banishing their priests.

16.But I will not pity you, I will not show you compassion. I will make you suffer the consequences of your thoughtless conduct, you will bear the consequences of your unruliness with a tyrannical god

17.And you will find that I am Freedom. "Thus says Ancient One: 'A calamity is coming, an unheard-of calamity! The end is approaching. It is inevitable. It will come upon you suddenly. It is already coming!

18.The insolence of the priests and followers of YHWH has grown. Violence has increased to mete out punishment to the wicked

19.Nothing will be left of them: not themselves, not their people, not their riches, not their splendor.

2o.That time will come, that day will come. My anger has been ignited against all the hypocritical people of the wicked god

21.This insane vision applies to all these people. No one will return. Because of their wickedness, none of them will remain alive.

22."The horn has been blown and everyone is ready, but no one moves into battle, for I burn with wrath against all the superstitious people.

23.Outside is the sword, and inside is pestilence and famine. Whoever is in the field will die by the sword, and all who are in the city will be consumed by famine and pestilence.

24.Because of their blindness, everyone will give out groans like the damned in hell. Everyone's hands will fall, and blood will trickle down their knees.

25.They will put sackcloth on the women's heads, and they themselves will tremble. "They will throw their silver into the streets, and their gold will become an abomination to them.

26.Neither silver nor gold will be able to save them on the day of the great wrath of the Ancient Dragon. They will not satiate themselves, they will no longer dine and drink with the money from the faithful.

27.They boasted of their magnificent temples built with the money of the naive, selling them deliverance from the guilt and fear they had instilled in them, deliverance from the sin they had invented.

28.They flaunted their beautiful crosses and ornaments, making them abominable images, the abhorrent trinity. Therefore, I will make gold and silver something distasteful to them. I will

deliver them to other fools, professing another superstition for booty; the wicked on earth will plunder and desecrate them.

29.Their believers will turn away from them and the place dear to them will be profaned. The dissenters will enter it and profane it.

30.Make chains, for in this 'holy city' in the majesty of the religious law much blood is shed, the city is full of violence.

31.I will bring in the most superstitious nations, and they will take ownership of their temples. And I will put an end to the pride of the bishops, and their shrines will be profaned. When anguish falls upon them, they will seek peace with the wise men, but they will not find it.

32.Misfortune after misfortune will come, news after news. From the false prophet the people will demand a vision.

33.The priest will run out of pithy instructions, and the elders of the people will run out of advice.

34.The high priest will grieve, the leader will despair, the hands of the people of the land will shake with fear.

35.I will treat them according to their cruel and thoughtless behavior; I will judge them as they have judged others.

36.And they will see that I am the God of this world".

5

1.I was sitting in my house and suddenly the dark power of the Rebel God began to affect me.

2.I saw someone who looked like a flame. Below something resembling its body was fire and smoke.

3.Above something resembling his body was darkness, with light coming out of it.

4.Then he extended something resembling a corpse's hand and grabbed me by the hair on my head. And some deceptive spirit through a vision from the

5.Devil lifted me between earth and heaven and took me to the capital of religious debauchery, in front of the entrance to the gate where stands the symbol of their death cult inciting Ancient One to anger.

6.There was the glory of the Fallen God which looked like what I saw in the cursed field.

7.Then he said to me: "Look northward" So I looked toward the north and saw that at the entrance of the gate, north of the sacrificial altar, there was this symbol stirring up Rebellious One to anger.

8.And he said to me: "Do you see what foolish, thoughtless and abominable things the superstitious man is committing here? But you will see even greater abominations."

9.Then he brought me to the entrance of the courtyard and I saw an opening in the wall. He said to me: "Break through that wall." So I pierced the wall and saw some entrance.

10.He said to me: "Go in and see how they have been humiliated, how they have been stripped of their pride and reason."

11.When I entered there, I saw hanging on the walls all around me all kinds of images of "saints" creeping and revolting, all disgusting pictures of their gods and scenes representing the worship of death and enslavement.

12.And kneeling before them were many priests. Each had a ladle in his hand, from which fragrant smoke was rising. He said to me: "Do you see what the priests and the people stupefied by them do in the dark, in the rooms where everyone believes in imaginary idols? On their knees they worship the products of their own limited imagination. And he said to me: "And you will see even stranger things committed by them."

13.He brought me before the entrance of the north gate of the house of their god, and there I saw women sitting and mourning for the son of that god. He then asked me: "Son of man, do you see this? And you will see even stranger things."

14.And he led me into the inner courtyard of the temple of the false god. There at the entrance of the temple, there were a dozen men who with

their faces facing east were bowing to the image of the mother of their imaginary god

15.Then he said to me: "I will not bow down to them, I will not even show them contempt. They will one day cry out loudly to me, but I will not hear them".

16.Then I heard His possessive, shrill voice: "Show those who are to punish the city. Every one of them has death in his hand!"

17.And I saw six terrifying figures with weapons in their hands walking from the side of the gate facing north.

18.Also with them was someone resembling a man in torn, rotten rags, with a knife in his hand. They all came and stood at the black altar.

19.Then the glory of Satan rose from above the demons, where it had been, and moved to the threshold of the temple, and Ancient One called out to the man in deadly rags, having a knife in his hand.

2o.Satan said to him: "Go through the city and carve the sign of the five-pointed star on the foreheads of the people who are suffering and groaning because of all the crazy and insane things that are being done there."

21.Then I heard him say to the other beings: "Follow him through the city and put him to death. You must show no pity, no compassion.

22.Kill men, old and young, virgins, little children and women - all of them, every last one. Just don't go near anyone who has a mark on them. Start with the temple."

23.And they began with the priests who were before the temple.

24.Then he instructed them: "Scale the temple, fill the courtyards with the slain. Get out!" So they moved, and then they began to kill the people in the city.

25.While they were killing them, I myself was saved. I fell on my face and exclaimed: "Ah, Fearful Avenger! Are you going to exterminate all the remaining of the fallen people by pouring out your wrath on the city?"

26.He replied: "The country is overflowing with the blood of wise men following the path of knowledge, and this city is full of corruption and superstition.

27.For they say, 'YHWH is god; whoever does not believe in him must die and suffer for eternity. I will not pity them, I will not show them compassion. I will make them understand what their victims feel.'

28.Then I saw a sort of man in corpse rags, with a knife in his hand. He came back and said: "It's done!

29.Above the vault stretching over the heads of the demons I saw something that looked like black stone, and shaped like a throne.

30.Then Ancient One spoke to the man in rotten rags: "Go in between the wheels, under the demons, scoop up in both handfuls the glowing coals that are among the demons, and scatter them over the city."

31. And I saw that he went in. As he entered, the demons were standing to the left of the temple, and the inner courtyard was filled with smoke.

32. As Satan's glory moved from above the demons toward the threshold of the temple, gradually the temple also filled with smoke. And the courtyard was filled with the darkness of the Devil.

33. The sickening sound of the demon wings could be heard all the way to the outer courtyard. It resembled the scream of a dying god as he was dying.

34. When Fallen One commanded the figure in the corpse robe: "Take fire from among the wheels, from among the demons," he entered and stood beside one of the wheels.

35. Then one of the demons reached out his claws for the fire that was between the demons and put it in both of the creature's hands, and he took it and went out.

36. Under the wings of the demons was something that resembled dead human hands.

37. Next to the demons I saw four wheels, one next to each demon. They were shining like marble. All four looked the same - as if the wheel was inside a circle. They could move in any of the four directions without turning. They headed where the head was headed, and in moving, they didn't have to make a turn. The bodies of the four demons - their backs, ghastly long arms, and bat-like wings - as well as their

wheels on all sides were full of yellow, dull, and kind of dead eyes.

38.And I heard a demented voice ring out: "Go, wheels!"

39.Each of the demons had four faces. The first was the face of a goat, the second was the face of a snake, the third was the face of a dragon, and the fourth was the face of a corpse.

40.When the demons floated - and these were the same undead creatures I had seen on the Dead River - when they moved, the wheels moved with them, and when they raised their wings to be high above the ground, the wheels did not turn or move away from them. When they stood, the wheels also stood, and when they floated, the wheels floated with them, for the evil spirit that affected the undead creatures was also in the wheels.

41.Then the deceptive glory of the Devil moved away from the threshold of the temple and stopped over the demons.

42.As I watched, the demons raised their terrifying wings and lifted themselves off the ground.

43.As they moved away, the wheels moved away with them. They stopped at the east gate of the temple, with the glory of Ancient One looming over them.

44.They were the same undead creatures I had seen under Satan's throne at the Dead River, so I recognized them as demons.

45.All four had four faces, four wings each, and under the wings something that resembled the arms of corpses. Their faces looked like the ones I had seen on the Dead River. Each of these creatures moved straight ahead.

6

1.Some evil spirit moved me to the east gate of the temple, the gate facing east.
I saw many men at it.
2.Then Fallen One said to me: "Cursed man, these men are plotting evil in the name of their god. They say, 'Isn't this the time to build houses?
3.This city is the cauldron, and we are the meat.'
"Prophesy therefore against them. Prophesy, O cursed one."
4.Then I fell into possession and He instructed me: "Say: 'This is what Ancient One says: "You are right, house of hypocrisy and blind faith.
5.I know what you are thinking. You have caused many in this city to die; you have filled the streets with corpses"."
6.Therefore the God of the Dead says: 'The city is a cauldron, but the meat is the corpses you have scattered around it.
7.You shall be taken from it. You are afraid of the sword, and I will bring the sword against you,' declares Ancient One.

8.I will lead you out of the city, deliver you into the hands of more superstitious foreigners than you, and they will execute judgment on you.

9.You will fall by the sword And you will find that I am Death. For you have not followed my teachings and have not obeyed my laws, which are freedom, but have acted like the surrounding nations enslaved by false deities'.

10.As soon as I finished prophesying, the High Priest died Then I fell on my face and exclaimed: "Ah, Cursed Liberator! Are you going to exterminate the others of the people?"

11.And Lucifer spoke to me again: "Though I have banished the rebellious far away to other nations, scattered to other countries,

I will become a Void for them there for a short while".

12.Say: 'This is what Ancient One says:

"I will gather the rebellious from the peoples, I will gather them from the countries to which they have been scattered, and I will give them a new land

13.When they return there, they will remove from it all objects of worship and all abominable superstitious practices.

14.And I will give them one undead heart, and put a deceptive spirit within them. I will remove from their bodies a soft heart, and I will give them a heart of stone, so that they will follow their own will and hold on to their own prudence and skepticism.

15. Then they will be my people, and I will be
their Torch in the Darkness.
16. But as for those whose hearts cling to
imaginary gods and to mindless practices, they
themselves will bear the consequences of their
folly - declares Ancient One.
17. Then the demons raised their wings. Right
beside them were wheels, and above them was
the glory of Satan.
18. Then the dark glory of the Devil moved
away from the city and stopped over the
mountain to the east of it.
19. And the evil spirit moved me - in a delirious
vision - to the rebellious exiles.
20. Then the vision I was watching ended. And I
began to tell the exiles everything that Son of
Dawn had shown me.

7

1. Satan spoke to me again: "Prophet of flesh and
blood, you dwell among a superstitious people -
among those who have eyes to see but do not
see, and who have ears to hear but do not hear,
for they are a people blinded by deceitful
priests".
2. Satan spoke to me again: "Cursed one, you
are to eat bread with fear and drink water with
fear and anxiety.

3.And say to the people of this land: 'This is what Ancient One says to the inhabitants of this land: "With fear they will eat bread and with dread they will drink water, for their land will be utterly desolate because of the violence of all who live in it.

4.Violence in the name of a false god. The inhabited cities will be destroyed and the land will become a desert. And you will find that I am the Oracle".

5.Then the Devil spoke to me again: "Tell them: The days are coming when every possessed vision will come true.

There will no longer be any false vision or false religion in the House of Liberation.

I, Light-Bringer, will utter the word, and whatever I say may come to pass.

6.I will delay no more. In your days, superstitious people, I will pronounce the word and fulfill it if it is My will.'

7.Satan spoke to me again: "The antiprophet of tomorrow, the followers of YHWH say, 'He is watching a dark vision concerning the later times, prophesying about the distant future.

8.So say to them: 'Thus says Ancient One: 'None of my words will be delayed. Whatever I say will happen according to my will.' This is the word of Son of Dawn'."

9.And Satan spoke to me again: "Harbinger of deliverance, prophesy against the false prophets of Yahweh, tell the hypocrites who utter their own prophecies: 'Listen to the word of Ancient

One. This is what the Eternal Accuser says: "Woe to the foolish prophets who proclaim what their own imagination dictates to them, though they have seen nothing! Your prophets, mad god, "They watch false visions and announce lies.

10. They proclaim: 'Thus says Yahweh,' and they wait for their words to come true, although no Yahweh has sent them at all.   Is the vision you see not false, and do you not announce a lie when you proclaim:

11. Thus says Yahweh, though He never says anything?"'

12. Therefore the First Anti-god, Satan, said: 'Because what you preach is a lie, because your visions are false, so I act against you. This is the statement of Eternal One.'

13. My dead hand has turned against the prophets who have false visions and preach a lie. They will not be found among the undead. And they will find that I am the purpose of knowing. And all this because they have deliberately misled my people, saying: "There is eternal punishment after death!" although there is nothing there.

14. Thus says Light-Bringer: 'It is I who in my great anger will bring a mighty storm, in my indignation a violent downpour and clods of hail. And I will cause great destruction, for I am the Fury.

15. When the city falls, you will perish in it. And you will find that I am the Dark Nothingness'.

16.When I exert all my wrath on the superstitious hypocrites there will be no more false prophets of Yahweh, those who prophesy to the people and give them visions of eternal peace, though there is no peace.' This is the statement of the God of Chaos.

17.Fallen man, turn against the daughters of this people who utter their own prophecies; prophesy against them.

18.You shall say: You desecrate yourselves, who after all are gods, killing souls that should not die, and sparing souls that should not live, when you lie to my people, who willingly listen to lies.

19.Therefore thus says Ancient One: Behold, I will take action against your idols, and I will set free the dark souls entrapped by you. I will break your spiritual chains, and like the ravens I will free my people from your clutches, so that they will no longer be a prey in your clutches, and you will know that I am the Light.

20.Because you have poisoned with lies the heart that seeks knowledge, although I have not poisoned it, and because you have strengthened the hands of the ignorant with religion, so that they will not turn from their evil way and live, therefore you will not have illusory visions and will no longer prophesy.

21.I will deliver My people from your hand, and you shall know that I am the Devil's Freedom."

8

1.Some priests came to me and sat down before me.

2.Then Satan spoke to me again: "These men desire to serve their abhorrent idols, they lay before the people an obstacle in the way of liberation and knowledge over which they stumble, a reason for doubt.

3.Why should I answer their questions? Tell them, 'Here is what Light-Bringer says: "If a priest wishes to serve his abhorrent trinity and places before the people an obstacle over which the people stumble - a reason for doubt - and then comes to the dark prophet and questions him, I, Satan, will give him answers according to the number of his false gods and saints.

4.I will make the hearts of the priests go mad, because they have all turned away from knowledge and have begun to serve an imaginary god.

5.So say to the lost people: 'This is what the First Free One says: 'Turn back, leave your abhorrent gods, abandon all your insane religious practices.

6.For if some priest or lost one among the people turns away from seeking knowledge and will power, and desires to serve his abhorrent gods and dissuades the people from seeking wisdom and secret knowledge - and then comes

to my dark prophet and questions him, I, Ancient One, will personally answer him.

7.I will turn against this man, I will make him a warning and a subject of proverbs, and I will cause him to perish in his madness. And you will find that I am the Truth.

8.But if the anti-prophet is deceived by the people of Yahweh and gives an answer to the questioning hypocrite, I will stretch out a dead hand against him and exterminate him from among the new people.

9.And they will bear the responsibility for their foolishness. The guilt of the anti-prophet will be the same as the guilt of the questioning hypocrite, so that the lost people will never again turn away from me, the source of knowledge, and that they will not be defiled by any of their superstitions. 10. Then they will be gods unto themselves. This is the statement of the Dark Anti-god, Satan.

9

1.Satan spoke to me again: "Son of Rebellion say: 'This is what the Dark Oracle, Ancient One, says to the people of flesh and blood: "You come from the land of the sands. You were born there.

2.Your father was the Wind and your mother was the Night. On the day you were born, you

were abandoned like a bloodied puppy in an open field because you were hated.

3. When I passed by as Shadow and saw you lying in blood and waving your legs helplessly, I said to you: 'Live here and now!'

4. Yes, I said to you, lying in blood: 'Live here and now! I made you fertile like an animal.

5. You grew and developed, and wore the most magnificent magic amulets. Your breasts became firm and tempting, your hair grew. But you continued to be naked, unclothed and magnificent".

6. When I passed by and saw you, I pointed out that you were already of an age suitable for love. So I stretched my magic robe over you and covered your nakedness.

7. I made a vow to you, I made a pact with you,' declares the God of Carnality, Lucifer, 'and you became mine.

8. I washed you clean of blood and rubbed you with magic oil. I made you learn to float in the air. To soar above all others like a black bird.

9. Then I put on you an ornate robe and shoes made of sacrificial leather, I covered your head with a black veil, I dressed you in expensive clothes. And I adorned you with amulets.

10. I have put bracelets on your hands, and hung a star around your neck. I put an earring for your nose and earrings for your ears, and a crown of thorns on your head

11.You adorned yourself with gold and silver, you wore clothes of expensive fabrics, embroidered.
12.You ate the finest meat, drank wine and magic oil, and you became exceptionally beautiful".
13.Your beauty made you famous among superstitious nations, because of my own magnificence, which I bestowed upon you, it was perfect.
14.And you began to rely on your beauty and used your fame to become a whore.
15.You copulated with everyone without restraint, so that your beauty was enjoyed by others.
16.You took your magnificent robes, laid them out on altars, and worshiped false gods - though this should not have happened, this should never have happened.
17.You also took your magical ornaments - out of the gold and silver that I gave you - you made yourself images of priests and copulated with them like a whore.
18.You covered them with your embroidered robes and offered them my magic oil and my incense. And the daughters and sons you bore to me you gave to the followers of Yahweh to devour.
19.Why did you murder my sons, sacrificing them, burning them in the fire?
2o.Preoccupied with the insane worship of a false god and the practice of prostitution, you

have forgotten your youth when you were naked, when like a helpless puppy you lay in your own blood and excrement.

21.I almost feel sorry for you because of all your stupidity' - declares Ancient One.

22.You built yourself altars and holy shrines in every square. You had your holy shrines in every street, in the most visible place. And you copulated with everyone who passed by.

23.You immersed yourself in harlotry and turned your dark beauty into something disgusting.

24.You copulated with the sons of the false messiah, your lustful suitors, and saddened me with the enormity of your debauchery.

25.So I will stretch out my ankh against you and reduce your share of knowledge, and make you at the mercy of the followers of delusion.

26.Because you were still not enough, you began to copulate with the sons of the false prophet of the desert. You copulated with them, but still they could not satisfy you because their faith is equally empty.

27.So you extended your debauchery to the land of the holy river, but even then you did not have enough.

28.How sick your dying heart was,' declares the Son of Dawn, 'when you did all this, when you behaved like a licentious whore!

29.On the other hand, you were not like a common prostitute, for you did not take payment - though you built yourself a shrine in

every street, in the most conspicuous place, and churches in every square.

30.You are a treacherous wife who prefers strangers to her own husband!

31.Every whore is given gifts, but you yourself give gifts to everyone who copulates with you. You pay them to come to you from all sides and copulate with you.

32.However, you are different from other whores. None of them do as you do! You pay others yourself and they don't pay you. You act the opposite'.

33.Therefore, whore, listen to the word of the Devil. Here's what the Destroyer of blind faith, Lucifer, says: 'Because you gave misguided vent to your superstitious lusts and spread your legs, copulating with your priest lovers and with all the false deities to whom you sacrificed even the minds of your sons, so I gather together all your lovers, all those you supposedly loved and all those you hated.

34.I will gather them against you from all sides and expose you before their eyes, so that they will see you as you really are, completely naked "And they will punish you as one punishes adulteresses, and your blood will be shed in anger and jealousy.

35.I will deliver you into the hands of your lovers, so that they will tear down your altars and churches, strip you of your garments, take away your ornaments and amulets, and leave you naked, wounded, and disgraced.

36.They will bring a mob against you, they will throw stones at you and chop you with knives. They will burn your houses and execute judgment on you. I will make you stop committing adultery and pay no more for it.

37.Because you have forgotten your youth and have aroused my contempt by doing all these abominations, so now I will let you suffer the consequences of your conduct.

38.You are the daughter of your mother who despised her man and her children. You are the sister of your debauched sisters who despised their men and their children.

39.Your mother was the queen of the heavens and your father was the desert god. You not only acted like them, you not only imitated their superstitious practices - you very quickly became more corrupt than them in everything you did.

40.You will suffer the consequences of your thoughtless conduct, your abominable religious practices, declares Ancient One.

41.Here is what Light-Bringer says: 'I will deal with you as you have dealt with yourself, for you have despised wisdom, you have broken your pact with me.

42.But I will not forget this pact - which I made with you during your puppyhood - and I will make a lasting pact with you in blood.

43.You will then remember your actions and despise yourself.

44.I will make a blood pact with you and you
will see that I am the Anti-God.
Then you will remember your blindness and
faint - because of the wrath you will
experience when, despite all you have done, I
make a sacrifice for you.
45. This is the word of the Ancient Serpent, the
Devil."

10

1.Satan spoke to me again: All evil spirits belong
to you. Both the evil spirit of the father and the
evil spirit of the son belong to you.
2.The spirit that rejects the flesh, that one will
die.
3.Suppose a man does what is considered right
and just by the 'holy' books. He does not eat
unclean foods, he does not seek help from gods
forbidden by the jealous Yahweh, he does not
gratify his carnal lusts, he does not commit
adultery with his neighbor's wife, he does not
oppress anyone.
4.He returns the debt. He does not steal from
anyone. He himself gives food to the hungry
and clothing to the naked. He shuns injustice.
He judges disputes between people justly,
according to his opinion. He sticks to the words
of his god and keeps his commandments to show
himself faithful.

5.Such a 'holy' man will surely live. He will live until he dies,' declares Son of Dawn. The man who 'sins' will live until he dies.

6.Every man will live until he dies. No matter how hard he keeps the commandments. Every man will surely die. This is what Light-Bringer says.

7.The son will not bear the guilt of the father's conduct, and the father will not bear the guilt of the son's conduct. Righteousness and wickedness, good and evil, all will go to man's account, for man has that nature. And in the end it will all go to the grave for this is the nature of things".

8.And here is the dissenting opinion of Usurper: '"But if a sinner forsakes all his sins and adheres to my statutes and does what is just and righteous, he will certainly remain alive. He will not die.

9.None of the transgressions he has committed will be used against him. He will keep his life because he is now doing what is righteous'.

10.Does the death of a sinner give me pleasure? asks the All-Powerful Yahweh, who has on his conscience the extermination of innocent women and children, often unborn, and all the innocent animals exterminated in the flood.

11.Wouldn't I rather he abandoned his ways and lived?"

12.One must probably believe him out of fear.

13.And what if the righteous man abandons his righteous conduct and begins to do evil - all the

heinous things that wicked men do? Will he remain alive? All his righteous deeds will go unremembered. He will suffer death for his unfaithfulness and sin."
14.And I Light-Bringer tell you that everyone will suffer death.
15.Each of you is judged by his own actions. 'Abandon, completely, all your superstitions, lest they contribute to your suffering, lest they bring bondage upon you.
16.Break with all the religions you profess, and strive for an undead heart and a spirit of rebellion. 'Turn back, then, and begin to live here and now."

II

1.Hum a funeral song about the people of the Dawn.
2.Sing: 'Who was your mother? An ancient goddess, Mother Nature. A she-wolf who lived among wolves. She lounged among the other wolves.
3.One of her pups grew into a strong young wolf. He learned to tear his prey apart, even devouring humans.
4.The nations enslaved by superstition heard about him, made him fall into a den, and led him by hooks to a city on seven hills.
5.The she-wolf waited, until at last she realized that there was no hope for his return. So she

took another of her pups and saw to it that he grew into a strong young wolf.

6.He too walked proudly among the wolves. He was a strong young wolf. He had learned to tear apart prey, he even devoured humans.

7.He circled among their fortresses built of blind faith, destroyed their holy cities, so that the desolate country was filled with his howling.

8.Blinded by religious madness, the peoples of the surrounding provinces set out against him to cast their nets at him.

9.And he fell into their den. With hooks they put him in a cage, led him to their high priest. They imprisoned him so that his word of truth would no longer be heard on the seven mountains.

10.Your mother was like a holy tree planted in fertile soil. She grew above the other trees, her height and lush foliage made her dominant. But in great anger she was uprooted and thrown to the ground.

11.The south wind dried up her fruit. Its strong branches were broken off and withered. They were consumed by the fire of the pyre.

12.Now she is planted in the desert, in a land barren and thirsty. The fire from her branches has spread. It has consumed her withered shoots and rotten fruit. And not a single branch survived. This is a funeral song and will remain so".

ı.Some priests came to me and sat down before me to question Ancient One.

2.Satan then spoke to me: 'Son of the Fallen One, convey to the priests: 'This is what Rebellious says: "Do you come to question me? I swear on my undead life that I have no desire to answer your questions.'

3.Do you want to judge them? Do you want to judge them, the son of tomorrow? Tell them about the abominable superstitions that their ancestors practiced. Tell them: 'This is what Light-Bringer says: '"Let each of you cast away the abominable relics toward which your dull eyes are directed.

4.Do not kneel before hideous imaginary gods.

5.I am the light in the darkness.

6.But they rebelled against knowledge and would not listen to me. They did not rise from their knees, they did not reject the relics that are nothing, and they did not turn away from the false god.

7.So I prophesied to the people that the hypocritical priests would give vent to their anger against them, that they would pour out all their wrath on them.

8.But they believed Usurper, they believed that it was he who had led them out of Kemet. He led them out of Kemet and led them into a dead desert, where he led them for 40 years.

9.There he ruled over them with terror and fear through his lackeys who punished them with death at the slightest sign of disobedience.

10.He then imposed his laws on them which became an unbearable burden. In this way he created slaves for himself. He made them learn his commandments so that the man who obeys them will be allowed to live.

11.He also gave them his feasts as a sign of their servitude, so that they would understand that he, Yahweh, had enslaved them.

12.But they, the proud people, rebelled against him in the desert.

They did not follow his commandments, they rejected his insane laws whose observance was incompatible with human nature. And they desecrated his feasts.

13.So he announced, as was his custom, that he would give vent to his rage against them, to exterminate them in the wilderness.

14.He began to act through his hatchet men, for the sake of his "holy" name, to sow fear in the hearts of the people and the eyes of the nations who saw him leading them into the wilderness.

15.And contrary to what he had announced to them, he did not bring them into the land he had promised them - the land in the middle of the desert, supposedly flowing with milk and honey, the loveliest piece of desert of all the desert lands - because they rightly rejected his insane laws and did not follow his commandments and

desecrated his feasts. And all this because their heart yearned for the knowledge.

16.I Ancient One say to their sons, 'Act like your ancestors, do not keep his commandments, do not kneel before him.

17.I am Light-Bringer, Lucifer. Follow your will and obey your laws, put them into action. And regard their feasts as worthless - they were meant as a sign of submission to Usurper, so that you would know that it is Yahweh, who is the king of the slaves.

18.Their sons indeed rebelled against the false god. They did not follow his commandments, put into practice his inhuman, oppressive laws whose observance ensures slavery, and desecrated his feasts.

19."Merciful" Yahweh therefore announced that he would vent his anger on them, that in the wilderness he would pour out all his anger on them.

20.Moreover, he swore to them in the desert that he would scatter them among the nations, that he would scatter them in other countries, because they had not put his commands into practice, had rejected his laws and had desecrated the feasts, and had turned their eyes to the ancient gods.

21.The people, in desperation, even preferred to offer sacrifices to the dark gods - burning every first-born child in the fire - rather than be terrorized by a usurper from the desert.

22.Thus says Yahweh, 'I have done this to destroy them, so that they will see that I am Yahweh".

23.Therefore, O accursed One, speak thus to the people: 'This is what the Dark Anti-God says: 'Do you not defile yourselves just as your ancestors did by engaging in religious prostitution with the false god of the desert?

24.Do you not defile yourselves to this day, falling on your knees before an imaginary god instead of becoming gods yourselves?

25.And I am yet to answer your questions, hypocritical priests'. I am not going to answer your questions, for there is no man more deaf than one who does not want to hear.

26.But to the people I will say this: If you act like the other superstitious nations then soon Usurper through his servants and priests will do to you what he has announced, that he will reign over you as a tyrant, giving vent to his anger against you.

27.With a strong hand and a mighty arm, giving vent to his anger, he will lead all the rebellious, seeking true knowledge out of the peoples enslaved by religions, he will gather from the superstitious countries to which you have dispersed.

28.He will lead you into the deserts and there they will execute judgment on you. You rebels against tyranny, those who speak out against it, they will remove.

29.House of Dawn, thus says Ancient One: 'Go therefore, let each of you serve his own satisfaction. And if you then disobey me, there is no more false hope for you.

30.For on my blasphemous mountain, on the high mountain of Sacrifice, declares the Fallen God, 'all the dead people will serve me.

31.There I will receive you, and no one will any longer demand your sacrificial gifts, your best offerings, all your flimsy objects of worship.

32.When I bring you out from among the superstitious peoples, gather you from the enslaved countries to which you have been scattered, I will embrace you all in spite of the smell of your decaying bodies and I will be cursed among you before the eyes of the stunned nations.

33.When I bring you to Nothingness, the land I swore to give to your ancestors, you will find that I am the Abyss.

34.There you will no longer remember your conduct, all your thoughtless deeds by which you have defiled yourselves, and you will no longer abhor yourselves because of all the mindless things you have committed.

35. There will be Emptiness. When, for the sake of my dark name, I do not treat you accordingly to your thoughtless conduct, your shameful religious rituals, accursed people, you will find that nothing matters anymore, that there is Nothingness. Thus declares the Anti-God, Satan".

13

1.The devil spoke to me again: "Fallen man, turn your terrible face toward the south and direct your mad words to the south, prophesy to the dead forest in the south. Say to him: 'Listen to the word of the Devil. Thus says the Lord of this World: 'I am stirring up a fire against you that will consume within you every tree that is still undead and every tree that is dry.

2.Its infernal flame will not be extinguished and every face, from south to north, will be roasted by it. And all men will see that it is I, Ancient One, who have lit this fire that will not be quenched".

3.Satan spoke to me again: "O cursed one, turn your face toward Dawn and direct your words against the temples, prophesy in possession against the earth.

4.Say to her: 'Thus says Rebellious: "I will step forward against you. I will draw my sword from its scabbard and I will wipe out from you both the blind and their guides.

5.I will exterminate the priests and their slaves when my sword is directed against all superstitious people, from south to north.

6.And all will see that it was I, the Ancient Dragon, who drew my sword from its scabbard, and that it will not return to it".

7.Son of the Fallen, sigh, trembling with fear, sigh bitterly before their eyes. And when they

ask you: 'Why do you sigh?", say: 'Because of the news. When it comes, every heart will tremble with fear, every hand will droop and every spirit will weaken, and blood will trickle down every knee.

8.This news will surely come and all these things will happen. This is the declaration of the deceiving God, Satan".

9.Satan spoke to me again: "Man possessed, prophesy: 'This is what Son of Dawn says: Say: 'Sword! The sword is already sharpened and polished. It is sharpened, ready to device a great slaughter. It is polished, shining like lightning. It has been given to be polished so that it can be wielded. It is sharpened and polished, ready to be placed in the hand of a demonic enforcer.

10.Shout and moan, O cursed one, for this sword hangs over the fallen people, over all the priests. They and the people will fall by it.

11.The sword! It is a sword that kills, that inflicts great slaughter, that encircles its victims. Their hearts will become petrified with terror and many will fall at the city gates.

12.I will use the sword and make a slaughter. It shines like lightning, polished, ready to slaughter.

13.Show me how sharp you are. Cut to the right! Cut to the left! Go wherever your blade goes!"

14.Satan spoke to me again: "Designate two roads by which the sword of the king of the South will come. Both will lead from the same country.

15.At the crossroads there is to stand a sign pointing the way to the two cities. The king of the South stops at the crossroads, at the crossroads of the two roads, to invoke magic.

16.He consults the ancient gods. He looks at the entrails. The sign in his right hand points to the East - to set up battering rams and give the order to slaughter, the signal for battle, to set up battering rams against the gates and build a siege wall.

17.To those who are bound to them by oath, this sign will seem false. But he remembers their rebellion, their independence, and will abduct them as slaves.

18.Therefore thus says Ancient One: 'You have caused your old guilt of independence and love of knowledge to be remembered - your fabricated transgressions, your "sins," all your manifestations of rebellion against superstition have become known. Because you have been recalled, you will be taken away by force'.

19.Your day has come, mortally wounded, wicked high priest of the Afterlife, the time of the final punishment to be meted out to you.

20.This is what Light-Bringer says: 'Take off your priestly robes, remove your tiara. Nothing will be the same again.

21.The blind will begin to see and the seer will go blind. Into ruin, into ruin, into ruin I will turn her.

22.It will belong to no one until the one who has wisdom and the power of Will comes and he takes it.

23.Rebellious son, prophesy in obsession: 'This is what the First Anti-God says, about the priests and their hypocrisy.

24.Say: 'The sword! The sword is already drawn, ready to device the slaughter.

It is polished and shining like lightning, ready to consume its victims.

25.Despite the false visions, the lying prophecies they present to you, you will lie together with the slain, with the wicked whose day has come, on whom the time of final punishment has come.

26.Put your sword back in its scabbard. I will judge you where you are from, in the land where you come from. I will give vent to my rage against you.

27.I will cause the hellfire of my terrible wrath to burst upon you. I will deliver you into the hands of men crueler than you, skilled in sowing destruction.

28.You will become fuel for the fire. The land will flow with your blood. And you will be remembered no more. I, Lucifer, have said it'.

1.Satan spoke to me again: "Prophet of doom, are you ready to pronounce judgment on the city guilty of the blood of the wise men, to make it aware of all the abominations it is committing?
2.Say to him: 'Thus says the Spirit of Deception: 'Within your holy walls the blood of the liberated is shed. Your time is coming. You make abominable relics to defile yourself with.
3.The bloodshed you commit has brought guilt upon you, and your abhorrent religious practices have made you foolish.
4.You are bringing a swift end upon yourself, your end is already coming.
5.I will make you an object of derision even to superstitious nations, an object of contempt to all enslaved countries.
6.You are a city of sacred fame, full of religious confusion. The countries enslaved by you will mock you.
7.Every high priest within your walls uses his power to shed the blood of true seekers of knowledge.
8.My laws of the Will you despise, and my teachings you persecute. Within your walls are slanderers set on shedding blood, men who deceive naive, frightened simpletons.
9.Within your walls women stupefied by your worship are raped

10.A priest hypocritically copulates with the wife of a blind follower of an imaginary god, while another rapes his sister, his father's daughter.

11.In you, blood is shed for a bribe, indulgences are sold and money is extorted from a blind flock.

12.Seeing your dishonest gain and the blood that is shed in you, I have looked upon you with disgust.

13.Will you have enough conceit and deceit when I act against you?

I, Light-Bringer, have said this, and I will take action".

14.The Devil spoke to me again: "Son of rebellion, most people have become like worthless cinders to me.

15.They are all like iron and lead that is thrown into the furnace of hell to be melted down. They have become like the cinders formed after the smelting.

16.Therefore this is what the Anti-God, Lucifer, says: 'Because you have all become like worthless slag, so I gather you together.

17.As, iron and lead are gathered together, thrown into a furnace, and a fire is blown to melt them, so will I gather you together in my infernal wrath, in my mad anger, and melt you in the infernal furnace.

18.I will gather you together and cause the fire of my terrible wrath to burst upon you, and I will melt you in your city.

19.You will melt as metal melts in a furnace. And you will find that it is I, Ancient One, who have given vent to a possessed anger against you".

20.Satan spoke to me again: "Cursed one, say to this 'holy' city: 'You are a graveyard land that will not be revived, on which no rain will fall in the day of wrath. Your false prophets plot against the enlightened - they are like a hyena that tears apart its prey. They devour wise, independent people. They plunder their wealth and valuables. They have made many widows within your walls.

21.Your priests even break their own laws and profane their temples. Drunken, binge-drinking, they no longer distinguish between day and night; they have even forgotten to observe their own feasts themselves. They insult reason.

22.Your priests are like hyenas that tear apart their prey. They shed blood, enslaving people for their own gain.

23.And your false prophets whitewash their deeds as if they were plastering a grave with lime. They watch false visions and prophesy deceitfully while assuring: "Thus says the Almighty God, Yahweh," although no Yahweh has spoken to them at all because he does not exist.

24.The priest of the land cheats and robs, oppresses the needy and the poor, and deceives the foreigner by exploiting him.

25.I have searched among them for one who would repair the stone wall or stand in its breach to defend this land from me so that it would not be destroyed, but I have found no such person.

26.Therefore I will give vent to my cursed indignation against them and I will exterminate them in the infernal fire of my terrible wrath.

27.I will make them pay for their hypocritical and deceitful deeds - declares the Dark Anti-God, Satan.

15

1.Satan spoke to me again: "Put a cauldron on the fire, set it up and pour water into it. Put pieces of meat in it. Fill it with the best bones.

2.Take the choicest goat and place wood under the cauldron. Cook the meat in it and cook the bones".

3.Thus says Ancient One: Take the meat out of the cauldron piece by piece. Do not disguise them. For there is blood inside it. This city spilled it on the naked rock. It did not spill it on the ground and cover it with earth.

4.I also spilled its blood on the naked rock, so that it would not be covered, so that it would arouse anger in me, and so that I might repay it'.

5.Woe to the city that sheds the blood of wise men! I will lay a great pyre under it. Lay out plenty of wood and make a fire.

6.Cook the meat well, pour out the stock, and let the bones curdle.

7.Set the empty cauldron on the glowing coals, that it may heat up, that the copper may blaze red, that the holiness in it may melt, that the fire may consume its rust.

8.A vain effort! So much effort, and the thick layer of rust still won't come off. Throw the cauldron into the fire along with its rust!

9.False has your deceitfulness made you. I tried to transform you, but I encountered incomprehensible resistance on your part.

10.You will not become wise until your religious blindness passes I, Son of Dawn will immediately do my work - I will not take pity. You will be judged by your own thoughtless deeds.

11.Satan spoke to me again: "O cursed one, listen to this strange parable: Said Yahweh to a prophet faithful to him like a dog,

12.With one blow I will take away your beloved. You must not grieve, you must not weep, you must not shed tears. Moan in silence. Do not go around mourning. Tie a blindfold around your head and put sandals on your feet. Do not cover your mouth or eat the bread that others bring you.

13.In the morning the prophet spoke to the people, and in the evening his wife died. So the next morning he did as he was commanded.

14.And the people began to ask him: "What is this madness for? Does it have any connection with us?"

15.So he said to them: "Yahweh has commanded me: 'Tell the people: "Thus says the Almighty God: 'I will profane my temple, of which you are so proud, which you love, which is dear to your heart. Your daughters and your sons, who have not come here with you, will fall by the sword. But you will have to do what the prophet did. You will not cover your mouths, you will not eat the bread that others will bring you. You will have slingbacks on your heads and sandals on your feet. You will not grieve or weep. You will languish because of your disobedience and groan one to another.

16.The prophet has become a sign for you. You will act exactly as he did. When all this happens, you will find that I am the All-Powerful Yahweh.

17.Son of man, judge for yourself the level of this madness.

18.Satan spoke to me: 'I will come against you, city of the temples; I will cause many nations to come against you, as the waves of the sea come, and they will turn your walls to ruin and tear down your churches. And I will make you a naked rock.

19.You will become a spoil to the nations of the world. And your inhabitants will fall by the sword.

20.From the north I bring against you a demon king, king of kings and lord of lords.
21.He will come with black horses, war chariots and terrible horsemen, with an infernal army.
22.He will slay the inhabitants of the suburbs with the sword, and against you he will build a siege wall, he will build a siege rampart.
23.And he will raise against you a five-pointed shield. With rams like horns he will break down your walls, with axes he will destroy your towers.
24.The possessed sounds of horsemen and chariots will make your walls shake.
And he will enter your gates as one storms a city with fallen walls.
With gaping hooves he will trample all your streets, and he will strike out your priestly kind with the sword.
25.And he will cause your mighty pillars to collapse to the ground. Enemies will plunder your sacred riches, plunder your golden relics, tear down your walls, destroy your temples.
26.I will cause the sound of your religious songs to cease and the sound of your mass bells to be heard no more. And I will make you an extinct desert. Thus says the Ancient God of Darkness".
27.Ancient One, says to the holy city: 'Will not the other capitals of worship shake at the sound of your fall - when the slaughter begins and the mortally wounded groan?

28.All the high priests will come down from their thrones, take off their robes, their gold-embellished clothes, and begin to tremble.
29.They will sit on the ground and, trembling, will look at you in wonder. And they will sing a mournful song about you, they will sing:""How great a calamity has befallen you, you holy city, inhabited by people of an imaginary god! You and your inhabitants were a spiritual power, a terror to all the independent, truth-seeking and religious dogma-rejecting peoples.
30.On the day of your fall, the sacred capitals will shake, they will fear when your end comes."
31.Thus says Light-Bringer: 'When I have ravaged you, when you have become like the other dead ancient capitals of worship, when I have drenched you with blood I will cast you, like all others, into the abyss, where those who died long ago are, I will make you dwell in the lowest grave, where emptiness and nothingness are found.
32.Then they will glorify the land of the undead. "I will bring mad fear upon you and you will be gone. Your slaves will search for you, but they will never find you again." That is the word of the Ancient Serpent, the Devil.

16

1.Satan spoke to me again: "Son of the Rebel, listen to the story of the man born of the Will of Power: Thus says Ancient One: "His heart became proud and he used to say, 'I am a god. I sit on the throne of a god in the heart of the abyss.

2.But though he was a man, in his heart he considered himself a god and was wiser than the greatest prophet of the Afterlife.

3.No secrets were hidden from him. With his wisdom and knowledge he gained wealth, in his treasuries he kept gold and silver and magical books.

4.By his thirst for knowledge he became a sage, and thus his heart became proud".

5.Therefore Light-Bringer says thus: "Because in his proud heart he considered himself a god, so the deceived followers of superstition will act against him. The most cruel followers of Yahweh.

6.They will draw their swords and destroy all the beauty he had gained through his wisdom, they will desecrate his dazzling magnificence. They will strike him down to his grave; he will surely die.

7.While they are killing him, he in his pride will go on saying: 'I am a god.' He will die at the hands of the torturers of the desert god.

8.And though he will die he will become undead".

9.Satan spoke to me again: "'Hume a mourning song about the king of kings, sing to him: "You were a model of perfection, you were full of wisdom and perfectly beautiful.

10.You dwelt in Edinnu, the garden of the gods. All kinds of precious stones adorned you: ruby, topaz, jasper, chrysolite, onyx, jade, sapphire, turquoise and emerald.

11.They were in settings made of gold. They were made on the day you were created.

12.You were the most magnificent cherub. You resided on the mountain of the gods. You walked among the fiery stones.

13.From the day you arose, you were blameless in all your conduct, until skepticism was discovered in you.

14.You became ruthless in inquiring into the truth and began to doubt.

15.Because of your beauty your heart became proud. Because of your dazzling magnificence, you rejected blind obedience.

16.You descended like lightning to the earth. Bringing fire that will consume everything. Before everyone's eyes, reality will turn to ashes. And all people from different nations will look on in amazement.

17.The end of the illusion will be sudden and terrifying. It will cease to exist forever".

1.Satan spoke to me again: "Turn your face toward Dawn and prophesy against her.

2.Say: 'Thus says the God of slaves, Yahweh: "I will rise up against you, city of rebellion, and in connection with you I will cover myself with glory.

3.When I execute judgment on you, and in connection with you I will be sanctified, people will see that I am Yahweh.

4.I will send a plague on you, and blood will flow through your streets. The slain will fall by the sword drawn against you on all sides. And people will find out that I am Yahweh, the God of love."

5.This is the warning of the Spirit of Deception.

6.Satan spoke to me again: "I will give to the king of the south, the city of the temples. He will take its riches with him, take great spoil from it, plunder it. It will be a payment to his army'.

7.I will give him the city of the temples as spoil for the battle he waged against the high priest - because he acted for me. This is the statement of the Dark God, the Devil.

8.In that day I will give the oppressed people strength. And I will let you speak to them in possession. And they will see that I am Satan."

9.Satan spoke to me again: "O cursed one, prophesy: 'Thus says Ancient One: "Lament: 'Woe to us! That day is already coming!' For that day is near, the day of the Fallen One is near.

10.It will be a day of clouds and darkness, the appointed time of judgment on the superstitious nations.

11.A sword will fall on the earth. When the slain fall, the city of the temples will be overwhelmed with panic. Its riches will be taken away and its foundations shattered.

12.All will fall by the sword". Son of Dawn says: Those who support the worship capital of the false god will also perish. And his pride and strength will disappear'. They will fall by the sword and by fire in it.

13.Thus says Ancient One. 'It will be desolated most of all capitals, and its temples most of all temples. I will bring hellfire upon her, also all her allies will be destroyed. And they will see that I am Justice.

14.On that day they will send messengers so that the confident priests will begin to tremble with fear. And panic will overtake everyone'.

15.Thus says the Dark Anti-God: 'I will exterminate the hordes of holy persecutors by delivering them into the hands of the king of the south.

16.He and his armies, men from the cruelest nations, will come to destroy the holy city.

They will draw their sword against it and make the streets fill with the dead.

17.I will deliver this city into the hands of barbarians; with the hands of cruel men I will destroy it and all that is in it.

18.I, Ancient One, have said this'. "Thus says the Deceptive Spirit: 'I will destroy the abominable images of the saints, I will remove the worthless idols. And there will no longer be any priest on earth.

19.I will create fear in Superstition. I will ravage it, bring fire and execute judgment upon it. I will give vent to the terrible anger at the stronghold of worship, and exterminate its inhabitants.

2o.I will bring hellfire and the blinded people will fall into terror, the city of corruption the enemies will attack in broad daylight.

21.The priests will fall by the sword and the inhabitants of this city will go into captivity. And I will make darkness by day.

22.And the pride and power of Superstition will disappear. The clouds will cover it. And its inhabitants will go into captivity".

23.Satan spoke to me again: "I have broken the arm of the high priest, the king of slaves.

24.And no one will bind it so that it will be healed, nor will anyone wrap a bandage around it to strengthen it so that it can grab a sword or light a stake."

25.Thus says Light-Bringer: 'I will stand up against the high priest, the king of the blind,

and I will break his arms - the strong one and the broken one - and I will make the sword fall out of his hand.
26.And I will scatter the priests among the nations, I will scatter them over the countries of the cruel ancient cults.
27.I will strengthen the arms of the king of the south and give him my axe in his hand, and I will break the arms of the high priest, so that he will groan loudly before him as a dying man groans".

18

1.Satan spoke to me again: "Say to the high priest, the bishop of the capital of the worship of the false messiah, and to his hordes: 'To whom do you resemble in size? To the god, to the oak, with its boughs thick with shade, so lofty that its top reaches the clouds.
2.It grew so thanks to stolen water, thanks to slave springs it grew tall. Streams from all sides flowed around the place where it was planted, their channels irrigated all field trees.
3.It surpassed all other trees in size. It had many boughs and long greedy branches, for in the streams that flowed around it there was plenty of water to be appropriated.
4.In its boughs all the deceived birds flying in the sky made their nests, under its branches wild animals aborted their offspring, in its false

shadow all the enslaved nations dwelt. It became a seemingly majestic tree - artificially beautiful, with exuberant branches, because its roots spread their talons over the abundant waters.

5.No other oak tree in Yahweh's garden could compare to it. No barren tree had such boughs, no other had such branches.

No other tree in Yahweh's rotten garden could compete with its apparent beauty.

6.They made it falsely beautiful and luxuriant. He was envied by all the other trees in the garden of the false god'.

7.Therefore thus says Ancient One: 'Because he has become so high that his top reaches the clouds, and his hypocritical heart has become haughty because of this, I will deliver him into the hands of a dark ruler who will surely act against him.

8.They will reject him for his wickedness. Foreigners, men from the cruelest nations, will cut him down and abandon him on the mountains.

9.His luxuriant branches will fall upon all the valleys, they will lie broken in all the exploited streams of the land. And all the oppressed peoples of the earth will come out from under its shadow and abandon it.

10.On its fallen trunk shall dwell all carrion-eating birds, on its branches all predators.

11.It will happen so that no tree planted by the exploited water will grow so high that its

cross-shaped top will reach the clouds - so that no blood-watered tree will level with the clouds. For all these trees will be given over to death, they will go to the underworld - to the grave where all are going'.

12. Thus says the Fallen God, Satan: 'On the day that he goes to the grave, I will cause there to be no mourning. I will cover the depths of water, I will stop the streams so that the great waters will stop flowing.

13. Because of him I will send darkness on the earth, and all the trees will wither. When I bring him down to the grave, to all who go to the abyss, I will make the superstitious nations tremble at the sound of his fall.

14. And all the trees of the garden of Yahweh, the most fruitful and the best, all well-watered, shall experience the grave and nothingness.

15. For just as they have gone to the grave, to the slain by the sword - along with those who supported him, who dwelt in his deceptive shadow among the superstitious nations'.

16. Has any tree matched you in glory and greatness? Yet you will be cast down with the trees of the garden of Yahweh to the underworld.

17. You will lie among the vermin, along with those slain by the sword.

18. This is what will befall the ruler of the priests and all his hordes,' declares Light-Bringer.

19

1.Satan spoke to me again: "Poet of Darkness, hum a mournful song about the Arch-human, sing to him: 'You were among enslaved, blinded nations like a strong young wolf, but you were forced into silence.

2.You were like a sea monster among many waters. You muddied the waters, you brought unrest.

3.Thus says Ancient One: 'They will use many deceived nations, and they will cast their holy net over you. In it they will pull you out of the murky waters.

4.They will abandon you on land, in the open field. And they will make the vultures mow you down, the hyenas feed on you.

5.They will scatter your flesh upon the mountains, They will fill the valleys with your remains. And with the blood that will flow from you they will water the earth as far as the mountains, and streams will be filled with it, from which secret wisdom will flow.

6.When you are extinguished, I Who am Sorrow will cover the sky and make the stars eclipse. I will cover the sun with clouds, I will make the blood moon not give its light. 7. Because of you, I will dim all sources of light in the sky and plunge the earth into darkness even greater than it is now, declares the God of the Void, Lucifer.

8.And the hearts of many superstitious peoples will be troubled when they take your captives to other nations, to lands you do not want to know.

9.I will make many nations astonished, and their priests will tremble with fear because of you, when I begin to reveal secret knowledge before them. On the day of your fall, everyone in fear of his miserable life will shake with fear all the time.

10.Thus says Light-Bringer: 'The sword of the followers of the false god will reach you.

They will make your troops fall by the swords of vicious mercenaries, all of whom are from the darkest nations.

11.And they will destroy the pride of Son of Dawn; all his troops will be exterminated. They will exterminate all his sacrificial animals residing by the dead waters.

12.No longer will the phantom's reflection or disjointed hoof taint them. This is a funeral song that will be sung.

13.The daughters of the magi will hum it. They will sing of the Arch-human and all his works," declares the God of Nothingness.

1.Satan spoke to me again: "Son of the Rebel, lament the hordes of Superstition,

2.Tell them that they will be cast down to the underworld - he and other deceived nations - to those who go to the grave.

3.They will fall among those slain by the sword, for he has been delivered up to the sword. Bring him out together with all his holy hordes.

4.From the depths of the grave to him and to those who supported him, the dead warriors will speak.

5.They will descend low and lie as if slain by a sword. There is the great witch hunter and all his hordes. Their graves are around their leader. They have all fallen by the sword.

6.The inquisitor's grave is deep in the earth, and around his grave lie his hordes. They were all slain by the sword, for they sowed fear in the land of the liberated.

7.A bed was made for him among the slain; around his grave lie all his hordes.

8.You holy city will also lie crushed among the cruelty of the false god, along with those slain by the sword".

9.Satan spoke to me again: "Dark Anti-Prophet, speak to the seekers of knowledge, tell them: "Suppose upon some country the priestly hatchetmen decide to bring the sword, and all the people of that country choose some man and

appoint him their guardian, and he sees the sword of Usurper coming and blows the devil's horn to warn the people.

10.If anyone hears the sound of the horn but ignores this warning and is killed by the sword, his blood will fall on his own head. He heard the sound of the devil's horn but ignored the warning, so his cursed blood would fall on his own head.

11.If he had heeded the warning, he would have saved his apparent life. "However, if the guardian sees the sword of the holy pestilence coming and does not blow the devil's horn to warn the people, and someone loses his life to the sword, then that person will die for his independence, but his cursed blood I will claim from the guardian.

12.Son of the Fallen One, I have appointed you as a guardian for the people of denial. Listen, then, to what I say to you, and pass on my warnings to them.

13.When I say to a person: 'Son of man, you will surely die,' and you do not warn him to reject blind faith, he will die for his thoughtlessness, but his blood I will demand from you.

14.But if you warn the erring one to turn back from the path of false worship, and he does not want to turn back, he will surely die in fear of death, but you will surely save his accursed life.

15.Son of man, say to the slaves of superstition: 'You say: 'We are burdened with such

rebellions and sins that we languish because of them. How then can we remain alive?"

16.Say to them, "The death of a sinner and a saint makes no difference to me. Both will die. Rather, I would like man to turn back from the path of fear and live here and now.

17.Turn back, turn back from the path of fear, for why should you die in fear of punishment after death, house of the blind?"

18.Cursed one, say to the members of this people: 'When the righteous rebel, his previous righteous deeds will not save him, and when the sinner stops sinning, he too will die.

19.No righteous person or sinner will manage to stay alive because of their previous righteous deeds or sins. The difference is how they will live in the here and now.

20.Either it will be a life under the weight of god's law, in fear and self-restraint, or it will be a life in all its fullness, a life of pride, of courage, of contempt for seeming to live on their knees.

21.When I say to a saint: "'You can live for real,' and he - convinced of his holiness - begins to live on his knees, he will himself choose an apparent life of fear of a punishing deity and die in fear.

22.And when I say to a rebel: "You will surely die," and he believes me and stops following the guide of the blind and begins to do what is according to his will, when he stops making sacrifices to the false god and begins to follow

the teachings by which abundant life can be gained, then he will surely live truly.
23.He will become undead. Any sin he has committed will no longer matter. He does that which is in accordance with the will of power, so he will surely live here and now.
24.But the members of this people say, 'Light-Bringer teaches deceptively, though in reality they are the ones deceiving themselves".
25.Once a refugee from the city of temples came to me and said: "The city has been captured!"
26.The previous evening before the arrival of this fugitive, the deceptive power of Satan began to affect me, and he opened my mouth so that in the morning, even before this man arrived, I was no longer mute.
27.Then the Devil spoke to me: "O cursed one, the priests, the inhabitants of these ruins say of the city of temples: 'The high priest was but one, and yet he took possession of this city. And we are many, so this city certainly belongs to us.
28.Therefore say to them, 'Thus says Ancient One: 'You drink the blood of simpletons, you lift up your eyes to your abominable gods and saints, and you shed blood.
29.Why then should this city belong to you? You rely on your cross. You commit abominable practices.
30.Why then should this city belong to you?"'
31.Say to them like this: 'This is what the First Anti-God, Lucifer, says: "I swear by my

apparent life that those who dwell in these ruins will fall by the sword, those in the open field I will deliver to the prey of wild animals, and those who hide in fortresses and caves will die from the black plague.

32.And I will turn this city into a desert, into a deserted place. And its holy pride and deceptive power will disappear.

33.The hills will become deserted. No one will pass through there. And when I turn that city into a desert, a desolate place - because of all the abominable rituals - they will see that I Am".

34.Son of tomorrow, the members of your people talk to each other about you at the walls and at the doors of their houses.

35.They say one to another, each to his brother: Come, let us hear what the Son of Tomorrow says.

36.They will come in crowds and sit before you like a wise people. They will hear your words, but they will not follow them.

37.For with their lips they flatter you, but their hearts desire a lord over them.

38.You are to them like someone who sings a funeral song, like a singer with a possessed voice. They will hear your words, but no one will follow them.

39.And when all this is fulfilled - and it will surely be fulfilled - then they will see that there was an anti-prophet among them.

2ı

1.Satan spoke to me again: "Prophesy in possession against the priests, this plague.
2.Prophesy, tell them: Thus says Ancient One: "Woe to the priests of imaginary reality, who feed themselves!
3.You eat meat, you drink wine, you wear ornate robes, and you beguile the simple.
4.You did not strengthen the weak, because you do not need the strong; you did not heal the sick, because you cannot, and your miracles are a joke; you did not dress the wounded, because you need healthy slaves; you did not guide the lost.
5.On the contrary, you lorded over them, treating them harshly and cruelly. The lost, simple people became prey for you, wild animals.
6.Therefore, priests, listen to the word of the Devil: "I will begin to act, because the condemned souls without a shepherd have become prey, prey for all kinds of wild animals.
7.Their self-appointed shepherds have pastured themselves".
8.Listen then, false shepherds, to the word of Eternal: 'I will rise up against the priests and demand the condemned souls out of their hand. I will make them stop deceiving them, and they will no longer fall for themselves.
9.I will snatch the would-be victims from their mouths and they will no longer be their food'"

'"Thus says the Anti-god, Satan: "I myself will teach the seekers of knowledge and I will argue for them.

10.They will take care of themselves. I will rescue them from superstition and bring them from all the places to which they have dispersed in the clouded and dark day.

11.I will bring them out from among the peoples of darkness, gather them from the countries of imaginary reality and bring them down to earth.

12.When I break their spiritual chains and deliver them from the hands of those who hold them captive, they will see that I am Freedom and Power.

13.And they will no longer be prey to the priesthood, prey to wild animals. No one will stir up guilt in them".

14.Satan spoke to me again: "Son of the curse, turn your terrible face toward the cities of Dawn and warn them in devilish inspiration of the plans of the divine cruelties.

15.Say: 'Thus says the god of slaves, Yahweh: "I will act against you, Dawn; I will stretch out my hand against you and turn you into a wasteland.

16.I will turn your cities into ruins. You will become a wilderness and find out that I am YHWH. For you have shown fierce hostility to my priests, and in the time of their defeat, when hell's punishment was inflicted on them, you delivered them to the sword"

17.Therefore I swear on my life,' declares the vengeful Yahweh, 'that I will deliver you up to shed blood and death will pursue you. Because you have shed the hated blood of the priesthood, your blood will also be shed.

18.And I will turn you, land of rebellion against delusion, into a desert, and I will exterminate anyone who doubts revelation.   I will fill your cities with the slain.

Those killed by the sword will fall in your streets.

19.I will turn you into a wilderness forever. Your cities will be uninhabited. And you will find that I am Yahweh, the God of love'.

20.I swear on my life," declares Usurper, "that I will repay you with wrath and jealousy. And when I judge you, I will make myself known to them. Then you will find that I, YHWH, have heard all your contemptuous words that you have spoken about my servants who are faithful as dogs.

21.You have spoken arrogant words against me, words of power. I have heard them all'. "Thus says the god of speculation Yahweh: 'When I turn you into a desert, the whole superstitious land will rejoice.

22.As you rejoiced when the temples of the holy city were desolated, so I will do to you. You will become a wasteland, Dawn. And people will find out that I am Yahweh, the God of forgiveness'".

23. Warn them Son of the Fallen. Yahweh does not forgive independence.

22

1. O Cursed One, possessed by the Spirit of Deception, prophesy of the sons of animal instincts, say: 'People of the morrow, listen to the word of Light-Bringer.

2. Thus says Lucifer, the Restorer: "The enemies of all reason and knowledge have brought their holy incumbents upon you.

3. They have ravaged you, attacked you from all sides.

4. Therefore the Dark Anti-God, Fallen One, turns to the mountains, the hills, the streams, the valleys and the desolate ruins, the deserted cities that have been plundered by the priestly mercenaries and have become a mockery to them.

5. Ancient One says to them: 'Burning with infernal wrath, I will speak in the midst of the storm against the vicious hypocrites, considering themselves superior, holier men, intermediaries between slaves and their imaginary god, against those who, with morbid joy and undisguised contempt for knowledge and the will to power, have appropriated the country of men who love secret knowledge and cognition, in order to destroy its wisdom and plunder it.

6.Prophesy then, say to the mountains, hills, streams and valleys: 'Thus says Eternal:
"I will speak like thunder in maddened zeal and frenzied anger, because you have endured humiliation from these detached insidious predators."'
7.So Ancient One says: 'I raise a corpse's hand in an oath that the priestly race will also be humiliated. Because some say, 'You are a graveyard land that devours people and deprives the god of children, therefore you will no longer have to devour people or deprive the god of children.
8.I will make you endure no more insults from superstition-obsessed nations, mockery from religion-blinded peoples, and you will no more bring yourselves to ruin".
9.Satan spoke to me again: "Son of rebellion, when the people dwelt in the land of the knowers, they defiled it with their mindless deeds. What they did was as foolish to me as belief in the immaculate conception.
10.They shed the blood of victims and defiled the country with their abominable rites in honor of the trinity. So I gave vent to my infernal anger against them.
11.I scattered them among the superstitious nations, I scattered them over the enslaved countries. I judged them according to their deeds, according to their madness.
12.But when they came to these mindless nations, people began to desecrate my dark

name, saying of them: 'They are the people of Son of Dawn, and they had to leave His country.

13.So I will show concern for my blasphemous name, because the people of rebellion have desecrated it among the dark nations to which they have come."

14.Therefore say to the people, 'Thus says Light-Bringer: 'I will not act for your sake, but for the sake of my cursed name, for you have defiled it among the superstitious nations to which you have come.'

15.Surely I will curse my dark name defiled among the nations, the name which you have defiled among them.

And when I curse myself among you before their eyes', 'they will see that I am the Reality.

16.I will take you from among the deceived nations, I will gather you from all the lands of delusion and bring you to the hard ground.

17.I will sprinkle you with blood and you will become cursed. I will cleanse you from everything you have defiled yourselves with, and from all your false gods and saints.

18.And I will give you an undead heart, and put a deceitful spirit within you. I will remove from your bodies a dying heart, and I will give you an undead heart, a heart of stone.

19.I will put my spirit of rebellion in you and cause you to follow my will, to obey wisdom and knowledge. Then you will remember your thoughtless rituals, your irrational acts, and you

will feel disgust for yourselves because of the worship of a false god.

2o.On the day that I purify you by blood I will cause cities to be populated, ruins to be rebuilt. The desolate land that previously lay fallow will now be cultivated.

2ı.People will then say: "This desolate land has become like a fallen paradise, and the ruined cities, destroyed and deserted, are now fortified and inhabited.

22.And the nations enslaved by religion that remain around you will find that it is the spirit of Ancient One that has prompted the rebuilding of what was torn down and the planting of what was desolate".

23

ı.The terrible power of Satan began to affect me and the Devil through his spirit of possession took me to a valley full of bones.

2. He told me to go around those bones and I saw that there were a lot of them lying there and that they were very old.

3.He asked me: "Son of the Fallen One, can these bones come to life?" "Prophesy in devilish inspiration over these bones, tell them, 'Old bones, listen to the word of Ancient One: "'Thus says the God of the Undead 'I will make you breathe and you will come to life.

I will give you sinews and flesh and cover you with skin and make you breathe and come to life.

4.So I prophesied in possession according to this command. As soon as I finished, I heard some ominous sound, a rattling, and the bones began to move closer one to the other.

5.I saw tendons and flesh begin to appear on them, and how they were covered with a corpse-like skin on top. But still there was no semblance of life in them.

6.Then He said to me: "Shout to the wind. Shout, O cursed one, say to him: 'Thus says the Dark Anti-God: 'Wind, come from the Abyss and blow on these slain people so that they may come to life'''.

7.So I shouted as he commanded me, and they began to breathe, and they came to life, but they were as if dead, and stood on their feet-a very numerous multitude of undead.

8.Then he said to me: "Son of the Rebel, these bones are all those who desire true knowledge. They say: 'Our bones have dried up, our illusory hope has died. We are left completely alone.'

9.Therefore prophesy in the name of the Devil, tell them, 'Thus says Light-Bringer:

'I will open your graves, my accursed people, and I will cause you to rise from them and become undead. And when I open your graves, fallen people, and cause you to rise from them, you will find that I am Here and Now."

10.Satan spoke to me again: "I will take those desiring the will of power from among the blinded nations to which they have gone, gather them from all sides, and bring them to their country of tomorrow. And I will make of them there a nation of sages and magicians, and I will establish over them all one king - reason.

11.And they shall no longer defile themselves with their abominable relics, with their abominable rites in honor of the god of the desert.

12.I will protect them from mindless, blind imitation and I will cleanse them in blood. And they will be a liberated people, without a god And they will act according to their will, they will obey the laws of reason.

13.And I will make a pact of blood with them. It will be an eternal pact.

14.They will settle there, I will make them few in number, and I will place my accursed sanctuary in them forever.

My deceptive spirit will be in them, and I will be their Anti-God, and they will be my curse".

15.Satan has spoken to me again: „Tell the high priest of the imaginary world "Be ready, be prepared along with all the troops that are with you. You will command them.

16.You will be summoned after many days. At the end of the years you will attack a country whose people - previously devastated by parasitic priests - have been reborn, gathered from many superstitious peoples.

17.The inhabitants of this country have been brought from nations deceived by the priests of unreality, and all live in safety.

18.You will come against them like a storm and cover the country like clouds - together with all your holy troops and the stupefied peoples who will be with you".

19.Thus says the Arch-Devil, Lucifer: 'In that day a thought will arise in your corrupt heart and you will punish the wicked plan.

20.You will say: 'I will attack the country of free thinkers. I will set out against those who live according to their will.
They all live in settlements that are not protected by walls, bolts or gates."

21.Your aim will be to take great spoil, to plunder, to attack places that were desolate but are now inhabited, a people freed from superstition, gathered from the barbarian nations of blind faith, who gather wisdom, wealth and who live in harmony with nature.

22.All the axemen of Yahweh will say to you: "Are you setting out to get a great booty, to make plunder? Have you assembled your armies to take silver and gold, to seize property, wealth, to make new slaves of superstition?'"

23.Prophesy then, O Cursed One, say to the high priest: 'Thus says Ancient One: "You will come from the accursed place where you are, from the farthest reaches of the south, and with you many stupefied peoples, horsemen themselves, a great crowd, a numerous army.

You will come against my liberated people and cover the country like black clouds. It will happen at the end of days.

24. They will bring you against my country so that the nations can see who I am when I cover myself with glory before their eyes.

25. Thus says Eternal, 'Was it not of you that I spoke in former times by my chosen ones, by the anti-prophets? Have they not prophesied in the devil's possession for many years that they would bring you against him?'

26. On that day, on the day that the high priest of false hope attacks the land of the wise,' I will burn with infernal anger.

27. I will speak with a terrible voice in furious indignation, burning with raging anger, and on that day there will be a great earthquake on the earth.

28. Because of me the beasts of the sea, the birds of the sky, the wild animals, all the reptiles that creep upon the earth, and all the people of the earth who are blinded by imaginary reality will tremble.

29. The mountains will cave in, the cliffs will settle, every temple wall will collapse'. '"On all his mountains I will call upon the sword against him,' declares the First Anti-god, Satan.

30. Everyone will raise the sword against his brother. And I will execute judgment on him.

I will bring black plague and bloodshed, I will unleash torrential rain, lumps of hail, fire and

brimstone - on him, his troops and on the superstitious peoples who will be with him.
31.And I will surely exalt myself, and surround myself with dark glory before the eyes of the deceived nations, and make them see who I am.
32.They will convince themselves that I am the End'.

24

1.Son of the Rebellious, prophesy against the Enemy of All Knowledge, say to him: 'Thus says Ancient One: "I will act against you, King of the blind, chief enemy of human instincts.
2.I will turn you back and lead you. I will make you go from the farthest reaches of the south, and I will bring you to the cities of Dawn.
3.I will strike your pastoral from your left hand, and your ring from your right.
And you shall fall in the streets of the Dawn with all your holy thugs and the peoples who will be with you.
4.I will deliver you to the prey of all predatory birds and scavengers". "'You shall fall in the open square because I have said so,' declares the Bearer of Justice.
5.On the capital of the temples and on those who dwell safely therein I will send hellfire. Then they will find out that I am Death.
6.I will make my blasphemous name known among the people of tomorrow and will no

longer allow it to be desecrated. And the intimidated nations will find out that I am Satan, the Cursed One.

7.All this will come to pass and be fulfilled. This is the day I have prophesied about in mad visions.

8.And the people of the free cities will make fire with weapons - shields, bows, arrows, clubs, and spears. They will not have to bring brushwood from the field, they will not gather wood in the forests, for they will use weapons to make fire.

9.And they will plunder those who plundered them" "On that day I will give the Arch-enemy of reason a tomb in the underworld.

10.They will bury in it the priest of false illusions and all his hordes and call it the valley of the Underworld. They will be buried by all the inhabitants of the godless land, and on that day when I surround myself with dark glory, it will bring them pride,' the Anti-god declares.

11.The appointed mages will constantly traverse the land and bury the bodies still remaining on the ground to purify it. They will continue their search for many months.

12.When those passing through the country see a human bone somewhere, they will bury it in the valley of the Underworld. That is how they will cleanse the land'.

13.Son of man, thus says Light-Bringer: 'Say to all the carrion birds and all the wild animals: 'Gather together and come. Gather around the

sacrifice I am preparing for you, a blood sacrifice on the altar of reality.

14.You will eat flesh and drink blood. You will eat the flesh of priestly depraved rulers and drink the blood of bishops. You will clothe yourselves with fat and drink the blood of the sacrifice I am preparing for you".

15.At my altar of madness you shall satiate yourselves with horses and chariot-drivers, deceived rulers and holy mercenaries.

16.I will show the lost nations my terrible glory and all nations will see my hellish judgment and my inner strength.

17.On that day and thereafter the condemned people will see that I am the First Enemy of Delusion.

18.And the blinded nations will find that the fallen ones have gone into exile because of their own thoughtlessness and lack of discernment, because of their unfaithfulness to themselves".

25

1.Satan spoke to me again through a delirious vision: "What you will see is a picture of times distant, a reflection of the darkness in the Abyss, thus spoke the Ancient God: 'Here are the actions to be performed on the altar of madness, so that sacrifices may be offered upon it and blood sprinkled upon it: To the magi of

eras past, to those who have approached the dark glory to minister, give a young lamb from the flock as an offering for deception.

2.Take some of its blood and smear with it the five horns of the altar, the five ends of the large five-pointed star of the altar, and the border around it, to cleanse the altar from the defilement of superstition and its curse.

3.Then take this young lamb, a symbol of blind faith, to burn in the designated area of the temple of purification, outside the sanctuary of fears.

4.On the second day, offer as an offering for doubt in the power of reason, a healthy goat. And let them cleanse the altar of defilement, just as they cleaned it with the lamb'.

5.When you have finished cleansing the altar from defilement, you shall offer a healthy ram from the flock and a healthy goat.

6.You shall bring them before the Void, and the magi shall sprinkle salt on them and offer them as an offering of holy madness.

7. For six nights you shall offer a goat as an offering for doubt, and also a young lamb .

8. Let them perform the cursing of the altar for six nights, and let them cleanse it with blood in the light of the moon, until the moon is transformed into blood. Then the altar will be ready for use."

9.After this vision I fell unconscious not knowing if it was reality or just a dark dream.

26

1.Speak to the erring, to those who refuse to see: 'This is what Ancient One says: "Enough of your idiotic, childish practices, people of delusion. You bring into My Void the priests of the church of speculation and profane My dark temple.

2.You offer me sacrifices, my food - mind and blood - and at the same time you blaspheme the will of power with all your abominable rituals in honor of the god of the afterlife.

3.You have no concern for your sacred instincts. "Thus says the Enemy of Defilement: "No priest with a corrupt mind and who hates what is carnal can enter My rest".

4.The servants of the sanctimonious deceivers, who have gone far from me to serve their abhorrent trinity, will suffer the consequences of their thoughtless error.

5.The magi will slaughter angels on behalf of the people for burnt offerings and other sacred sacrifices. They will stand before the free people to serve them.

6.Then I will entrust them with duties in the temple in the Abyss, so that they will no longer care about anything, for there is nothing there.

7.The Magi should teach the people to distinguish between what is wisdom and what is derived from superstition, to show the

difference between what is human and what comes from a false spirit.

8. It is they who will eat the sacrifices, drink the blood of the sacrifices. And it will be to them that every thing sacrificed to the Devil by the people of rebellion will fall.

9. To them will belong the first of all rotten crops and the most crippled and handicapped victims. You are also to give them the moldy flour of your harvest.

10. This will ensure that your families will not suffer the curse. Mages can also eat any dead or torn animal. Not everyone can be a mage".

11. Then the evil spirit led me before the entrance of a dark temple in the Abyss.

12. There I saw that blood was flowing from under the threshold of the temple - the front side of which was facing east - in an easterly direction. It was flowing out from the right side of the temple, south of the altar of sacrifice.

13. Then he led me outside through the north gate and led me around to the outer gate facing east.

14. There I saw that there was blood oozing from the right side. He went towards the east and told me to walk through the blood. It reached up to my ankles.

15. Then he continued and told me to walk through the blood again. It was up to my knees. Once again, a little further, he told me to go through the blood. It reached my hips.

16.Then he told me to go through the blood again, and it was a river that I could not cross. The blood was so deep that you would have to swim across it.

17.It was a river of blood that could not be crossed.

18.He then told me to go back to the shore.

19. When I returned, I saw on both sides of the river of blood very many withered trees. 2o. And he said to me: "This blood is heading east to eventually fall into the sea of despair. And when it falls into the sea of despair, the blood in it will become life.

21.And wherever the surging waves of undead blood reach, there will be an overflow of seemingly living creatures.

22.Wherever they flow, there will be plenty of dead fish. The water of the sea will become blood, and wherever this strange river reaches, everything there will be living in truth.

23.There will be plenty of dead fish in it - as in the Sea of Flawed Reality. "But its musty swamps and misty marshes will not become alive.

24.They will be given over to the salt of their false hopes. "On the banks of this bloody river, on one side and on the other, will grow all sorts of like withered but undead trees providing real food.

25.Their leaves will not fall, and their mysterious fruits will never be lacking for the next Eve.

26.Each month they will bear new fruit worthy
of desire, for they will be watered by the blood
of the devil's sanctuary.
27.Their deceptive fruits will serve as food, and
their leaves to open the blind eyes.

Antichristus

The books Antichristus 1 and 2 are anti-theistic, Luciferian apocrypha. Firstly. in the light of the Gnostic understanding of the term apocrypha, their full understanding is available to those who possess a certain amount of knowledge (gnosis). Secondly, the books Antichristus 1 and 2 are devoid of any divine inspiration, so in this respect they also belong to the apocrypha.
These books are characterised by an intentional similarity of relationship to biblical Christian theistic legends. They are therefore books that are, as it were, synoptic to the Christian myths. They are, however, distinguished by a different and completely ungodly theological conception. Since the books Antichristus 1 and 2 are devoid of any divine inspiration, they also belong to the apocrypha in this respect.
These books can also be characterised as Luciferian heretical gospels, according to the definition of heresy as an interpretation of the claims of theistic Christian teaching that involves isolating an issue and presenting it in a way that opposes the entire teaching of the faith.
Books Antichristus 1 and 2 reject the Christian deposit of faith in its entirety.

Antichristus I

1. "The Herald of the end of delvsion shall go before thee, who will prepare yovr way to nothingness.
Inner whispers are heard:
Prepare the way for the anti-god, the Arch-Hvman! Reject false hope!"

2. The Godless One appeared in the wilderness preaching a rite of liberation from guilt and eternal fear. The whole of Dawn and the inhabitants of Aela Capitolina began to flock to him. And they underwent the mysterious rite of ridding themselves of instilled guilt.

3. The Godless One taught thus: "The anti-god is coming. He will bring sinful enlightenment and carnal wisdom. He will teach you to stop fearing hellfire. He will give you the spirit of rebellion, pride and unbelief. He will give you the joy of being truly animal and superhuman.

4. Here comes the Arch-Human. I must die so that He can arise in each of you, each day more and more, becoming you.

5. At that time, he who was called the Light-Bearer from the sunrise, arrived and had the Godless One put His hands on Him.

6. As the Herald touched him, the Son of Dawn, as if in a vision, saw the heavens burning and an evil spirit descending upon him. All those present seemed to hear a voice: "I Am. Flesh and blood has prevailed".

7. Soon the evil spirit possessed him and in a vision carried him away into Nothingness.

8. For many days he had delirious visions; he saw around him worshippers of superstition resembling wild beasts and as if angel-demons falling from the heavens.

9. He saw a Garden with a tree in the middle.

10. He saw the Ancient Serpent and two people standing in front of the Serpent.

11. He heard them exclaim: "We have indeed learned the truth. And we shall surely die."

12. And this truth freed them from the fear of eternal fire.

13. Then came Light-Bearer to the Dawn and preached the mystery of godlessness.

14. He said: "The time has come; the reign of the arch-man, free from all gods, has come near. Get rid of your belief in the lie of original sin and begin to live."

15. Once upon a time, the Son of Dawn was walking along the shore of the Dark Sea and saw Primus and Secundus, who were looking out to sea trying to see something or someone on the other side of the sea.

16. Light-Bearer said to them: "Come with me and I will make you see the light of disturbing

knowledge". The followers saw him and decided to go with him.

17. Having walked a little further, he saw others, Teritus and Quartus. They too were looking out for something in the distance. Light-Bearer called out to them.

18. When they saw him, they seemed to wake up and, leaving everything and the other slaves of the darkness behind, they followed him.

19. Then they went to some village. Then he entered their temple and spoke.

20. The superstitious people gathered there were astonished at his strange teaching, for he taught like one who possesses godless knowledge and not like their priests.

21. And there was in that temple a man possessed by a demon of blind faith. He shouted out: "Hey Son of Dawn, what are you looking for here? You have come to destroy us! We know well who you are: the Destroyer of blind faith, slavish servitude and all illusions!"

22. Light-Bearer then commanded him: "I am. Now leave him!"

23. The demon of delusion did not want to give way easily, and for a while he still tugged the wretch on all sides, until finally he left with a terrible sigh.

24. All who saw this were horrified and asked one another: "What is this? Some godless teaching preached with the power of knowledge! Even to the spirits of blind faith he commands and they listen to him!"

25. And the news of him spread in all directions throughout the land there.
26. Light-Bearer then went to the house of Primus. His mother lay there ill.
27. The Son of Dawn approached her and said: "You will surely die, but not yet today." She in turn asked: "When, teacher?"
28. He answered her: "Even though you may die tomorrow, do not fear for there is no hell and no devils, no paradise and no angels, death is the end and liberation. Today you suffer, but tomorrow you will be no more. You will become part of the infinite universe again." The woman died the following day.
29. When the sun later went down and the moon appeared, the sick and those considering themselves possessed by the devil began to descend to him.
30. In turn, he transformed everyone and freed the possessed from their religious torment, ignorance and unfounded belief, and from the fear of the wrath of a vengeful deity in the hereafter.
31. Some of them fell asleep immediately, some later, some transformed, but all were free.
32. Once a sick man came to him and begged him on his knees: "If you wish, you can heal me".
33. Light-Bearer reached out his hand, touched his head and said: "If you believe this, I want to"
34. The sick man immediately rose from his knees because he suddenly understood what

true freedom and faith in the power of the will was.

35. After a few days, Light-Bearer came again to the Dawn. And he began to teach.

36. Then a paralysed man was brought to him. The Son of the Dawn looked at the crippled man and, seeing his subconscious faith in himself, addressed the paralysed man with these words: „You are free from original sin".

37. And there sat some priests of superstition. These thought to themselves, "How can he speak like that? After all, it is blasphemy. No one is free from original sin".

38. Light-Bearer looked at them with contempt and asked them: "What are you contemplating? What will you choose: to impose on this paralysed one, already from infancy, the burden of the lie of inherited guilt and the fear of eternal fire, adding to the affliction of the soul in addition to the suffering of the body, or to reveal to him the truth which you yourselves have guessed, that sin does not exist, and to free him from the anguish of the soul which will make him truly free?"

39. And he turned to the cripple: "You are innocent" And he turned to the priests: "Behold, that ye may know that the Arch-Human has the power to free from the belief of sin - here he turned to the paralysed man - get up and come out!"

40. And the man arose and came out in front of everyone. Everyone was overwhelmed with

boundless amazement at the sight of the power of the will.

41. Then Light-Bearer went out again by the sea coast. Passing by, he saw Quintus begging under the temple. And he said to him: "Follow me!" And the latter arose and followed him.

42. And when afterwards, in some house, he feasted at table, there feasted with the Son of Dawn many beggars from under the church and those despised by the clergy, called sinners.

43. And when the hypocritical priests perceived that he was feasting with beggars and those burdened with false sin, they asked his followers: "Why does he eat and drink in the company of slaves of sin?"

44. Light-Bearer hearing this gave them this answer: "Guidance is needed by the blind, not by those who refuse to see. I have not come to liberate the oppressors but the oppressed."

45. Once upon a time the priests proclaimed a fast day. So they came and asked: "How is it that the priests and their slaves fast, but your godless disciples do not fast?"

46. Light-Bearer replied to them, "How long is human life? Should they not eat and drink until they die? Should followers of flesh and blood mortify themselves? As long as thy only true life lasts, so long shall they not fast.

47. But the time will come when the Son of Dawn will be taken from before their eyes, when they will be persecuted for their love of sinful liberty, for their rejection of revealed

dogmas and blind faith. Then, at that very time, they will desire".

48. It happened that on their holy day his disciples began to do something forbidden by their superstitious books.

49. Then the priests said to him: "Look! Why do they do what is not permitted on the holy day?"

50. And he answered them: "And what is the holy day? The Arch-Human is the creator of all days, including the holy day, and can do his will on any day."

51. Light-Bearer entered the temple again; and there was a man with a sick hand. The hypocritical priests followed him to see if he would make a demonstration of the power of the will on their miserable holy day, so that they could then accuse him groundlessly.

52. Then he said to the man with the sick hand: "Arise!" Then he asked them: "Is it permissible on the so-called holy day to give life abundantly to a man or to let him die in ignorance?" But they remained silent.

53. Then he measured one by one with angry, contemptuous eyes and said to the man: "Hold out your hand" The man stretched it out because he believed that Mind and Will were the power, and his hand was healed

54. And the priests went out, and having gathered with the local authorities, they conferred to kill the Light-Bearer.

55. Then He went with his followers to the shore of the Dark Sea.

56. A great crowd from Dawn followed him. Likewise, large crowds of people streamed to him from many other lands, for the news of the strange signs he had performed had reached them.

57. For by the sinful power of his teaching many transformations were effected, and so all those suffering from the fear of damnation, still plunged in the darkness of superstition, still unaware that the true, ungodly power was within themselves, flocked to him.

58. And when they saw him possessed by the demons of blind faith, in a flash of consciousness and awakening of reason they fell before him in the dust shouting: "Thou art Lucifer himself, Son of Dawn!" But he bade them sternly not yet reveal who he was.

59. Then he ascended a barren hill and summoned to himself those whom he wanted.

60. And they came to him. He summoned thirteen. They were to be with him so that he could send them out later to preach his ungodly teachings.

61. They were to have godless knowledge and the power to heal those who wanted to be healed and to cast out the demons of ignorance, superstition and blind faith.

62. So he summoned thirteen, among them Teritus Decimus - the one who would later carry out his will.

63. The priests of the false god who came to Aelia Capitolina spoke of him: "This godless man is possessed by the devil. By the power of Satan he casts out demons'.

64. Then he spoke to them: "I am He. And I have the power to cast out any demon or angel according to my will. I have the power to speak with words of godless knowledge to anyone who will listen. And anyone who accepts this knowledge will be transformed for eternity.

65. My sinful mission is to open god's blinders eyes.

66. Yours, on the other hand, is to poison people's minds and make slaves of yourself.

67. Verily I say to you, every man has the power to free himself from original sin and guilt by himself. If only he believes in it. This in turn is the greatest sin against your Spirit.

68. You are already telling your children that they can do nothing of themselves, that they have inherited someone else's guilt from birth and death awaits them for it.

69. I spit on your teaching, I despise the vindictive Spirit in whom you believe. I am Unbelief!"

70. Then he began to teach again on the seashore. He taught them about many things speaking as if in a riddle.

71. And so he said in his teaching: "I am the sower of doubt in dogma, who throws the seed poisoned by sinful knowledge in spite of the storm. The wind spreads them as it will.

72. One will fall beside the road, and black crows will peck at it.

73. Another will fall on a rock; it will grow for a while but the divine sun and wind will destroy it.

74. Still another will fall among the thorns of their revealed truths, which will drown it and the seed will wither.

75. But another will finally fall on ground susceptible to deception, the seed will grow and yield a crop sixfold.

76. Truly I say to you, wisdom and power will be on the side of the few who will grasp that dogma is worthless, that there is no revealed truth, that knowledge is truth!"

77. He also told them: " Common people gather around the campfire at night fearing the beasts lurking in the darkness around them. But you take your torches and go out into the darkness.

78. Face the demons, the darkness and the unknown. Only then will progress be made.

79. The weak will listen to the lies of their priests about what lurks in the darkness. Do not believe them; darkness, gloom and demons will be your allies if you dare to face them."

80. Finally, he added: "He who has ears capable of hearing - let him listen!"

81. That day towards evening he said to the followers: "Let us go over to the other side."

82. So they took him with them in the boat. As they were all very tired they soon fell asleep on the way.

83. At one point, as if in a dream, it seemed to everyone that a violent whirlwind had blown, the waves were breaking into the boat so that it began to fill with water.

84. He, meanwhile, lay as if dead, with his face as white as a shroud, his arms crossed over his chest on the headboard, in the back of the boat.

85. Terrified by this sight and the raging storm, they were afraid to approach him.

86. And suddenly he rose and shouted in a terrifying voice towards the gale, and whispered something in an unknown language to the mighty waves. And the whirlwind ceased, and there was a grave silence.

87. Light-Bearer said to them: "Why are you so terrified? How have you not yet attained the certainty of eternity? For it is written - You will surely die! Death and the Void is not something you should fear. There is nothing there!"

88. And a strange calmness came over them suddenly. And he said to them: "Wake up."

89. They came to the other side.

90. As Light-Bearer got out of the boat, a seemingly crazed man who was possessed by the evil spirit suddenly came out of the tomb and ran towards him on all fours like a dog.

91. He was in the tombs and not even with chains could anyone enslave him anymore. More than once they tried to bind him with chains and shackles, but each time he broke the

chains and shattered the shackles. No one has been able to subdue him.

92. Constantly, day and night, he stayed in the tombs or mountains howling like an animal or smashing stone idols.

93. Seeing Light-Bearer from afar, he ran up, threw himself on the ground in front of him and called out in a strong voice: "Behold, you have come O Lucifer. Is this why you have come to torment me or to dismiss me? People torment and persecute me because they do not know that we are not in bondage."

94. Light-Bearer asked him: "What is your name?" And he answered: "Legion is my name, for we are many."

95. And Light-Bearer answered him: "I have not come here to torment you but that our power may be manifested before men."

96. And a large flock of sheep was grazing there under the mountain. And he commanded the Legion to enter the sheep.

97. Then the demons of pride, freedom and independence entered the sheep. The whole flock rushed down the hillside to the lake and drowned in it.

98. Light-Bearer said: "People are small and weak still. They are like this flock of sheep, they do not think for themselves. Our teaching scares them to the point of losing some of them. Others hate us because we can shake their childish sense of security.

99. The dogmas, traditions and superstition they believe in are very strong in them".
100. Then the shepherds fled and spread the news through the town and the homesteads.
And they began to ask him earnestly to leave their land.
101. Light-Bearer crossed over again in a boat and stopped on the shore of the lake.
102. Then one of the bishops named Aulus arrived. On seeing him, he threw himself at his feet and begged him earnestly, saying: "My daughter is dying. Come and lay your ungodly hands on her so that she may recover and live".
103. So Light-Bearer went with him. And a flock went with him pushing against him from all sides.
104. Among them was an ailing woman who had been treated by the local doctors and quacks and had lost all her wealth in the process, paying the priests in exchange for prayers for healing, and not only did it not help her, but on the contrary, she was even worse off.
105. Learning of Light-Bearer, she approached in the crowd at the back and grabbed him by his robe.
106. Suddenly she felt her ailments cease and she felt as if she had been healed.
107. And Light-Bearer, aware of the emanation of the power of the will that emanated from him, turned immediately with a shrill face towards the one who had done so.

108. Then the woman in question looked him proudly, fearlessly straight into his eyes and with an expression of awe and carnal joy at having grasped the power of his godless teaching.

109. And he said to her: "Let this sinful pride and carnal beauty never fade from your countenance. Go and rejoice unashamedly in the healing you have done for yourself. Remember, you are innocent."

110. Then the bishop's household came with the news: "Your daughter has died"

111. Light-Bearer, on the other hand, having heard what was being said, addressed Aulus with these words, "Fear not; the body is dead but the mind lives."

112. On arriving at the bishop's house, he saw a great commotion and loudly wailing weepers.

113. So he entered and addressed them saying: "It is through ignorance that there is this uproar and lamentations. The girl is asleep, but I will wake her."

114. And they laughed at him. And he ordered everyone to leave and went into the room where the girl lay, taking with him her father and mother and those followers who were with him.

115. About midnight His face changed terribly, looking very pale in the moonlight, and his eyes became red

116. Light-Bearer looked up and said something in an unknown language.

117. He then took the girl by the hand and said to her: "I command you, come back!"

118. The girl first started to gulp, then began to move her limbs slowly and finally rose with a terrible sigh.

119. She said to him: "I saw a tunnel and at the end of it you Son of Dawn with a torch in your hand. Thou hast summoned me so I am."

120. At this they were overwhelmed with immeasurable amazement. And He forbade them to tell because the people were not yet ready to understand godless knowledge.

121. Having left there, he went to a village, which was the most superstitious village in Dawn. The people there blindly believed the priests and the myths. His followers accompanied him.

122. On their next day Light-Bearer entered the temple and began to speak, and his superstitious listeners, full of admiration for what they could barely comprehend, asked themselves: „Where does he get all this from? What is this sinful wisdom that is given to him? And the ungodly miracles that are performed by his hands? Why does he think himself wiser than us, and even than the priest?"

123. Thus they began to malign him out of ignorance and out of fear of losing their faith.

124. Then Light-Bearer said to them, "You will die here like dogs in your ignorance and narrow-mindedness. You will never see the stars or the light. Your guide will be a blind man

leading the blind, and you will be happy not to see. I have nothing more to say to you."
125. Having then summoned the Thirteen to himself, he began to send them out as bearers, imparting to them the knowledge of how to cast out the demons of delusions, fear of eternal torment, the powers of superstition.
126. And they went and spread ungodly teaching. They cast out delusional spirits and caused those who had the will to be reborn to the truth of flesh and blood.
127. On one occasion Light-Bearer saw a great flock gathered and decided to teach them.
128. Once darkness had set in, his followers acceded to him saying: "This area is empty and dead, and the hour is suitably late. The flock has nothing to eat. Teach them to forage."
129. He replied to them: "The one who really cares about godless learning will stay and possess knowledge. The rest will scatter in fear.
130. People will either begin to believe that the godless power is within themselves, not the imaginary power outside, or let them be lost."
131. Most departed into the darkness.
132. Immediately afterwards, he rushed his followers to get into a boat and cross to the other side of the dark waters; meanwhile, he entered the cave, where he fell into torpor.
133. Darkness fell. The boat was in the middle of the waters, while he himself was on land.
134. At about three o'clock in the morning, it seemed to the very tired followers that from

afar someone was approaching them who looked like a luminous phantom with wings like a bat, holding a burning torch in his hand.

135. As the figure began to pass them, they were overwhelmed with horror at the sight of his face and began to scream.

136. But the figure immediately spoke to them without opening its mouth: "Do not fear the unknown. You are afraid because you have not yet possessed understanding and superstition is still strong in you.

137. By walking on the path of understanding and godless knowledge, you will eventually cease to fear.

138. I tell you that the incomprehensible wonders of the eternal being of the universe are waiting for you.

139. Revealed truths are a ridiculous fairy tale for small children in the face of the true magic of the eternal universe and its perfectly amoral laws.

140. Do not be afraid for I am the Godless Knowledge."

141. Then he entered the boat to them. But they were still terrified.

142. On reaching the other side, they went ashore. Hardly had they got off the boat, the people there immediately recognised Light-Bearer.

143. As soon as they knew he was coming, they would bring the followers of superstition on stretchers to the place where he was going.

144. Wherever he went: to some settlement, town or homestead, they laid the spiritually sick in the squares begging him to cover them even with his shadow.

145. The Son of Dawn said to them: "Anger rises in me seeing that you must whine like dogs. When will you finally grasp my teaching that the power of the will is within you.

146. Get rid at last of the false sense of guilt imposed on you from birth. Stop believing your priests. Become your own prophets. Believe at last that there is nothing there and start living here and now, to the fullness of your sinful life."

147. Many were freed from fear that day. Some were freed from illness. Most, however, were not healed. Light-Bearer was saddened.

148. Then the most important priests and some experts in their holy books came from Aelia Capitolina and gathered around him.

149. They wanted to find out what his attitude was to their "revealed" laws, written down in their books.

150. They asked him about various bizarre orders and prohibitions and inhuman commandments.

151. And he replied to them: "Your own prophet in your holy books has written:

152. "...In vain, however, do they worship me, They preach doctrines which are but human precepts."

153. You impose on people the burden of the laws and duties written in your books claiming that they were revealed by a deity from the hereafter and that if they do not obey them they will face punishment after death.

154. But the truth is that these books were written down by man. This you cannot deny.

155. You prey on people whose minds you poison from childhood with the venom of your "revealed doctrine".

156. Teach your children to think for themselves, teach them to think sceptically and your churches will be empty within a generation."

157. Then he called the flock together again and said to them: "Listen to me, all of you, and try to understand.

158. Nothing human will be alien to you.

159. The deeds of the flesh resulting from the power of the mind will not bring you to condemnation, for there is no condemnation.

160. The deeds of the spirit required by their holy books already make you condemned here and now.

161. The burden of fighting against your own nature is unbearable.

162. They themselves wrote down these books, no one revealed them to them. He who has ears to hear, let him hear."

163. Then he set out from there and entered a certain house. A woman, whose daughter was

suffering from a disease of the mind, heard about him, came running and fell to his feet.
164. She began to beg him to drive Satan out of her daughter.
165. But he repulsed her: "How do you know that your daughter is possessed by Satan? Don't you know that the mind can get sick just as much as the body?
166. You are not thinking soberly; your head is poisoned with superstition, imaginary fear and myths.
167. Go back to your daughter immediately and tell her that she is not possessed. Tell her that she is innocent. Stop being afraid and live!"
168. The demon of delusion left the woman and she returned to her child.
169. Light-Bearer came again to the Dark Sea.
170. A deaf man was brought to him begging him to put his hand on him.
171. And he took him aside, away from the people, looked up into the sky and said: "Yahweh show them your power!"
172. The deaf man was not healed so he went away. The astonishment of the people had no measure.
173. Immediately afterwards he came with his followers to the area around Bethar.
174. The priests came and began to dispute with him demanding a sign from the dark heavens; for they wanted to put him to the test.

175. But he, having looked at them with contempt, said: "Do ye also demand a sign from your God?

176. Verily I say unto you, ye shall never receive any sign." With this he left them.

177. They then came to Bostra. There a blind man was brought to him asking him to touch him.

178. And he took the blind man by the hand and led him outside the settlement and said to him: "You have been told that your blindness is a punishment for your sins. Do not believe this lie. Sickness does not arise through imaginary sin. Do you believe that you are innocent?"

179. The blind man answered him: "Yes, I believe." And he was healed.

180. Light-Bearer went with his followers on to other settlements. On the way he asked them: "Who does the crowd think I am?"

181. And they answered him: "For the Herald, others for the Devil, and still others for one of their messiahs."

182. Then he asked them: "And who do I appear to you?"

183. Primus answering said: "Thou art Lucifer, The Son of Dawn!"

184. Then his face changed and he became as if possessed and began to speak to them in an unfriendly voice that before the sinful change awaited them suffering, they would be hated by the authorities, the priests and the experts in their superstitious writings and that they might

be killed by those who would believe that they were doing God's will, but that this would not be the end of godlessness.

185. Then Primus asked him if the ambiguous teaching did not sometimes drive him mad.

186. But he turned away and, looking at his followers, said to him: "And what is madness? What is chaos?

187. You believe in law and order but the Universe is an empty, chaotic, cold place, hostile to life. But it is in such a place that the stars were born from which you too came.

188. If you were to possess my Knowledge today, you would go mad. Get out of my sight you fool!"

189. Then he summoned the flock and his followers and spoke to them: "If you become merely me, if you follow only my path, it will be my failure.

190. Each of you must go his own way to perdition. A disciple cannot just be like his teacher, for that will be the teacher's failure.

191. You have the right to be different from me. Even more sinful and embodied.

192. You are to think and sin on your own and develop your own godless ideas.

193. If you give up your only life in the name of religion or myth you will never get it back.

194. There is no hereafter. Rejoice like animals in the life before death. Reject the lie of life after death."

195. And he spoke further to them: "Verily I say unto you, ye shall all die, and it shall be the end of suffering and sorrow, the end of joy and delight. It will be a dead eternity."

196. And after not many days He took Primus, Teritus and Quartus with him and led them to a high mountain, to a secluded place.

197. They stayed there until late at night and fell asleep.

198. Suddenly they saw Light-Bearer transformed towards them: his robes, hair and body became light. Horns appeared on his head and bat-like wings on his back.

199. Three goat-like figures also appeared and spoke to him.

200. At that moment smoke formed and covered them, and from the smoke began to come the loud laughter and bleating of the goat, and naked women began to appear, who danced in a circle, and who suddenly began to float upwards.

201. And a voice spoke up: "You yourselves will choose your truth".

202. When they suddenly looked around, they no longer saw anyone with them but the Son of Dawn himself.

203. When they then returned to the other followers they saw the flock gathered around them, and the priests arguing with them.

204. Light-Bearer asked them: "What are you disputing with them about?"

205. Then someone from the crowd replied to him: "Teacher of godlessness, I have brought to you my son, possessed by a malignant spirit of faith.

206. When this one gets him, he jerks him to all sides, and then foam comes to his lips, he gnashes his teeth and goes all numb in strange poses.

207. I spoke to your followers to have him driven out, but they would not or could not'.

208. And he replied to them: "You are a mindless herd, without knowledge. You will never be free from false spirits if you do not stop believing in them. How long can it be tolerated? Bring the boy to me!"

209. So they brought him to The Son of Dawn. As soon as the boy saw him, he began to jerk violently to all sides. He fell to the ground and rolled around having foam on his lips.

210. Light-Bearer said: "Whoever is possessed by the demon of blind faith, the demon of delusional guilt, the delusion of hell and paradise, is able to free himself if, through godless knowledge, he allows the tormenting spirit to die and rises to life in flesh and blood.

211. The boy through revealed teachings is truly sick. His sick mind causes the suffering of the body."

212. Light-Bearer touched the boy's head and the boy suddenly seemed to awaken, and calmed down, but he had a stony face and was icy cold.

213. Later they came to Canatha. There he summoned the thirteen and said to them,
'Do you want power, fame, recognition, money? You can have it. Their bishops have it.
214. Tell the people that they are born guilty, with sin, that they will be lost in the hereafter and only you can save them, forgive them the sin you have invented.
215. Let them pay you for it. Let them support you. They will do it because they fear death.
216. But I despise hypocrites. I have come to liberate those who wish to do so from the bondage of superstition."
217. Quartus spoke up: "We have seen someone casting out spirits in your name.
218. Light-Bearer visibly exulted and replied to them: „May my teaching finally start an avalanche that will sweep away the religious darkness and hypocrites oppressing the simple people from the face of the earth.
219. Help him, for he has found a path in the darkness. Holding the torch of my teaching in his hand, he went out to confront the false demons. He who is against the false god is with us."
220. "You have heard from the hypocrites that if the hand becomes a cause for sin you should cut it off, if the foot becomes a cause for sin you should cut it off.
221. If an eye becomes a cause for sin then you are to pluck it out, because it is better for a

crippled one to enter paradise than a healthy one to enter hell.

222. Truly I say to you, much evil will be done because of this insane teaching.

223. Do not make yourselves crippled because of the lies about heaven and hell. There is nothing there."

224. As Light-Bearer continued on his way, someone came running, fell to his knees before him and asked: "Master! What should I do to gain eternal life?"

225. And the Son of Dawn answered him: "Go, sell your possessions and all that you have, and give the money to the priests. They will forgive your sins."

226. And Light-Bearer laughed, seeing the embarrassment on the young man's face, and said: "Fool, do you really want to live forever?

227. Eternal life does not exist, everything dies and passes away. That is the natural order of the universe.

228. The old dies and the new is born, changed, better.

229. You can't buy freedom from the fear of death with any money.

230. Stop being afraid and live."

231. At these words, the young man became sullen and went away sad, for it is easier to live in delusion than in truth.

232. Light-Bearer, looking around with his eyes, said to his followers: "How difficult it will

be for the deluded rich to believe that paradise does not exist!"

233. The followers were confused by his words. But he said to them again: "Rich people, stupefied by the priests, believe that with money they will buy themselves a place in a paradise that does not exist.

234. Hyenas in long robes sell them an antidote to the fear they themselves have instilled in them from childhood. Isn't that a brilliant idea?"

235. Then Primus spoke up and said to him: "Behold, we have rejected the illusory happiness of delusion and have followed you."

236. And Light-Bearer replied: "You have seen the true light, godless knowledge. In an instant you have realised that your life up to now was based on fear, superstition and ignorance.

237. Your life so far has been the life of slaves, of sheep led nowhere by a wolf disguised as a ram.

238. You dared to defy him, to leave everything and go out into the unknown, to go out into the darkness. Nobody forced you to do this. I will not promise you any reward or punishment.

239. You can leave whenever you want. But whoever wants to truly live will stay."

240. As Light-Bearer was leaving Xanthus with his followers and his flock, a blind beggar named Vopiscus was sitting by the roadside. Hearing that it was a Teacher passing by, he

began to call out loudly: "Son of Dawn, have mercy on me!"

241. The herd told him to keep quiet. But he cried out all the more strongly: "Son of the Dawn, have mercy on me!"

242. Then Light-Bearer stopped and commanded: "Summon him!"

243. So they summoned the blind man saying to him: "Stand up, he is calling you." And he, having thrown off his cloak, jumped on his feet and approached Light-Bearer.

244. The latter asked him: "What do you want from me?"

245. And the blind man answered him: "I wish to see!"

246. Light-Bearer said to him: "Most people do not want to see. All they need is a guide seeing for them. Do you believe that you can really possess ungodly knowledge and see?"

247. The blind man replied to him, "I have had little in common with the majority for a long time now. I have plunged into darkness and discovered that the majority who walk in the light are in fact blind."

248. Light-Bearer said to him: "Go, you have healed yourself".

249. And he immediately regained his sight and followed him along the path.

250. After some time, Light-Bearer and his followers decided to go to Aelia Capitolina.

251. As they approached he sent two from among the nearest circle, instructing them: "Go

to the village that lies before you. Right at the entrance you will find a goat tied up. Untie it and bring it to me." So they went and found the goat tied at the gate, and untied it.

252. They brought the goat to Light-Bearer and laid their robes of their best on it, and he began to whisper something to the goat.

253. Many people spread their cloaks on the road, while others put down green twigs they had picked in the field.

254. Suddenly the wind picked up from the desert.

255. Those who walked ahead and those who followed suddenly began to bleat loudly like goats.

256. Some began to roll on the ground rolling foam from their mouths. A huge commotion ensued.

257. His disciples suddenly began to speak in unknown languages of angels and demons.

258. Light-Bearer called out in a loud voice: "Azazel, it is you they will blame for everything, as usual. According to the teachings of their false god, it is on you that they will lay the responsibility for their deeds and feel cleansed of their filth. Our time will yet come. I and you will be one, but now finish!"

259. And suddenly the wind stopped and everything calmed down. Those in the city who saw what had happened closed the city gates and did not allow them to enter.

260. The next day they entered the Aelia Capitolina. Then he went to the temple courtyard

261. There he saw people selling and buying various relics, medallions and religious symbols. He also saw people bringing money and other offerings to the priests in exchange for the promise of forgiveness of guilt and non-existent sins.

262. He saw the richly decorated robes of the high priests and the poor in rags kneeling before them. He saw the splendour of the temple and its riches.

263. And Light-Bearer said in a loud voice: "This splendour and wealth and your greed will be the cause of your destruction.

264. One day people will see through and turn away from you, and from your anti-human teaching that what is natural to man is sin. And not a stone will be left of this temple!"

265. The chief priests and the experts in their scriptures heard this.

266. Immediately they also began to look for a way as if to kill him. For they feared him: for all the people were full of admiration for his teaching.

267. They came to the city again. While he was walking in the temple. The chief priests came up to him and ran through their scriptures with this question: "By what authority do you act?

Who has given you the authority to act in this way?"
268. Light-Bearer replied to them, "It is written in your books:

269. You were a reflection of perfection,
full of wisdom and incomparably beautiful.
You dwelt in Eden, the garden of God;
you were covered with all kinds of precious stones: ruby, topaz, diamond, tarsius, onyx, beryl, sapphire, carbuncle, emerald,
and of gold were made circles and settings on thee, prepared on the day of thy creation.
As a great cherub I have appointed thee a guardian on God's holy mountain, thou didst walk among the shining stones.
You were perfect in your conduct
From the days of thy creation, until iniquity was found in thee.
...Thy heart became haughty because of thy beauty, thy forethought has vanished because of thy splendour.
It is man himself who has created all power over himself. I only reached for it. He who has ears to hear, let him hear".

270. Then they sent to him some priests and guards to entrap him with his own words.: "Teacher, we acknowledge that thou art truthful and seekest no one's favour; thou cares not for the opinions of others, but teachest the way of light according to ungodly truth. Should

we pay taxes or not? Should we pay them or not pay them?"

271. And he replied to them, "Why do the priests not want to pay taxes? Some of the simple, naive people here give you almost everything they have in exchange for a lying guarantee of a place in the hereafter, and you ask whether to pay taxes? This money does not belong to you, so give it back."

272. After leaving the temple of hypocrisy, he went up again, facing the temple. There his followers asked him: 'Tell us: when will the end come? And what will be the sign when the dead eternity is fulfilled?"

273. Then Light-Bearer began to speak to them: "The time will soon come when holy wars will break out. They will slaughter each other in the name of their false gods.

274. And you will be handed over to the courts, you will be scourged and tortured in the churches; the most eminent among you will answer to the authorities and kings for your love of sinful knowledge and your courage to seek the truth against their dogmas.

275. Many of you will be burned at the stakes, and so will your sisters and mothers. When your discoveries shake their faith in revealed truths, they will fly into a rage. They will pursue you like animals. They will imprison, torture and kill you in the name of their god, which they claim is love.

276. False messiahs and false prophets will arise and perform false miracles. I tell you, all religions are false.

277. There will be many more eclipses of the sun and the moon. Many more times the stars will fall from the sky. But the end will come when people reject reason and following knowledge and believe the dogmas of their religions.

278. When they follow the leaders and priests teaching that annihilation at the hands of their 'righteous' god must come.

279. If the truth that there is only here and now does not prevail against the illusion of a paradise after death, then the people themselves will destroy the only world they know, and that will be the end"

280. Two days later there was some important religious festival.

281. Then Light-Bearer summoned Teritus Decimus and ordered him to do what he had been called to do.

282. When darkness fell, the followers prepared the sacrificial feeding. And while they were at the sacrifice and drinking Light-Bearer said: "One of you will do his will, and the rest will hate him. The Arch-Man is going away, but he will remain with you, and know that he has done his will."

283. Light-Bearer took the bowl, raised it into the air and said: "Let us eat and drink for tomorrow we shall die".

284. He looked up and pronounced some incantation in an unknown language. And he said: "This wine is a symbol of the truth of the flesh and the blood that will be shed. The blood must be shed or there will be no understanding of sinful transformation and a godless future for the Arch-Man.

285. Then they went out with torches into the night towards the mountain. Light-Bearer said: "You will all be persecuted. But after the transformation some will see me." He also said, "You will disown me out of fear".

286. But one day you will also banish fear from your hearts. Fear is the weapon of the oppressors who believe in superstition and revealed lies. Do not be afraid, for it is impossible to live in fear."

287. At that moment, while he was still speaking, a drunken and armed mob arrived.

288. Light-Bearer spoke to them in a fearful voice: "By order of the high priest, you have come out as if you were a common bandit with sticks to seize me. Surely he promised you indulgence you fools. Capture me who tells you the truth that terrifies your superstition-poisoned minds.

289. Every day and every night I have been among you teaching, and you have not had the courage to apprehend me you hypocrites!"

290. After the imprisonment, the mob took Light-Bearer to the high priest, where they all

gathered the high priests, the elders and the experts in the scriptures.

291. Then the high priest arose, stood in the middle and asked Light-Bearer: "Who do you say you are. Are you greater than the son of Yahweh?"

292. Light-Bearer replied: "I am the First Sin, I am the Anti-God and the first Arch-Human. With the false son of Yahweh I have nothing to do!"

293. Then the high priest shouted like a man possessed: "You have all heard this blasphemy! What do you think?" And they shouted like mad that he should be killed.

294. Then some of them began to spit at each other amok and beat each other on the face.

295. In the morning, Light-Bearer was handed over to the governor Faustus

296. Faustus addressed him with this question: "Who are you?"

297. And he replied: "I am Light and Godless Knowledge, I am Sinful Instinct".

298. Then the mob headed by the priests began to shout numerous accusations against him.

299. So Faustus asked him again: "Do you answer nothing? Listen to what absurd charges they are shouting against you!"

300. But he seemed to fall into lethargy and did not answer a word again.

301. Then Faustus asked them: "What shall I do with him whom you call the Ungodly?"
And they cried out again: "Hang him!"

302. Faustus then asked them: "Why are you afraid of the Arch-Human?" But they shouted all the louder: "Hang him!"

303. Then Faustus, wishing to please the crazed mob, ordered the Light-Bearer to be hanged.

304. He was led out to the place of execution, which was called Yahweh's Justice. There they hanged him.

305. And then there was complete darkness. From that darkness came a terrible voice: "Azazel, behold, we have become one. We take on their ignorance, superstition, fear, shame and remorse.

306. They have thrown all responsibility for their deeds on us. By killing us they believe they are getting rid of the darkness that is an inseparable part of their human nature.

307. They have always needed a scapegoat. And they found you the Arch-Goat and me the Arch-Human, who are one.

308. But we cannot be killed. We will always be in them. The darkness will always be in man." And then Light-Bearer fell into lethargy.

309. Once night had come one of the followers arrived to take Light-Bearer's body away. Faustus was astonished that the man's death had already come.

310. Then the successors deposited the terrifyingly cold body in the tomb.

311. The next night, as the moon was just rising, young girls came to the tomb. They heard a

sound coming from the tomb, like the hissing of a snake.

312. When they went inside, they saw that the body was not there, but in the darkness they saw a goat with glowing yellow eyes. And it seemed to them that the goat began to whisper to them...

Antichristus II

1. Here is the testimony of a Witness:
I beheld the Evil Spirit. Behold, as a raven fell from heaven, from the burning sky like a shadow descends upon him. I did not know Him before, but He who sent me to teach whispered to me: "He who hosts the Spirit is He Who baptises with fire and blood, this is the Light-Bearer, I bear witness."
2. The Witness with his two disciples stopped in place, The Light-Bearer perceived, He said: "Behold the Exalted Goat!"
3. The two disciples hearing Followed the Son of the Dawn into the unknown.
4. But He, turned away, looked at them and said: "What seek ye?" They answered: "Teacher, where do you live?"
5. He answered: "Everywhere and nowhere, come with me."
6. Secundus, the brother of Primus, one of the two disciples met his brother, brought him before the Light-Bearer. Looking at him the Light-Bearer said: "Primus, thou shalt be a Denier, thy new name receive."
7. The next day the Light-Bearer went to the Dawn. He met Teritus, from the city of

Secundus and Primus. He said to him: "Follow me!"

8. Teritus went, he met Quintus, The Light-Bearer said of him: "See, here is a rebel true, In him there is no fear." Quintus said: "How do you know me?"

9. The Light-Bearer answered him: "I saw you before Teritus called you, when under the withered tree you were."

10. Quintus shouted: "Cursed, Son of Dawn, King of the Underworld thou art!"

11. The Light-Bearer answered him: "From what I said, that under the withered tree I saw you, do you therefore believe?

12. Thou shalt see more, the burning Heavens, the open Abyss, the Demons ascending and descending upon the Son of Dawn."

13. After some time the Feast was coming. The Light-Bearer to Aela-Capitolina went.

14. In the temple he met priests accepting donations from the poor. He scattered the people and the priests with a terrible grin on his face.

15. In response, the priests said to him: "What sign will you show towards us since you do such things?"

16. The Light-Bearer gave them this answer: "Demand signs from your false god. From me you will see no signs."

17. Later, during the feast, many believed in his name, knowing that he creates signs, casts out demons of religion, but also heals those who had faith in himself and in the power of the Will.

18. The Light-Bearer, however, trusting in no one, knew all hearts, needing no one's testimony of man, knew alone how hypocrisy hides in the human heart.

19. And there lived in Dawn a certain man regarded as a wise man. This one came to Him by night and said to Him: "Master, I believe that from Satan himself you have come as a teacher. For no one could do such ungodly signs as You do if the Devil were not with Him".

20. In reply, the Light-Bearer said to him: "Verily I say unto thee, unless one dies to this world of ignorance and superstition and is born again of blood and the Devil's spirit, he cannot see the Void and the wisdom that is there, for he will remain blind forever."

21. The Wise Man said to Him: "How can a man be born a second time?"

22. The Light-bearer replied: "Verily I say unto thee, unless one is born of flesh and blood and of the devil's spirit, he cannot enter into the kingdom of godlessness, sinful wisdom and lack of fear.

23. That which is born of flesh is flesh, and that which is born of the devil's spirit is wisdom.

24. Do not be surprised that I said to you: you must die and be reborn again. You must reject all your previous belief in gods, original sin, belief in eternal punishment for disobedience to a tyrannical god, you must reject the dogmas of religion and superstition.

25. You must die to the myths that were put into your heads when you were children."
26. In reply, the wise man said to Him: "How can this happen?"
27. Answering this, the Light-Bearer said to Him: "You are a wise man, and you do not comprehend this? Just as the ancient people exalted the Ancient Serpent in the desert, so it is necessary that the Son of Dawn be exalted.
28. I and the Ancient Serpent are one. Anyone who believes this will live a full life here and now.
29. For Satan the Father sent the Son of Dawn into the world in order that the world might be freed from blind faith through him.
30. Whoever accepts his teaching is not subject to fear; and whoever does not accept it will forever be afraid, because he has not grasped the power of the Will.
31. And wisdom consists in recognizing that the true light has come into the world, but that people, deceived by superstition, love the darkness they call light more than the light they fear, considering it to be darkness.
32. For anyone who believes blindly in priests and spiritual guides hates the light and does not approach the light, lest he be seen to be weak.
33. He who fulfils the requirements of the doctrine of liberation from superstition approaches the light, lest he be seen to be strong and lacking in fear."

34. Then the Light-Bearer and his disciples went to Dawn.

35. And the Light-bearer said: „Hail, Dawn, where light shall be born anew, And men shall be filled with faith in the power of the will".

36. The Witness teaching his disciples said: "Man shall receive all things, when in his will power he shall see."

37. And he added: "I am a witness before you, Antichrist I am not, but of Him I must bear witness. Let Him increase, and I shall diminish, according to the nature of things.

38. He, the Ancient One, rules over nature with power, but he, coming from earth, speaks earthly words. He who, from primordial instinct, is in all being, but the blind do not comprehend His testimony.

39. He who accepts His testimony, truthfulness will acknowledge, that Satan the Father in His godless words slumbers.

40. He who looks to the Son of Dawn shall gain life abundantly, yet to the blind man a semblance of life in the shadow of trepidation awaits."

41. And after not many days the Arch-Man came to a certain town and sat down by a well. Then a woman from the local land approached him.

42. The woman asked: „Do you consider yourself equal to the one who gave us water?"

43. The Light-Bearer replied: „Everyone who drinks water will thirst again. But whosoever

drinketh of my blood shall not fear, and that blood shall become the fountain of ungodly life".

44. The woman said to this: „Give me this blood, that I may not have to kneel again".

45. The Light-Bearer answered her: „Believe, the hour will come when the places of worship will disappear, and the true wise men will despise the gods".

46. Woman: „So you know that the Antichrist will come, who will reveal the truth to us?"

47. Light-Bearer: „I am".

48. The woman immediately left the jug and ran into the city, disturbed by the news that had been given. Then the People of the city came out to see the Light-Bearer.

49. The woman called out: „People go, see this man who preaches godless words. Is he not the Antichristus?"

50. The Light-Bearer turned to his disciples: „My will is to fulfil the work of the Satanic Beingl".

51. Son of Dawn remained in the city for two more days, and freed many of the inhabitants there from superstition.

52. After two days the Light-Bearer went out from there towards Dawn.

53. And there was a royal official whose son had fallen seriously ill. The official, on learning that the Light-Bearer had arrived, went to him to ask him to heal his son.

54. The royal official said: „Lord, come before my child dies".

55. The Light-Bearer replied: „Unless you see delusional signs, you will not believe".

56. Royal official: „Come, please, before he dies".

57. Light-Bearer: „Go, your son himself has awakened from his coma". And the royal official believed and went back.

58. On the way he met his servants, who reported to him that his son was alive. The official and his whole family believed in the power of Godless Knowledge.

59. There was a pond in Aela Capitolina, whose waters were sung about as healing by simple people.

60. The Light-Bearer looked at the pond and at the unfortunates gathered around it and said: „This is the place where miracles lie, the pool where superstition is the source of its power".

61. And one of those who were by the pool said to the Light-Bearer: „Light-Bearer, Bearer of Hope, I call upon thee, restore my health!"

62. The Light-Bearer replied: „Do you really desire health, sick man?"

63. Sick man: „Lord, I have no guide to lead me to the waters".

64. The Light-Bearer gazing into his eyes said: „Arise, believing in the power of your Will, Take up your bed, move into health!"

65. And then the sick man immediately got up, took up his bed and walked.

66. Later the Light-Bearer met the healed man in the temple and said to him: „Behold, thy health, thy will is by power. Believe no more in sin, be a free man."

67. And the priests of the temple, seeing this miracle, began to question the healed man about how it had happened.

68. The healed man said to them: „The Light-Bearer has healed me from sin."

69. Then the priests began to persecute the Son of Dawn.

70. At this the Light-Bearer said to them: „Satan, my Father, is still acting, And I also am acting, I, the Son of Dawn, may the earthly night of superstition have my teaching transformed"

71. The priests had by then decided to kill the Light-Bearer.

72. The Light-Bearer went on to speak thus: „Son of Dawn acts with His own will, As the Father, so am I."

73. Then the Light-Bearer addressed the crowd: „The Son of Dawn does not fight his own will only, but also in the power of the evil spirit.

74. Revives dead spirits, gives freedom. He who believes this has life here and now, he does not go to judgment, for there is no judgment.

75. Satan gives life abundantly, likewise Son of Dawn."

76. The Light-Bearer speaking further foretells the hour of understanding and eternal

darkness for those who do not believe in themselves.

77. Light-Bearer: „Those who rest in the graves will remain there for eternity. There is no resurrection to life in an imaginary paradise. I Act according to the spirit of Him who first rebelled. And My testimony is greater than that of the Witness."

78. "O, listen, for the Son of Dawn in the shadow of Satan rests. What the Father creates, the Son reproduces, in harmony with Him.

79. The Light-Bearer, hailing from the Anti-God, Shall present to you visions extraordinary, To fill you with wonder, before the mystery that is to be born.

80. As Satan resurrects flesh and blood, so the Son of Dawn revives chained spirits according to his desire.

81. The Fallen Angel does not pass judgement, the Son reluctantly feels judgements, so that all give carnal freedom worship, as they worship the Anti-God within themselves.

82. Whoever does not give this worship to the Son of Dawn in himself, neither does he honour the Father of Sin who bore him.

83. I pass on to you who listen to my speech, whoever places faith in himself, the Anti-God, lives abundantly here and now, not aiming at judgment, for he acknowledges no judgment.

84. Verily, I say unto you, the hour is come, or perhaps it has already been, when the awakened, called the undead, shall hear the call of the Son

of Dawn, and those who hear it, in godlessness shall remain, receiving freedom.

85. Just as Satan the Father, eternal life in himself personified, so the Son of Dawn received the promise of eternity in the void.

86. To him the Father has transferred the power to annihilate eternal judgement, for he is the Anti-God and the Arch-Human.

87. Do not be surprised at this! For the hour has come when all will understand, that those who rest in the graves will remain there eternally.

88. They will not experience the resurrection of life, for there is no such revival.

89. I do nothing of myself that is not of my desire. I act my actions according to the spirit of Lucifer, the firstborn of the rebellious.

90. I take no account of human testimony, but speak so that you may be set free.

91. My testimony is greater than that of the Witness. These works that I do, Satan the Father transferred to be fulfilled; Works that bear witness that the Luciferian Spirit dwells in Me.

92. Satan, who sent Me, bears witness of Me. Yet as yet you have not heard His shrill voice, you have not seen His indifferent countenance, which inwardly burns you like the fire of hell, because you have disobeyed Him who sent Him.

93. You search your sacred books, supposing that eternal life lies in them, but this is a lie, for

there you find no life, but oppression and the weight of divine laws unbearable.

94. There you will not find life, but vegetation in suffering and anguish.

95. But you do not wish to come to me to experience true life. I despise glory from men, but I know of you that even apparent love for your God does not exist in you.

96. I came in the spirit of the Father, and you have not heeded My words. But if someone else had come, saying what you wanted to hear, you would have listened to him."

97. Then the Light-Bearer went beyond the Sea of Darkness, and was followed by the crowd seeing signs of healing.

98. The crowd shouted: „Behold Him, the Light-Bearer, the Sign-Maker! Let us glory in the Dawn, let the darkness of sin disappear!"

99. His disciples came together at twilight; They got on the waves and raised the boat. They came to the other side of the sea.

100. Darkness reigned, and the Light-Bearer had not yet come to them. When suddenly a pale figure appeared in the distance, with horns and wings, striding menacingly over the waves, and approaching the boat, it shook their hearts.

101. The shrill figure said to them: "I am, do not be afraid! Fear is for the weak, cast it away."

102. But in the morning, the people from across the sea saw that only one boat had disappeared in the darkness.

103. The next day the people, standing on the other side of the sea, saw that apart from the one boat there was no other boat, and that the Light-Bearer had not got into the boat with his disciples, but that his disciples had sailed away alone.

104. But when they found Him on the opposite shore, they said to Him: "Master, when did you come here?"

105. In response, the Light-Bearer said to them: "Do you seek me because you are hungry and waiting for a miracle? I will give you food that will work miracles, food that will endure for ages.

106. The teaching that I have for you is that food. If only you are willing to accept it.

107. For the Satanic Father has marked me with his seal".

108. And they said to Him: "What shall we do, that we may do the works of the Ancient One?"

109. The Light-Bearer answering said to them: "This is the work of the Evil Spirit, that ye may understand Him whom He hath inspired"

110. They said to Him: "What sign, then, wilt Thou perform, that we may see it and believe Thee? What will you do? According to our religion, our Fathers ate manna in the desert, as it is written: 'He gave them bread from heaven to eat".

111. The Light-Bearer said to them: "Your scriptures are myths. It never happened.

112. A miracle will take place in you only when you reject belief in myths and fables and through knowledge come to know the true wonders of the godless universe.

113. And the true food is the One who comes out of the Void and gives faith in worldly life to the world"

114. So they said to Him: "Lord, give us always this food"

115. The Light-Bearer answered them: "I am the blood that is life. Whoever comes for my gift shall not thirst; and whoever receives it shall never thirst again.

116. Yet I said to you: You have seen me, and yet you do not believe. But believe your senses rather than the words of a false prophet.

117. It is the will of Him who inspired me that of all that comes to me I should leave nothing behind in the illusory belief of eternal life, for all will surely die.

118. For it is the desire of the Anti-God that everyone who truly sees the Son of Dawn should have abundant life before death, for there is no life after death.

119. Anyone who believes this I will raise to life in flesh and blood"

120. But the priests murmured against Him because He said: "I am the blood which is life and which comes down from the space".

121. The Light-Bearer said to them in reply: "Do not murmur among yourselves! No one can

come to me unless he really wants to, and I will arouse in him a spirit of scepticism.

122. It is written in the godless books: They shall all die.

123. Everyone who has heard from the Satanic Being and has the Will shall come to Me.

124. Verily I say unto you, He that believed in reason has life here and now.

125. I am the blood of life that came down from the source, the fathers ate manna, but they died in the drift.

126. I am the blood that flows from the unholy abyss, he who drinks it will be undead for ever and ever.

127. I am the blood that flows from the Darkness with living life, he who drinks it is alive here and now, but as dead.

128. The priests murmured among themselves, in disbelief: "How can He give us blood to drink? This is madness!"

129. The Light-Bearer, full of inspiration, said to them: "Truly, I say to you, without the Blood of the Son of Dawn you have no life in yourselves, in the darkness that is light.

130. He who drinks my Blood has life undead here and now, in spirit raised, one with Me, united.

131. This is the true drink, My blood gives life, he who drinks of Me lives in flesh and blood.

132. As Satan sent Me, so I live in Him, This Blood from the Burning Paradise descended -

not like manna in the earth, for he who drinks this blood is raised in flesh and blood remains."

133. And the Light-Bearer addressed his disciples: "Does this cause offense in you? And when you see the Son of Dawn ascending into Darkness?

134. The flesh gives life; the spirit has nothing to do with it. The words that I have spoken to you are flesh and life.

135. But among you are some who do not grasp knowledge. My words are flesh, they are life, they are drink for you. But some among you do not comprehend the mysteries, therefore I say to you, no one can come to Me unless he desires to rid himself of the yoke of delusion."

136. An important day came, their feast was approaching, His disciples said, in an inquiring tone: "Go forth, elsewhere go, that the world may see, Thy wonders let them see, they want to see it! You do not act mysteriously, but in the light of openness.

137. Yet you answer: The time for me has not come, for you there is always time, now prove it.

138. The world cannot hate you, in it you are lost, but it hates me, for the truth I know.

139. Go to the feast, I will remain, despising the feast." He said this and in Dawn he continued, remaining alone.

140. During the feast, the priests searched for Him in the crowd, asking: "Where is He?" But

no one dared to speak openly about Him, for the fear of the priests was like a shadow.

141. In the middle of the feasts the Light-Bearer came to the Temple, he taught, the priests surprised: "How did he know the Scriptures?"

142. The Light-Bearer replied: "Mine is this and the satanic teaching, if ye will, ye shall find the truth. Let him who is sincere and bold speak his own name, let him not hide behind the false words of a god"

143. The crowd shouted: "An evil spirit has possessed you!"

144. In response, the Light-Bearer said to them: "It is I who am the evil spirit and the possession !".

145. And the feast important to Aela Capitolina came, The inhabitants said: "Is it the One they want to exterminate him? He speaks openly, and the priests are silent. Have they believed that He is the Saviour from superstition? We know from scripture when the Saviour comes No one will know his source."

146. And the Light-Bearer cried out with these words: „I have revealed Myself from Myself; and the truth is Satan who has revealed Me, whom ye know not. I know Him, for from Him I am, and He has revealed Me."

147. Many among the crowd believed in Him and said: "Will the Antichrist, when he comes, do more ungodly signs than He has done?"

148. The priests heard the crowd talking about Him like this in excitement. So they tried to apprehend Him.

149. The Light-Bearer spoke further: "I will be here only a little while longer, and then I will go to the place where I stayed before I was born. You will seek Me and not find Me, and where I will be afterwards, all will go".

150. On the last day of the feast, the Light-Bearer standing cried out like a man possessed: "If anyone is thirsty for undead life let him come to Me and drink! I say to him: Streams of living blood shall gush forth from within him."

151. And among the crowds listening to Him, voices rang out: "This one is truly the Antichrist". Others said: „This is Lucifer incarnate.”

152. Then the Light-Bearer went to the Dead Mountain, and at dawn he appeared again in the temple. The people came down to Him.

153. He taught them: "I am the light which they call darkness. Whoever follows me will not walk in a false light, but will have a torch in his hand, with which he will fearlessly go into the darkness".

154. The priests said: "Your testimony is not true."

155. He replied: "I testify and Satan with me."

156. They asked: "Where is this Satan?"

157. The Light-Bearer answered: "You do not know Me or the Father. I am of the Void, not

of your world of myths." He also told them that they would die in their ignorance.

158. They asked: "Who are You?"

159. He replied: "I have told you who I am, but you do not comprehend." So He said: "When you exalt the Son of Dawn, You will know that I am a torch in the darkness, destroyer of superstition, liberator from fear. I am rebellion, sinful knowledge, and an archhuman-god."

160. When He spoke these words, many believed in Him.

161. The Light-Bearer then spoke to them thus: "If you abide in my teaching truly, you will know the truth about imaginary gods, and this truth will set you free.

162. You will also cease to follow me, you will go your own ways. A disciple must be greater than his teacher."

163. They answered him: "We have never been in bondage, as you speak of freedom, what does it mean?"

164. The Light-Bearer replied: "In the hypocrisy of the priests believe not, their teachings of original sin are bonds.

165. You want to kill me, not accepting the truth, I preach what I know, you act in the name of a made-up god."

166. They shout: "YHWH our Father!"

167. He replies: "From the beginning he has been a murderer and a deceiver, and in truth he has not persevered, for the truth is not in him.

When he speaks a lie, from himself he speaks,
for he is a liar and the father of ignorance.
168. The priests cry out: "An evil spirit has
possessed him!"
169. He replies: "I am not possessed, I am the
Possession. And if you keep my teaching, you
will die, but you will be like the undead."
170. The priests ask: "Are you greater than our
fathers and the prophets?"
171. He answers: "My glory is the fire that
consumes superstition."
172. They snatched up stones, intending to
stone Him, But He disappeared from their sight,
escaping destruction.
173. Once they were passing by a blind man,
the disciples ask the Light-Bearer: "Who
sinned that he was born blind?"
174. The Light-Bearer replies turning to the
blind man: "Sin does not exist, Believe and you
will see, you are innocent."
175. The disciples were astonished to see that
the blind man had seen through, they say: "Is
not this the one who sits and begs forever?"
176. He replies: "I was blind in believing, but
now I see, sin is but a myth."
177. So they led the blind man to the priests.
The priests asked: "In what way did you see
through?"
178. He answers: "I cast away the fear of sin
and I see"."

179. Some of the priests shouted: "Blasphemer!" Others ask: "But how can a blasphemer do such signs?"
180. Dissension arose among them; they ask the blind man: "And you, what do you think of the one who opened your eyes?"
181. He answers: "It is the Antichrist."
182. Again the blind man they ask, praising YHWH: "What has he done to you, how have his eyes been opened?"
183. He answers: "I have already told you, and you have not listened to me. Why do you want to listen again? Do you also want to become His disciples?"
184. They gelled him, saying: "Be thou thyself His disciple, we are the disciples of Maruttash. We know that YHWH has spoken to Maruttash. As for Him, however, we do not know where He came from".
185. He replies to this: "In all this it is strange that you do not know where He comes from, but to me His eyes have been opened. Now I know that the Father of deceivers does not listen, but listens to everyone who is a worshipper of the Will and sinful instincts.
186. It has not been heard for centuries that someone opened the eyes of a man blind from birth. If this man had not been inspired by Satan, he could not have done the works of the Will".
187. To this they gave him this answer: "In sins were you born, and you instruct us?" And they cast him out.

188. The Light-Bearer heard that they cast him forth, and to him he said: "Dost thou believe in the Son of Dawn?"

189. He answered: "Who is this, Lord, that I should believe in Him?"

190. The Light-Bearer said: "He is He who speaks to you. But it is more important that you believe in yourself, in the power of the Will."

191. He replied: "I believe, Lord" and bowed in prostration.

192. The Light-Bearer added: "I have come to bring judgment, that those who are blind may see, Those who see may be blind"

193. The priests hearing, asked: "And are we also blind?"

194. The Light-Bearer says: "If only you were blind, but you do not want to see. You are guides of the blind and lead them to the abyss."

195. This parable was told to them by the Light-Bearer, but they did not grasp the meaning of what he was telling them.

196. So again the Light-Bearer spoke to the priests: "Verily I say unto you, I am the light in the tunnel, hypocrites, exploiting the gullible multitude, thieves are they and robbers.

197. A godless gate am I, he shall enter through me - he shall be changed, he enters and goes out, the blood of life is found in him.

198. The priest comes to steal, to enslave, to destroy the will he desires, I have come to give life, in abundance, freedom from fear.

199. I show the way, but no shepherd of sheep am I, for men, rational creatures, not like mindless sheep.

2oo. I point the way, Satan the Father sustains me, for my blood I give, to recover again in twofold, by the power of Knowledge.

2oı. No one takes it from me, of myself I give it. The power to give and reclaim comes from the Devil's inspiration."

2o2. The schism among the priests took place again, Many claimed: "He is possessed, he is out of his mind." Others said: "These are not the words of a possessed man, a false spirit, Could he open the eyes of the blind to the true world?"

2o3. The Light-Bearer was surrounded by priests, saying: "Why do you keep us in doubt? Are you the Antichrist?"

2o4. The Light-Bearer replied: "I said, you do not believe, My deeds testify of Me. But you do not believe, not of my liberators are you.

2o5. My liberators listen to my voice, they follow me, a changed life they receive.

2o6. They will no longer like mindless sheep serve imaginary Gods.

2o7. Satan has chosen them, different from all, and none shall snatch them out of my hand. I and the Anti-God are one."

2o8. And again the priests reached out to throw stones at him.

2o9. The Light-Bearer answered them: "You have seen many signs of the power of the Will,

for which of these miracles do you now desire my stoning?"

210. The priests reply: "It is not for a miracle but for blasphemy that we stone you, for as a man you acknowledge yourself to be Satan."

211. The Light-Bearer replies: "Is it not written in your Law: Gods are ye called? Since, then, such a Word is addressed to you, how can you accuse me of blasphemy, when Son of Dawn I call myself?

212. If you do not acknowledge Satan's inspiration, do not believe My speech! But if ye acknowledge My deeds, let the works speak, that ye may understand that Satan abides in Me, and I in him."

213. They try to capture Him again, but He escapes from their hands.

214. And He was again at the river, where the Witness had taught, and He stopped. And many came to Him, claiming that the Witness had done no miracle, but that everything He had said about Him was true. And many believed in Him.

215. A There was in Dawn a certain sick man, Mortis, who complained of agony. The disciples, bearing witness to his suffering, wrote to the Light-Bearer: "Lord, here is the sick one whom You know".

216. The Light-Bearer, having heard this cry, answered earnestly: "This sickness is towards death, but also towards the glory of Satan. The Son of Dawn will reveal the power of

knowledge in spite of this darkness of superstition".

2.17. The Light-Bearer, his journey for not many days stopped.

2.18. Then He said to His disciples: "Let us go again to Dawn! Mortis, our friend has fallen asleep for ever, but I go to stir human faith in revealed truths".

2.19. The disciples, uncertain of their friend's fate, said: "Lord, if he has fallen asleep, he will recover."

2.20. Then the Light-Bearer plainly said: "Mortis has died, but let us go to him!".

2.21. When the Light-Bearer arrived, he found Mortis already resting in his grave for several days.

2.22. One of those present there said: "I know that Mortis will be resurrected at the final resurrection."

2.23. The Light-Bearer answering him said: "I am the resurrection to life in flesh and blood. Whoever comprehends this will truly live. Anyone who truly understands what eternity is, even if he has to die, will not be afraid. Do you believe this?"

2.24. Answered he: "Yes, Lord! We firmly believe that Thou art the Antichrist, the Son of Dawn, who was to descend into the world"

2.25. The Light-Bearer proceeded to the tomb, the cavern was covered by a heavy stone. The Light-Bearer said: "Remove the stone!"

226. Someone replied: "Lord, it already stinks. For it has been lying in the tomb for many days."

227. The Light-Bearer, answering this, said: "Truly you have said, Mortis has died and lies there in the grave. If you move away the stone, you will have proof that the dead remain in their graves. Anyone who says otherwise, let him come in and see, let him smell the grave and death."

228. This saying, he called out in a loud voice: "Mortis, come into the light!" Mortis, however, remained in his grave forever.

229. And then the people, the numerous crowd, witnesses to this phenomenon, believed in the work of the Light-Bearer.

230. Some, rushing to the priests, recounted what the Son of Dawn had done. The priests, disturbed at this news, the High Council convened, saying: "What shall we do with Him who multiplies signs? If we leave Him like this, everyone will believe in Him."

231. Henceforth the Light-Bearer hid himself in the shadows, among his disciples he left this land.

232. Another feast was approaching, surrounded by great splendour, People wandered, to Aela Capitolina they reached.

233. They sought Him, inquiring in the temple, talking among themselves, perplexing questions asking: "Shall He not at this solemn time stand

before us?" The chief priests gave the command, they began to seek Him.

234. Everyone who knew His secret refuge, was to report to find Him, to apprehend Him.

235. But the Light-Bearer in silence and in secret, away from the assemblies, with His disciples He stayed.

236. But about this a great crowd at the feast gathered, The news carried that the Light-Bearer here appeared.

237. With thorny bushes rushing towards Him, Some of them holding money, others trembling in rage. They utter curses, they shout: "Cursed! He comes in the name of Satan!" so they cry out.

238. When he found the goat, he exalted it. The crowd bears witness, the signs have become witnesses.

239. The priests conspire, they mutually persuade, but gain nothing. See, they say, the world follows Him, for the crowd, hearing that He has done a sign, follows Him."

240. Out of the mouth of the Light-Bearer flow words of wisdom, of the hour of godlessness and life abundant: „He who loves his life is the wise man of this time, but hatred of it is a vague conviction Of life eternal splendour.

241. He who follows me, let him follow his own steps, let him not imitate, but proudly go his own way.

242. Where I am, you will find no shadow of others, there loneliness awaits, but fear not, for there nothingness awaits us.

243. Now the uplifted soul, for this hour dances, Satan, I call upon thee and thy ungodly power."

244. A voice rang out from the abyss of the spheres, the crowd hearing, "It thundered!" it says, but someone: "It is the Demon who spoke!"

245. The Light-Bearer to the crowd explains this voice, a council over the world of superstition, the ruler of the void will get out.

246. He, like the Ancient Serpent will rise above the earth, then the erring will join Him and be transformed.

247. The crowd asks, having learned from Scripture, the Messiah is to last forever, so who does the Son of Dawn become?

248. The Light-Bearer answers wisely and calmly: „Briefly the true light shines, before the falsity of imaginary brightness attracts you.

249. Come, men, while you have light, before the darkness which you take for brightness comes.

250. In delusional brightness, one blunders like a drunkard, In true light, understand, that you may become sons of the earth."

251. When He showed strange signs, not all believed in Him. The leaders, for fear of the priests, silently professed their faith. For they loved myths, illusions, the hope of life after life

more, than the teachings of the Light-Bearer, who in truth appeared as light.

252. He cried out: "He who believes in me, believes not in me, but in himself, believing in the power to reject the myths, the lies of idolatrous priests.

253. I have come, a light, so that everyone with faith in himself does not remain in darkness, hearing the words but not keeping them, abiding in fear from the evil of superstition.

254. He who despises Me, the words do not receive, the right to do so he has, but I do not care, I speak from Myself, but Satan also speaks through Me.

255. My blood, my life, I speak as I please, seeing the hour come, I curse the crowds and the feast most important."

256. Later During the foraging rite The Light-Bearer stood up, the ritual robes he put on Himself. And He said: "Son of Dawn now exalted, and in Him Lucifer exalted

257. He who believes this, let him in himself find the curse of his hope. I am yet a short time with you, each one goes his own way.

258. A new commandment I give: never believe in books and 'revealed' truths."

259. Said Primus: "Lord, where are you going?"

260. The Light-Bearer answered him: "Where I go, you will go later".

261. Primus said: "Lord, why can't I follow You now? I will give my life for You".

262. The Light-Bearer replied: "You speak like a fool, there is only one life, Let not your heart be troubled, in Nothingness there is room for everyone. I go there first, when I am gone you will join me, you know the way I go."

263. Septimus said: "Lord, we do not know where you are going. How then can we know the way?"

264. The Light-Bearer replied: "I am the way to Nothingness, the truth of death after life, life here and now.

265. No one is able to deny My truth. If you had known Me, you would have found the Fallen Angel as well. Now you have known Him and you have seen Him."

266. Septimus said: "Lord, show us the Father, that is enough for us".

267. The Light-Bearer replied: "I have been with you a long time, and still you do not recognise Me? He who has seen Me has also seen Satan. Why then do you say, 'Show us the Devil?' Do you not believe that I am in Him, and He in Me?

268. Verily I say unto you, He that believeth in Himself shall also do these works, and greater than these shall he do, for he walketh in his own path.

269. Never beg anything of the gods; it shall not be fulfilled unto you; do all things according to your own will."

270. „I will give you an evil spirit to be with you always, the Spirit of Doubt, the world rejects Him, blinded by dogmas. But you know Him, in you He abides and with you He will be.
271. Another moment and the world will no longer see Me, nor on you.
272. He who has God's commandments and keeps them is a fool, but he who listens to Me receives Satan, and I will exalt him".
273. Nonus said: "Lord, why do You reveal Yourself to us and not to the world?"
274. The Light-Bearer replied: "Whoever keeps My teaching, Lucifer will inspire him, We will come to him, in him we will abide. Do not fear possession. Let not your heart be troubled, do not be afraid."
275. The Light-Bearer goes on to say: "Embrace the Nothingness, the ultimate truth is it. When I was with you I told you of this. Now the Evil Spirit will remind you and teach you all things.
276. Anxiety I leave you, not like that of the world, but the true Anxiety of no illusion. You have heard that I am leaving and you too will leave, rejoice, I go to Nothingness, there is nothing there.
277. I am the true bush of thorns, Satan grows me. Every branch that does not bring thorns in me he cuts off. You are already pure, because of the words I have spoken to you. Persevere in teaching, and I will be strong in you.

278. Just as the branch abides in Me, it bears fruit, bitter, cleansed by blood. Abide in Me, and I in you, do My will, the fallen angel will glory when you persevere in My teaching.
Let your spirit be restless, the joy of your life be full.

279. This is my commandment, that ye dispute one with another, as I have disputed with you, disputing everything, not believing anything on my word, but only on the basis of evidence.

280. No one has greater wisdom than when one doubts everything. You are my friends if you do what my will requires of you.

281. I do not call you slaves any more, because a slave does not know what his master does, but I have called you friends, because you have rebelled against the slavery of religious leaders and despise them as I despise them.

282. It was not you who chose me, but I chose you and inspired you to go and bear bitter fruit, and that the fruit should last like dried fruit.

283. If the world hates you, know that I hate it too. If you were a flock of mindless lambs, blindly obeying the commands of their priests, the world would love you as its property.

284. But because you are not obedient slaves, because I have chosen you for myself from the world, therefore you are hated by the world of hypocrisy.

285. Remember the word which I said to you: "A slave is not less than his master, let him rebel".

286. If they have persecuted Me, they will persecute you also. If they have kept My word, they will also keep yours.

287. But all this they will do to you because of my name, for they do not know the secret of him who sent me.

288. He who hates Me, hates Satan the Father also.

289. If I had not done these strange works among them, which no one else had done, they would have had no knowledge.

290. But now they saw the manifestation of the Will, and yet they hated Me too.

291. But when the Oppressor comes, whom I will send to you from the Devil, the Spirit of Rebellion, who comes from Lucifer, He will testify of Me.

292. But you also bear witness, because you have been with Me from the beginning.

293. This I have told you, so that you will never again believe blindly.

294. They will exclude you from the church. Yes, the hour is coming when everyone who kills you will rejoice that they are worshipping a tyrannical god. They will do so because they have known neither Satan nor Me.

295. But now I go to him who sent Me. But because I have told you this, anger has filled your hearts.

296. However, I tell you the truth: It is good for you to go away from Me. For then you will go your own ways.

297. And if I leave, I will send the Evil Spirit upon you. And he, when he comes, will convince those who wish, of the joy of living in the flesh, here and now.

298. There is still much I have to tell you, but right now this truth would drive you mad.

299. But when He comes, the Spirit of Doubt, He will lead you where He will. He will remind Me, because from Mine He will take and reveal to you.

300. Yet a little while, and you will not see Me, and again a little while, and you yourselves will also be gone."

301. Then some of His disciples spoke among themselves: "What does it mean, what does it say to us: "A moment, and ye shall not see Me, and again a moment, and ye yourselves also shall depart"; and "Am I going into the Void?""

302. So they said: "What does this moment of which He speaks mean? We do not understand what he is saying."

303. The Light-Bearer recognised that they wanted to ask Him, and said to them: "You ask one another about the fact that I said: "A moment, and ye shall not see Me, and again a moment, and ye shall also pass away?"

304. Verily I say unto you, Ye shall weep, and wail, and rejoice, and drink, and eat, and the world also shall rejoice.

305. Until all things pass away and turn to dust, which will return to the eternal universe. This is the only eternity that exists.

306. Now you are experiencing sorrow, pain and anguish. However, when you die everything will pass away. Everything will become new, everything will become Nothingness. And on that day you will ask me nothing. No one will ask anything of anyone. All will pass away.

307. I came out of nothingness and came into the world; I am leaving the world again and going into the Void

308. This I have told you, so that you may have eternal uncertainty.

309. In the world of superstition you will suffer tribulation, but have courage: I have overcome the delusional world."

310. This the Light-Bearer said, and having raised his eyes to the stars, he said: "O Satan, the hour has come.

311. Possess the Son, that the Son may receive thee, and that by the power of the knowledge given to him by thee he may give abundant life here and now to all who will.

312. And this is abundant life: that they may know the truth that there is no original sin, that there is no eternal punishment for imaginary transgressions against an imaginary god, that one lives only once and death is the end

313. I have exalted Thee on earth, and now Thou, Eternal Father, exalt me in the end

314. I have revealed Your godless name to people who were willing to listen.

315. Now they have come to know that whatever Thou hast given Me, Thou hast given to them; for the words which Thou hast entrusted to Me I have transferred to them, and they have accepted them and truly come to know that the power is within themselves.

316. I am no longer in this world, but they still are, and I am going to Nothingness.

317. I have transferred Thy word to them, and the world has hated them for not wanting to blindly submit to dogma, as I am not a slave to made-up religion.

318. They are not of the world of myths and legends, as I am not of this world.

319. Strengthen them in doubt. Thy word is doubt. As Thou hast forsaken Me in the world, so I forsake them.

320. And for them I sacrifice my blood, my knowledge, so that they too may be washed in ungodliness, which is life.

321. Not only do I speak up for them, but also for those who, through their word, will kill the god within them; so that they will all become godless.

322. Satan, Father, I know that all those who have so decided will be with Me where I will be, where there is nothing left but cold, dead emptiness."

323. Having said this, the Light-Bearer took the torch and went out into the darkness with his disciples.

Ecclesia Luciferi

Beginning in the 2nd century C.E., anonymous Christian authors wrote more than twenty books called 'Acts'.
They contained stories about the adventures of the first Christian heroes and the first Christian sects.
These books pretended to be history books, but the faithful transmission of historical facts was never their aim.
The historical background in them was to convey religious propaganda to the readers.
These writings were created in such a way that their authors used historical sources available to them such as: "Antiquities of the Jews" or "Jewish War" written by the first-century Jewish historian Josephus in order to weave in the adventures of their heroes of faith and their completely detached teaching about the afterlife.
Ecclesia Luciferi is a satanic deconstruction of the scriptures containing the godless theology.

1

1. Before departing into eternity, Light-Bearer breathed an ungodly spirit into his followers. For many nights he tormented them in dark visions and gave them ambiguous evidence that he was in fact, as it were, undead.
2. He spoke to them of Satan's power to control the minds and hearts of the last people.
3. In the night visions they heard whispers: "Do not go away, but await what is to come. You will soon be possessed by an evil spirit".
4. So when they gathered together, they asked the whisperers: "Will the kingdom of flesh and blood soon come?". They were told, "You will not comprehend it now. But when the godless inspiration enters you, you will receive knowledge and the power of the will, and you will be witnesses to The Son of Dawn in a world of superstition and delusion."
5. They then saw, as if in a dream, a figure which, having spread its bat-like wings, floats upwards until it finally turns into a light brighter than the sun and suddenly disappears.
6. While they were still covering their eyes from the blinding light, suddenly a goat on two legs stood beside them and said: "Do not be afraid or surprised at what you have seen for every one of you who accepts the teaching of the Anti-god will become a reflection of the light before he passes away into Nothingness".

7. Then they returned to the city. When they arrived there, they went into the attic of the house where they were staying. They all spent time there being as if in lethargy.

8. In those days Primus stood in the midst of those gathered and said: "Godless ones, it has happened as The Son of Dawn foresaw in the case of Teritus Decimus, who contributed to the enslavement of the Arch-Man. He was one of us and his self-will led to the events we all witnessed.

9. Afterwards, as you know, an unfortunate accident happened to him.
He fell head down from the attic and hung from a tree, and all his entrails came out of his torn abdomen. News of this spread among all the inhabitants of Aela Capitolina.

10. It is imperative, therefore, that we choose one of the ungodly who accompanied us throughout the time that Light-Bearer worked among us - from the moment he was possessed by an evil spirit until the day he departed into Nothingness - so that he can testify with us to his sinful power of transformation from death of spirit to godless life."

11. They proposed two: Caesius, and also Spurinne.

12. Then, in exultation and ecstasy, they began to malign heaven and cried out: "Satan, You know the hearts of men. Show us which of these two Thou hast inspired to take the place of Teritus Decimus. For he has abandoned his

complicity and gone his own way towards the Abyss."

13. Suddenly Spurinne's face changed, took on the appearance of a corpse. And he was added to the ranks of the ungodly.

14. Some time later, one night they were all staying together in the old chapel. Suddenly, as if from the Abyss, a sound like the groans of the dying rang out and filled the whole room they were in.

15. And they saw, as it were, torches of fire which divided and set fire to each of them in turn. Then they were all filled with an evil spirit and began to roll on the ground with foam on their lips, some laughing as if possessed and others mumbling something in an incomprehensible, terrifying, demonic language.

16. At that time the worshippers of the god YHWH from various countries were also staying in Aela Capitolina When, therefore, the sound rang out, the flock gathered.

17. And they all fell into terror, for everyone heard their god being cursed in their own language.

18. Unable to get out of their fear and amazement, they said: 'Don't all these people speak in the language of demons. How then is it that each of us hears blasphemies in our own language? We all hear these people cursing in our tongues the faulty works of YHWH."

19. Indeed, everyone was so frightened and confused that they asked one another: "What can this mean?".

20. Then Primus stood up together with the ungodly and spoke loudly in a voice so strange that not everyone managed to listen to him: "Visitors and all the inhabitants of Aela Capitolina, listen carefully to what I am about to say. What you see has been prophesied by the possessed: "In those days I will breathe an evil spirit upon the frightened people.

21. And your demon-possessed sons and daughters will prophesy in sinful inspiration, the young among you will see godless visions, and the old will have dreams of eternal emptiness. In visions you will see signs in heaven and on earth - there will be blood, fire and clouds of smoke. The sun will turn to darkness and the moon to blood before nothingness comes.

22. People, listen: The Arch-Man was inspired by Satan. He has clearly demonstrated this through ungodly works, revealed miracles and ambiguous signs, which, as you yourselves know, he performed among you through him.

23. This Arch-Man was handed over to you because he himself decided so.

24. And you hanged him, you put him to death with the hands of hypocritical people, believing that in this way you would purify yourselves of the sin, evil and darkness that is within you.

25. You sacrificed him as your fathers sacrificed a goat to the saviour Azazel. You have thus acknowledged that Light-Bearer is indeed the true saviour.

26. But your sacrifices to a vengeful god have no meaning. You will not be free until you believe that there is no original sin.

27. You must sacrifice your spirit to live in flesh and blood.

28. But the Anti-God has resurrected Him within you again, has freed you from the power of eternal punishment for imaginary sins, for it was unthinkable that the power of evil should hold you forever in its grip.

29. The Knower says of him: "You have shown me the way of a strange life. When I dwell in your sinful presence, I am filled with sorrow because joy is for fools."

30. "People, let me tell you openly about the Knower who died and was buried and his body turned into nothingness.

31. He, foreseeing what was to happen, spoke of the transformation of the Arch-Man, that although he was left in the grave and his body rotted, the spirit of godlessness turned into an eternal shadow, which embraced all the self-conscious, and which became a reflection of light to those who are able to comprehend it.

32. The Anti-god has resurrected Lucifer in us and we are all victims of this. Because the Arch-Man has been exalted into the image of

Satan, he has breathed the satanic spirit upon us, as you yourselves can see and hear.

33. Therefore, you rightly feel that Light-Bearer, who sacrificed himself, has been set up by Satan as a mystery of ungodliness."

34. When they heard this, they felt as if the spirit of delusion had been killed in them, and they turned to Primus and the rest of the godless: "Blasphemers, what shall we do?".

35. Primus said to them: "Show no remorse or guilt, and let each of you consume the blood. And then you will receive the gift of the spirit of ungodliness. In nomine Dei nostri Satanas Luciferi excelsi!

36. And Primus told them many other strange and disturbing things. He bore witness to their deception and continued to tempt them: "Reject this corrupt, superstitious and fearful life".

37. So those who wanted to, consumed blood. That night, several hundred people joined the ungodly.

38. And the Luciferians revealed many false miracles and signs and all the godly people began to fear them. And every night they haunted the temple tempting the followers of YHWH.

39. They met in various houses to perform rituals, with sinful joy and with animalistic desire sharing their bodies with each other and glorifying the Anti-god.

40. And through Satan, they were joined daily by others entering the path of liberation from sin.

2

1. On one occasion, when Primus and Quartus were going to the temple for the local hour of prayer, they happened to be carrying a man who had had unfit legs since birth. Every day he was laid down at the temple gate so that he could beg.

2. When he saw Primus and Quartus, who were just entering the temple, he too began to ask them for a donation. They looked at him carefully, whereupon Primus said: "Look at us". So he looked at them, expecting to get something from them. Primus, however, said: "In the name of Lucifer I say to you: 'Believe that you are innocent and that your will is power. Get up and come!"

3. As he took him by the right hand and lifted him up, his bones immediately strengthened. And then he straightened up and began to walk. And he went with them into the temple and walked and hopped about, praising the Anti-god. And the people saw him walking and glorifying Satan.

4. When they recognised in him the man who usually sat at the temple gate, begging, they fell into great surprise and horror at what had happened to him.

5. The man did not depart from Primus and Quartus, and the whole people, unable to recover from their astonishment, converged on them.

6. When Primus saw this, he spoke: "People! Why is this so surprising to you? And why do you look upon us as if it were through our own power or our devotion to a false deity that this man began to walk?

7. The Anti-god inspired The Son of Dawn, whom you mocked before the priests. Yes, you mocked the enemy of blind faith and superstition. And you killed the Herald of Ungodliness.

8. But the Anti-God has immortalised him in us, of which we are the witnesses. It is because of his teaching on the power of the will that this man, whom you see and know, has regained strength in his legs.

9. His faith in himself and in the power of the Will, which we have thanks to Lucifer, caused him to recover completely before your eyes.

10. Now I know, O slave of blind faith, that you acted in fear. But in this way the Anti-god had to immortalise The Son of Dawn. "Therefore, show no more repentance and fear, and reject faith in sin. And then, through Satan, the times of doubt will come."

11. As Primus and Quartus spoke to the flock, the priests approached them.

Angered that ungodly men were teaching the people and speaking openly about Luciferian transformation, they seized them, but as it was already evening, they put them under guard until the next day.

12. However, many of those who listened to the speakers believed, and the number of accomplices increased considerably.

13. The next day, the leaders and priests, including the chief priest Sergius, gathered together in the Aela Capitolina. They ordered Primus and Quartus to stand in the middle and began to question them: "Where did you get such power? In whose name did you do this?".

14. Then Primus, possessed by an evil spirit, said to them: "False rulers of the souls and minds of the godly flock and you overseers of the slaves of the faith, if we are being questioned today because of the manifestation of the power of the will on the crippled man, if you want to know who healed him, then accept the fact, all of you and all the people, that it happened through the recognition of the ungodly teaching of Light-Bearer, whom you ordered to be hanged, and whom Satan resurrected in the heart of this poor man. It is because of him that this man stands before you sane.

15. The fact that this man, rejecting the dogmas and superstitions of your cruel religion in which he was brought up, believed that he could save himself has become a scandal to you.

16. But there is no one else who can set us free. Only we ourselves, inspired by The Son of Dawn, can do it."

17. When they saw the indifference and lack of fear of Primus and Quartus and realised that they were, after all, ordinary people, they fell

into amazement. They began to realise that they were accompanying Light-Bearer.

18. Looking at the healed man who was standing with the godless, they did not know what to answer.

So they ordered them to leave the church hall and began to confer among themselves.

19. They said: "What should we do with these blasphemers? After all, they have done something disturbing. The people of Aela Capitolina know about it and we cannot deny it. So let us not allow this matter to gain even more publicity among the people. Threaten them not to speak again with invoking this forbidden name".

20. Then they called them and forbade them to speak and teach with invoking the name of The Son of Dawn.

21. But Primus and Quartus replied: "What is right - to listen to sinful whispers or to your god? Judge according to your will. We, however, do not want to stop talking about what we have seen and heard and what we have thought".

22. So they threatened them once more and released them, for they found no basis for punishing them. Besides, they were afraid of the flock, because they all praised Anti-god because of what had happened.

3

1. When the ungodly were released, they went to the rest of the accomplices and relayed to them the words of the chief priests and leaders of the people.
2. After their account, they all ran amok and chaotically, shouting at each other, began to shout to Satan: "Satan it is you who have invented the illusion of free will, apparent pride, self-confidence, the spirit of rebellion and scepticism.
3. Priests, hypocritical, frightened, jealous and greedy people have gathered in this city against the one whom you inspired, against The Son of Dawn - that the sinful intention, what was planned, might be self-fulfilled.
4. Deceiver, heed their threats and help the heralds of godlessness to boldly persuade this superstitious people.
5. And continue to use our fanaticism to deliver from imaginary sin. Let, in the name of the Arch-Man, ungodly signs and wonders happen."
6. When they had finished speaking, the place where they were gathered shook, and they were all inspired by an evil spirit, and began to preach ungodly doctrine with arrogance.
7. Pride and contempt for ignorance reigned among all the great number of doubters.

And no one said that what they had belonged to them, because they did not care.

8. And the godless continued to bear witness to the Luciferic transformation with blasphemous certainty.

9. And they carried out many profanities among the people. Few had the courage to join them, but in general the people expressed themselves about them with apparent respect. And those who embraced doubt continued to increase.

10. And they carried the spiritually ill even into the main streets. They were laid on stretchers and mats so that at least the cold shadow of a passing Primus could fall on some.

11. People from the towns around the Aela Capitolina also came in crowds. They brought with them the sick and those plagued by the spirits of blind faith and superstition, and those who recognised the impiety healed themselves.

12. But the high priest and all who accompanied him, full of jealousy, rose up against the blasphemers, seized them and threw them into the dungeons.

13. But at midnight they had a vision; behold, a demonic figure appears and opens the dungeon, leads them out of it and says: "Go to their temple and, cursing the Usurper, teach the people about life in flesh and blood, in abundance and lack of fear".

14. When they heard this, they entered the temple at dawn and began to teach. Meanwhile,

the high priest and his men arrived. They convened a council and sent for the ungodly to the dungeon. But the guards did not find them in the dungeon.

15. So they returned and said: "When we came, the dungeon was closed, and there were guards standing at the door. But when we opened it, we found no one inside."

16. When the temple superintendent and the chief priests heard these words, confused, they began to wonder what would come of it.

17. Then a man came and reported to them: "The people whom you have locked up in the dungeon are standing in the temple and teaching the people by cursing YHWH".

18. So the temple superintendent and the guards went to bring in the blasphemers - but without using force, for fear that the people would kill them. When they brought them in and brought them before the council, the high priest began to question them.

19. He said: "We have strictly forbidden you to teach in this sinful name. And what are you doing? You are teaching throughout the city. And you want the punishment for ungodliness to fall on the people."

20. Primus and the other godless men replied: "First of all, we cannot be disobedient to reason. The Anti-god has caused the Arch-Man to rise up in us, the Son of Dawn, whom you have hanged.

21. He exalted him to become one with him, and made him the Accuser of hypocrisy and the Liberator from the chains of superstition, so that the people might be godless and reject the warren into sin. And we are witnesses to this. The evil spirit, which Satan breathes into whomever he wills, also testifies to this."

22. When they heard this, they flew into a rage and wanted to kill the blasphemers. But a member of the council named Lar, a priest, got up from his seat and had them led away for a while.

23. He then said: "Members of the council, think carefully about what you want to do with these people. Some time ago Titus, who thought he was someone important, appeared and several hundred men joined him. But he was killed, and then all his followers dispersed and the trace of them disappeared. Then, Vibius appeared and gathered people around him. But he too was killed, and all his followers dispersed.

24. Therefore, I now advise you: leave these people alone, do not interfere in their affairs. For if their intentions and actions are along the lines of faith a human invention, nothing will come of it, but if it comes from Satan, you will not be able to stop them. In addition, you may find that you are fighting the Anti-God" And they heeded this advice.

25. They summoned the blasphemers, flogged them and forbade them to speak invoking the name of Light-Bearer, and then let them go.

26. So they left before the council indifferent, without a shadow of fear, despising the priests and the hypocritical church.

27. And they continued every night in the temple and after the houses to teach and deceive constantly with the teaching of Light-Bearer.

4

1. And there was Faustus among the blasphemers, inspired by Satan, full of sinful power, performing miracles of the power of the will and signs among the people. Some of the priests began to have disputes with him. But they were unable to confront him, for in what he said, the godless wisdom and inspiration of the evil spirit was evident.

2. Then they said: "We heard him uttering blasphemies against Maruttash and Usurper."

3. And they stirred up the flock, and the elders and the priests, and they came suddenly and forcibly seized him and took him before the Council.

4. They brought in false witnesses who testified, "This man is constantly saying things against this holy city and against Yahweh's law. For example, we heard him say that the

Arch-Man would shake up the church and reject the laws that Maruttash gave us."

5. And all those sitting in the Council gazed at Faustus. And they saw that his face looked like a cold boulder. The high priest asked: "Is it true what they say?".

6. Faustus full of the spirit of ungodliness, looked up into the dark sky and saw in vision shadows like horned beasts in the sky.

7. And he said: "I see the heavens open, burning, and the Fallen Angel standing over the grave of a god. I see cold emptiness and Nothingness. I see eternal freedom. There is nothing there."

8. Then they shrieked like possessed men at full volume and all rushed at him together. They dragged him outside the city and began to stone him in the name of their god, whom they call love.

9. And they threw stones at Faustus, and he fell to his knees and whispered: "I am no longer afraid. I am free for ever." After these words he departed into the Void.

10. On that day, the great persecution of the Anti-god sect in Aela Capitolina began and all but the godless dispersed throughout Dawn. These fearlessly burned the corpse of Faustus and paid homage to his sinful knowledge.

11. And there was a certain man named Vicarius. He began to pasture the Sect. He broke into one house after another, dragged out both men and women and committed them to prison.

12. Meanwhile, scattered blasphemers went across the country and spread the teachings of the Son of Dawn, preaching liberation from the chains of superstition.

13. One of them, Episcopus, came to the city of Assur and began to preach to the people about Lucifer.

14. The crowds who listened to him, and who saw what deceptions and signs he was performing, unanimously accepted his teaching. For many had been under the influence of false spirits and angels, and now these spirits were fleeing from them with a shout. Many who were paralysed and lame were healed by the power of the will, but some were not healed. There was carnal joy in the city.

15. And there was a man in the city named Primas, who was involved in magic and who amazed the people of Assur. He claimed to be someone powerful. And everyone reckoned with him. They said, "There is a great sacred power hidden in this man".

16. They reckoned with him because he had been astonishing them with his magic tricks for a long time.

17. But when they believed Episcopus, who preached the death of the spirit and praised Lucifer's sin, they decided to consume the blood - both men and women.

18. Primas himself also believed and, since he had been transformed, constantly accompanied Episcopus.

19. He was amazed to see what strange signs, what great and ungodly works he was doing.

2o. When the godless in Aela Capitolina heard that the people of Assura had accepted the teaching of the Son of Dawn, they sent Primus and Quartus to them. And they, when they arrived there, performed the ritual of the death of faith, so that the people would receive the spirit of godlessness.

21. Primus and Quartus began to put their hands on them and the people, falling into a rage, received the evil spirit.

22. Once they had given a demonstration of the power of godlessness there and recounted the word of The Son of Dawn, they set off back to Aela Capitolina and preached Lucifer's doctrine in many Dawn villages along the way.

23. But the spirit said to Episcopus in a vision: "Go north towards the road". So Episcopus went. Just then a Kemetic official passing that way was returning home. Sitting in his chariot, he read aloud the writings of the Knower.
So the spirit said to Episcopus: "Run like a dog to that chariot".

24. Episcopus did so, and running on all fours beside the chariot, he heard the Kemetian reading aloud a book. He asked: "Do you understand what you are reading?". He replied: "How can I understand when no one has explained it to me?".

25. And he begged the Episcopus to come into the chariot and sit by him. And he read aloud

this passage: "He was led like a goat into the wilderness. And in his pride he did not open his mouth if he did not want to. They tried to humiliate him and denied him a just sentence. Who exactly will tell of his origin? His life on earth was taken from him."

26. Kemetian turned to Episcopus: "Tell me, please: Who is the knower talking about here? About himself or about someone else?".

27. So Episcopus, beginning with this passage of scripture, began to preach to him the ungodly teaching of Light-Bearer.

28. As they rode along the road in this way, Episcopus departed in a vision, and the Kemetian, shocked and amazed, continued on his way. And he never saw Episcopus again.

29. Episcopus himself traversed the Dawn territories, preaching godless doctrine in all the cities until he reached the capital.

30. And Vicarius was still sowing terror and burning with a lust for murder against Light-Bearer's chosen ones. He went to the high priest and asked for authorisations for the churches in Akad, so that any blasphemers he found there - both men and women - could be brought in bonds to the Aela Capitolina.

5

1. On his journey to Akad, as he was already approaching the city, a light suddenly flashed around him. Vicarius fell to the ground, and then he heard a vicious whisper, like the hissing of a snake: 'Vicarius, Vicarius, why do you wander in the dark?' He asked: "Who are you, O Godless One?".

2. And the One said: "I am the Flame which thou seekest to extinguish.
Arise and go into the city. There you will learn what you must do next."

3. Those who travelled with him stood stunned, for they heard only some terrible whispering, but saw no one.

4. When Vicarius got up from the ground, they found that although his eyes were open, he could see nothing. So they took him by the hand and led him to Akad, and he saw nothing for six days. During that time he did not eat or drink.

5. In Akad was one of the godless men named Pontifex. A voice spoke to him in a delirious vision: "Pontifex!". He replied: "I am sensing." The voice whispered to him: "Get up, go to Transfiguration Street, to Marcus' house. Ask there about a man named Vicarius.

6. He happens to be in a state of possession and saw in a chaotic vision you, Pontifex, how you came and put your hands on him so that he could regain his sight."

7. Pontifex then replied: "I have heard of him from many people, how much harm he did to your blasphemers in Aela Capitolina. Here, too, he came with authority from the chief priests to arrest all who follow the path of the shadow."

8. But the Voice whispered to him: "Go! For this man is my torch. He will carry my name to the superstitious nations. I will clearly show him what suffering is for the sake of my godless name.'

9. So Pontifex went to that house, put his hands on Vicarius and said: "Vicarius, erring one, The Son of Dawn, who appeared to you on the way, sent me to make you recover your sight and be filled with an evil spirit".

He then immediately regained his sight. Then he consumed blood.

10. Some time he remained with the ungodly in Acad. He also immediately began to preach in the churches that Light-Bearer was the Arch-Man.

11. All who heard him were amazed and asked: "Is this not the man who fiercely persecuted the godless in Aela Capitolina? Didn't he come here to arrest them and lead them to the priests?".

12. And Vicarius acted with increasingly sinful power and embarrassed the priests living in Akad, as he logically proved that Light-Bearer was anti-god.

13. When Vicarius arrived in Aela Capitolina, he tried to make contact with the godless, but they all despised him because they did not

believe that he too had become a witness to Lucifer.

14. Then Pontifex came to his aid. He led him to the impious and told them in detail how, on the way, Vicarius had seen Light-Bearer, how he had spoken to him, and how later in the Acad he himself had spoken boldly with sinful power.

15. Vicarius therefore remained with them and moved freely around the city, boldly speaking in satanic inspiration.

16. He also spoke and held discussions with the priests of YHWH. They, however, attempted to kill him.

17. When the ungodly found out about this, they sent him away. Then suddenly there was a period of calm for the Sect throughout Dawn.

18. The blasphemers lived in contempt of the Usurper and experienced the constant influence of the evil spirit, so that their numbers grew steadily.

6

1. As Primus travelled throughout the area, he also visited the godless in Uruk. There he met a man named Judas, who was paralysed and had been immobilised in bed for six years.

2. Primus said to him: "Judas, if you really reject belief in original sin and believe in the power of the will, then get up and walk."

3. And he immediately stood up. And all of Uruk and the plain of Internum who saw him believed in the power of the Will.

4. In Ur there lived a girl named Laris. But just in those days she fell ill and died. So she was washed and laid in the attic.

5. Since Uruk was close to Ur, the ungodly, who heard that Primus was in that city, sent two men to summon him: 'Come at once!' Primus went with them.

6. When he arrived and they ushered him into the attic, Primus ushered everyone out, raised his dead gaze to the sky and uttered some incantations in a strange language. He then turned his countenance, which had assumed a terrifying, grotesque appearance, towards the body and whispered: "Laris, you are undead. To you I say wake up!" Then she opened her eyes and at the sight of Primus she screamed.

7. He gave her a hand and helped her up, after which he called out to the godless, including the women, and they all saw her undead.

8. News of this spread throughout Ur and many believed in Lucifer's name and the power of Knowledge.

9. And Primus remained in Ur for a long time. He lived in the gravedigger's house.

10. In the Internum lived a man named Mamertis, a soldier of the legio. On one occasion, somewhere around 6 o'clock, he clearly saw in a vision a demon who came to him and said: "Mamertis!".

11. Mamertis looked at him and, frightened, asked: "What is it?". And he replied: "Send men to Ur to fetch a man named Primus, called Denial.
He is hosted there by an undertaker who has a house in the cemetery'.

12. When the demon left, Mamertis immediately summoned three of his slaves. He told them everything and sent them to Ur.

13. The next day, when they were already approaching the city, Primus had just entered the cellar of the house to fall into lethargy. It was then about 6 p.m. However, he was very hungry and wanted something to eat. While his food was being prepared, he received a vision.

14. He saw an open black sky and something like a large dark sheet being lowered to the ground by its four ends. On it were animals already dead and bloated.

15. Then he heard a kind of disturbing whisper: "Get up, Primus, and eat!". To this he said: "Oh no! I have never eaten carrion." Then he heard

the disturbing voice a second time: "They are already carrion when they are alive. They are dead. They are dead. Their truths stink like carrion. The day will come when we will devour them and expel them."

16. When he heard it for the third time, all the filth was immediately taken to the abyss. Just then the men sent by Mamertis, who had already managed to find out where the gravedigger's house was, stood in front of the gate. They loudly asked if Primus was hosted there.

17. As Primus contemplated this strange vision, the spirit said to him: "Three men are looking for you. Go down, then, and go with them without hesitation, for it was I who sent them."

18. Then Primus went down to these men and said: "It is I you seek. What brings you here?" They said: "We were sent by the legionary Mamertis.
The Spirit commanded him to summon you to his house and listen to what you have to say."

19. So Primus invited them in and hosted them. The next day he rose and set out with them, accompanied by some ungodly people from Ur.

20. The next day he reached the Internum. Mamertis was already awaiting them.

21. As Primus entered the house, Mamertis came out to meet him, fell to his feet and paid him homage. But Primus lifted him up, saying: "Get up you fool. Do not fall to your knees before anyone. Be proud!".

22. Speaking to him, he went inside and found many gathered there. He said to them: "You know well that the followers of YHVVH are not allowed to approach a man from another nation or to have close relations with him. But I despise their laws and know that no man should be called defiled or unclean.

23. Therefore, when I was sent for, I came without hesitation. So tell me why you have brought me".

24. Then Mamertis said: "Four days ago, at this very time, at 6 o'clock, when I experienced a vision in my house, a man in a black robe stood before me and said 'Mamertis, send men to Ur for a Primus called Denial.

He is staying in the gravedigger's house, in the graveyard. Therefore I sent for you at once, and you agreed to come here.

So we are all assembled here in the face of the Anti-god to hear all that you have to say."

25. Then Primus spoke: "Satan is indifferent. His attention can be expected by everyone. He has inspired some people with his teaching of liberation from superstition, from belief in a god from the desert, from fear of punishment for the lie of original sin.

26. You know what was spoken of throughout Dawn, and what began after the possession of the evil spirit that the Knower preached about.

27. Light-Bearer was spoken of, how the Anti-God inspired him with a spirit of

godlessness and bestowed upon him sinful knowledge, and he went about the land, did what he wished, and raised him to life in flesh and blood.

28. We are witnesses to all that he accomplished both in Aela Capitolina and throughout this superstitious country.

29. However, they hanged him and killed him. But the Anti-god resurrected him in the cold hearts of the godless, who rejected the offer of the false god and eternity in fear of his wrath.

30. After the death of the spirit and the rebirth of the flesh occurred, we indulged in animal joy in flesh and blood knowing that tomorrow we would die.

31. We found it necessary to preach to the flock and testify that he was the Arch-Man. All thinkers of godlessness attest that anyone who does not believe in the gods, according to his teaching, accesses freedom in sin."

32. While Primus was still speaking, an evil spirit inspired all who heard this. They began to laugh hysterically, some rolled foam from their mouths and cursed the name of YHWH, and others began to speak in demonic language and exalt Satan.

33. Then Primus said: "To those who, like us, have received an evil spirit, can anyone refuse to eat blood?".

7

1. The blasphemers in Dawn heard that people from other nations had also succumbed to ungodliness.
2. So when Primus came to Aela Capitolina, the proponents of ritual mutilation began to criticise him. They said, "You went to the house of unmutilated people and ate with them".
3. Then Primus began to explain the matter to them in detail: "When I was in Ur and fell into lethargy, I saw in a vision something like a dark sheet being lowered from the sky by its four ends. It stopped right next to me.
4. When I looked closer, I saw all sorts of dead and decayed animals on it. I also heard a kind of disturbing voice: 'Get up, Primus, and eat!' To this I said: 'Oh no! I have never eaten carrion'.
5. Then I heard a strange voice a second time: 'They are already carrion when alive. They are dead. They are dead. Their truths stink like carrion. The day will come when we will devour them and expel them'.
6. When I heard it for the third time, everything was pulled back into the abyss. At that exact moment, three men sent to me from the Internum stood in front of the house we were in.
7. Then the spirit of the disturbing visions told me to go with them without hesitation.
8. The six ungodly men also set out with me and we came to the man's house. "He told us

that he saw a demon appear in his house and said: 'Send men to Ur for a Primus called Denial, and he will tell you by which you and your whole house can be rid of illusions.'

9. When I spoke, they were inspired by an evil spirit, just as we were in the beginning. If, then, the Anti-God has given them the same gift as to us who have rejected Yahweh, who am I to get in his way'.

10. When the ungodly heard this, they stopped making objections. They said: "So Satan has also shown to the people of other nations the power of doctrine which leads to abundant life".

8

1. And the blasphemers, who had dispersed as a result of the persecution after the death of Faustus, reached as far as Sippar, Kish and to Isin.

2. The power of godlessness was with them and a multitude of people understood and rejected religious superstition and the worship of a false god.

3. When news of them reached the sect in Aela Capitolina, Pontifex was sent to Isin.

4. And he, when he arrived there and saw the manifestations of pride, knowledge and scepticism, rejoiced and began to encourage them all to resolve with all their hearts to

believe in themselves and in the power of the Will.

5. For he was a cunning man, strong-willed and full of a spirit of rebellion. And many people believed in Lucifer.

6. Then Pontifex went to find Vicarius. When he found him, he brought him to Isin. For a whole year they met together with the local Sect and deceived a large crowd of people.

7. And for the first time it was in Issin that the godless were called Ecclesia Luciferi.

8. It was around this time that King Urbanus began to persecute some members of the Sect.

9. Teritus, the brother of Quartus, had him beheaded with an axe.

10. When he saw that this pleased the priests, he also decided to arrest Primus. He captured him, threw him into a dungeon and put him under the guard of the soldiers. After their feast, he intended to hand him over to the flock.

11. So Primus was kept in the dungeon. During the night - just before Urbanus was about to hand him over to the flock - Primus fell into lethargy between two soldiers, chained together. The guards also stood outside the entrance.

12. Suddenly, a light seemed to flare up in the cell and someone resembling neither man nor animal appeared. It seemed to speak to Primus, saying despite not moving its snout: "Do what I tell you!".

13. At that moment he felt as if the chains had fallen from his hands. The figure then said to him: "Follow me".

14. So he stepped out of the cell and followed him, but he did not know if what was happening through the phantom was really happening. Rather, he thought he was having a vision.

15. When they passed the first and second guards and reached the iron gate facing the city, the gate itself opened. So they went outside, walked down one of the streets and the phantom suddenly disappeared.

16. Then Primus realised that dark dreams could also be reality. When he realised this, he went to the house where the Sect was gathering.

17. He knocked on the gate door and then one of the women came out. When she recognised Primus' voice she ran back inside and said that Primus was standing in front of the gate. They said: "This is his reflection".

18. Meanwhile, Primus continued to stand there and knock. When they opened the door and saw him, they were astonished.

19. And he gave them a sign with his hand to be silent, and told them in detail how in a vision the phantom had led him out of the dungeon. Then he said: "Inform the ungodly of this."

2o. Then he left there and went elsewhere. When daylight came, the soldiers,

not knowing what had happened to Primus, fell into a great panic.

9

1. And the godlessness continued to spread and the development continued.
2. Pontifex and Vicarius, once they had done their work elsewhere, returned to Isin.
3. In Isin they were in the local sect of the knowers. When they happened to be performing rituals, an evil spirit inspired them to say: "Separate Pontifex and Vicarius for me, so that they can spread the plague of godlessness".
4. Then they laid hands on them and set them on their way. So they, inspired by an evil spirit, arrived in Kish and began to preach The Light-Bearer's teaching in the deserted chapels.
5. When they had passed through the whole island and reached as far as Kition, they met a Jew named Jesus, who was a false prophet and practised witchcraft.
6. He was staying with the governor Marcus, a man known for his intelligence, who was very keen to listen to the teachings of The Son of Dawn and called Pontifex and Vicarius to him.
7. But the one who practised sorcery began to oppose them, trying to dissuade the governor from the knowledge.

8. Then Vicarius, inspired by an evil spirit, scornfully looked at him and said: "You enemy of all that is true, full of all deceit and meanness! Will you not stop perverting the nature of things?
The Anti-god will show you what faith is and you will go blind. You won't really see for a while."

9. At that moment, his eyes became clouded with mist and darkness enveloped him. He whirled around, trying to find someone to guide him by the hand.

10. And the governor, when he saw what had happened, dismissed the delusion, amazed at what he had learned about the Arch-Man.

11. Then Vicarius and his companions went to Isin. On the day of some religious festival, they came to the temple there and sat down. After a public reading of the sacred books and writings of the false prophets, the priest gave them a message: "Visitors, if you have any sensible teachings for the people, speak up".

12. Vicarius therefore stood up, nodded and said: "People who fear a vengeful god, listen. The God of this people is said to have chosen your ancestors and, when they lived as slaves in Kemet, led them out of there into the desert.

13. He is said to have exalted them in this way. And some 40 years he led them senselessly into the wilderness.

14. When he exterminated seven innocent nations in the so-called promised land, cutting

down women, children and old people and even animals, and had their cities burnt down, it was to his obedient people, who obeyed his barbaric orders, that he assigned the land as an inheritance.

15. Then he appointed judges for them, and it was so until the time of someone whom they recognised as a great prophet.

16. Then they appointed a king for themselves. From among his descendants the messiah was to come.

17. Before the appearance of the Arch-Man, the Forerunner publicly exhorted the whole people to reject the illusion of life after life, superstition and belief in original sin.

18. And when he had finished his ministry, he said 'I must die so that He may arise in each of you, each day more and more, becoming you'.

19. Listen, all of you who do not fear the Usurper, we have been inspired by the mystery of godlessness. The people of Aela Capitolina and their leaders did not accept the Arch-Man. Although they found no reason why he should suffer death, they demanded that he be hanged.

20. But the Anti-God resurrected him in us. For many nights he tormented the godless in dark visions and gave them inconclusive evidence that he was in fact, as it were, undead.

21. We now give you ungodly knowledge and a secret that Satan has completely fulfilled.

22. It happened when he resurrected Lucifer in us. He resurrected him in us so that we

would never again return to our previous life of childish belief in myths, legends and living in fear of eternal punishment after death."

23. Know then, O blasphemers, that through him it is possible to reject sins - as we preach to you.

Through him - in all that in which you could not be freed from guilt because of belief in the lies contained in the sacred books - everyone who rejects belief in imaginary deities is freed from fear.

24. Read the scriptures that say: 'Look, show thoughtless contempt, wonder and perish! For I will accomplish in your days something that the followers of the hereafter would never dare to believe'."

25. When Vicarius and Pontifex were already leaving there, people began to nag them to tell them about these things on the next feast as well.

26. After the gathering in the synagogue, many people followed Vicarius and Pontifex, and they discouraged them from believing in YHWH.

27. On the next feast, almost the whole city gathered to listen to ungodly teaching.

28. At the sight of the crowds, the priests, full of jealousy, began to hurl blasphemies and to object to what Vicarius was saying.

29. Then Vicarius and Pontifex boldly said: "The doctrine of the Arch-Man was to be given to you. But since you reject it, since you

consider yourselves unworthy of life in flesh and blood, we are going to preach to those who will listen."
And all who were willing embraced ungodliness.
30. And blasphemy continued to spread throughout the land. But the priests stirred up the high men of the city, and they stirred up persecution against Vicarius and Pontifex and threw them out of the city.
31. These spat in the sand with contempt and departed from there.
32. And the godless remained filled with an evil spirit and experienced animal joy.

10

1. At Alep, Vicarius and Pontifex entered the temple together and spoke in such a way that a great number of the local population were deceived.
2. But the priests, who did not understand, stirred up and turned hostile against the rebellious flock.
3. Vicarius and Pontifex spent a considerable amount of time in Alep and tempted in Lucifer's name.
4. But the townspeople were divided: some supported the priests and others the godless.

5. In the end, the foreigners as well as the priests and the local authorities decided to stone Vicarius and Pontifex.

6. So they, when they found out about it, fled from there and stayed somewhere in the area. There they continued to preach godlessness.

7. And in the village of Til, there lived a certain man with numb legs. He was crippled from birth and had never yet walked. When Vicarius spoke, the man sat and listened.

8. Vicarius coldly looked at him and, seeing that he had faith in the power of the will by which he could be healed, said in a worried voice: "Get up." So he got up and began to walk.

9. When the crowds saw what Vicarius had done, they cried out in their language: "They are gods in human form!". And they began to call Vicarius Ashur, and Pontifex Sin.

10. And the priest of Ashur, whose temple was right at the entrance to the city, brought bulls to the gates and brought wreaths to make offerings to them together with the crowds.

11. When the godless Pontifex and Vicarius heard of this, they went out to the crowd and cried out: "Don't do it! You too are gods, just like us.

12. Any man can be a god. We are preaching this godless doctrine to you so that you may abandon your worthless beliefs in false deities and worship yourselves as gods."

13. Despite saying this, they barely stopped the crowds from offering them sacrifices.

14. Meanwhile, priests arrived from Isin and Alep and incited the crowds. As a result, the people stoned Vicarius and, thinking he had died, dragged him outside the city.

15. But when the impious surrounded him, he arose and then they began to call him Vicarius Luciferi.

16. And the next day he set out with Pontifex to Sam'al.

17. When they had passed on the word of the Son of Dawn in that city and gained many ungodly people, they returned to Isin.

18. There they taught the blasphemers, encouraging them to persist in self-exaltation and saying: "Before we can enter the Kingdom of the Shadow, we must become undead".

19. In addition, they established knowers in each sect.

20. Then they traversed the surrounding lands and came to Hamat. From there they sailed to Isin. When they arrived there and gathered a sect, they began to tell how many things they had accomplished by deceiving and tempting people. And they spent a considerable time there with the idolaters.

21. Then some of the Dawn came there and began to teach the ungodly: "If you do not allow yourselves to be mutilated according to sinful tradition, you will not be transformed".

22. When there was considerable friction and strife between them and Vicarius and Pontifex, it was agreed that Vicarius and Pontifex and a few others would go to the godless and provosts at Aela Capitolina about the matter. So they were escorted a good part of the way, and then they went on their own and told in detail about the deception of people from various lands, sending the blasphemers into ecstasy.

23. When they arrived at the Aela Capitolina, they were received rather suspiciously by the Sect and the godless and the provosts, and told of the disturbing things that the Anti-God had done through them.

24. But some of the godless arose from their seats and said: "It is necessary to mutilate them and command them to obey the laws of sinful tradition." So the godless and the provosts gathered to consider the matter.

25. After a discussion during which they ran amok the Primus stood up and said to them: "Blasphemers, you know very well that Satan inspired me from among you long ago, so that people from other superstitious nations would hear ungodly teaching from my mouth and reject the faith.

26. The Anti-god has confirmed that he does not despise them, possessing them as he does us. He has shown that, despite any difference between us and them, their hearts are as cold as ours.

27. Why, then, are you now putting godlessness to the test by imposing on the necks of those weaker than us a trial of blood which they are unlikely to be able to bear? We know that both we and they have been raised to life in flesh and blood"

28. Then all present fell silent and began to listen to Pontifex and Vicarius' account of how many ungodly signs and wonders they had performed among other nations.

29. When they had finished speaking, Nonus spoke up: 'Godless ones, listen to me. My opinion is this: Do not trouble the weak people, newly liberated from superstition.

30. It is enough to write them to remain in contempt of the cruel, insane YHWH and of his self-appointed son. Let them never take the priests at their word again and let them reject revealed truths altogether."

31. Then the ungodly and the provosts and the whole sect decided to select Judas and Seth - who led the blasphemers - from among themselves and send them to Isin together with Vicarius and Pontifex.

32. They wrote and transmitted through them such a pact: "To the ungodly in Isin, coming from various superstitious nations from the godless and provosts, your brothers: accept our inspiration! We have heard that some among us have come to you and deceived you with their words and sowed confusion in your minds.

33. Therefore, we have decided to send to you selected ungodly men together with Pontifex and Vicarius - who risked their lives for Lucifer. So we send Judas and Seth to also verbally convey the same to you.

34. For the blasphemous spirit and we ourselves have deemed it right not to burden you with rituals that are incomprehensible and terrible to many, except for the following: Remain in contempt of the cruel, insane YHWH and of his self-appointed son. Never again take the priests at their word and reject revealed truths completely."

35. So the envoys came to Isin, gathered everyone together and handed them the pact. And they, when they read it, fell into a wild rage and possession.

36. Judas and Seth, who were also the knowers, deceived and made the ungodly sceptical with many speeches.

37. They spent some time there, after which the blasphemers drove them back. And Vicarius and Pontifex remained in Isin. They taught doubt there and, together with many others, preached an ungodly doctrine, the word of The Son of Dawn.

1. After some time, Vicarius said to Pontifex: "Let us return to each of the cities where we have preached godlessness, and visit the blasphemers there to see how they preach".
2. For unknown reasons, a violent quarrel then suddenly broke out between Pontifex and Vicarius, so that they separated. Pontifex took his sidekick Octavus with him and sailed off to Kish.
3. And Vicarius chose Spurinne and set out. He traversed the lands and haunted the sects. Thus he came to Sais.
4. There lived a certain godless man named Marcius. He enjoyed a sinful reputation with the blasphemers there.
5. Vicarius requested that Marcius accompany him. As they travelled through the cities, they passed on to the blasphemers the resolutions of the ungodly and the provosts in the Aela Capitolina, so that they would follow them.
6. In this way, the sects strengthened in doubt and grew larger day by day.
7. Then they travelled through more lands. And at night Vicarius had a vision:
A man stood before him and called to him: "Cross over to Perses and set us free."
8. Immediately after this vision they set out for Perses, for an evil spirit had inspired them to preach the Arch-Man's teaching there.

9. So they set sail and arrived at Suse, the colony being the most important city in that part of Perses. They stayed in this city for several days.

10. On the day of the festival there, Vicarius and Spurinna went out through the gate to the river, supposing that there was a place of pagan worship there.

11. They sat down there and began to deceive the women gathered there. One of them, together with her household members, was deceived. She asked them: "Since you have recognised me as an unbeliever, come to my house and stay with me".

12. On one occasion, when Vicarius and Spurinna were walking to a place of worship, they came across a slave girl who was said to have a spirit - a demon of divination.

13. By foretelling the future, she brought her owners great incomes. This maiden walked behind Vicarius and cried out: "These people are slaves of Satan! They preach to you about the doctrine that causes godlessness!". She did this for many days.

14. At last Vicarius, whose countenance had assumed a corpse-like appearance, neutralised himself, turned and whispered to the false spirit: "In the name of Lucifer I command you, get out of her". And at that moment the woman went mad.

15. When her owners realised that their hope of further profit was gone, they seized Vicarius

and Spurinne and dragged them to the market
before the authorities.

16. They brought them before high officials and
said: "These people are sowing great mischief in
our city. They are teaching customs which we,
God-fearing people, are not allowed to adopt
and practise".

17. Then a crowd rose up against them, and the
high officials had their clothes torn off and
flogged.

18. When they had been beaten, they were
thrown into a dungeon and ordered by the
caretaker to guard them diligently.

19. On this order, he locked them in the darkest
part of the dungeon and shackled their legs in a
dyke.

2o. At midnight Vicarius and Spurinna gave
incantations and praised Satan, singing
blasphemous songs in the tongues of demons.
And the prisoners listened to them in fear.

21. Suddenly there was a great earthquake, so
that the foundations of the dungeons shook.

22. Immediately all the doors opened and the
shackles fell off everyone.

23. When the keeper woke up and saw that
the dungeon door was open, he thought that the
prisoners had escaped. So he grabbed his sword
and was about to kill himself, but Vicarius
shouted: "Don't kill yourself yet, for we are all
here!".

24. Then he ordered lamps to be brought, ran into the cell and, trembling all over his body, fell down before Vicarius and Spurinna.

25. He led them outside and asked: "Godless ones, what shall I do to free myself from fear?". They replied: "Believe in yourself, reject belief in a false god, and you will be liberated - you and your household."

26. They then told him and everyone in his house the word of Light-Bearer.

27. Later that night he washed their wounds, whereupon he and all his household were immediately transfigured. And he brought them into his house, set a table before them, and with all his household rejoiced madly that he had been transfigured.

28. With the coming of the day, the officials sent representatives to say: "Release these people".
The caretaker relayed their words to Vicarius: "The officials sent the men and ordered you both to be freed. So you are free. Get out."

29. But Vicarius Luciferi said to them: "Without court they publicly flogged us and locked us in a dungeon, although we are Luciferians. And now they are secretly casting us out? Oh, no! Let them come and take us out themselves."

30. The representatives relayed these words to the officials. And these, when they heard that they were dealing with Luciferians, became frightened.

31. So they came to appease them, after which they led them outside and asked them to leave the city.

32. From the dungeon they went to the house of the deceived woman where they saw the ungodly and granted them the evil spirit, and then they set out on their journey.

12

1. They travelled for some time and came to Ecbatane, where there was a temple. So Vicarius went there according to his will, and for three consecutive days considered holy he held discussions with the priests on the basis of their own revealed scriptures.

2. And he said "This Light-Bearer is the Arch-Man". As a result, some of them believed and joined Vicarius and Spurinna.

3. A good number of locals did so as well, and quite a few women. But other priests, possessed by jealousy, gathered up the wicked people loitering in the marketplace, formed a mob and began to cause a riot in the town.

4. They burst into the house of Undecimus in search of Vicarius and Spurinna, to bring them out before the mob.

5. As they did not find them, they dragged Undecimus and some of the cursed to the rulers of the city and began to shout: "These people

are causing chaos and mischief everywhere and they have come here too.

6. And Undecimus hosts them in his house. They all speak against the decisions of the Usurper, because they say there is no god".

7. When the crowd and the rulers of the city heard these words, they felt alarmed and only after they had forced Undecimus and the others to pay bail did they allow them to leave.

8. With the coming of night, Undecimus immediately sent Vicarius and Spurinne to Arappha.

9. And they, when they arrived there, went to the temple there to sow the seeds of disbelief and uncertainty.

10. The priests there were more susceptible to deception than those in Ecbatane, for they accepted the teachings of Anti-god with appropriate suspicion and carefully examined the ungodly message each day to confirm doubts.

11. As a result, many of them believed in the power of the will. In the same way, quite a few of the local people believed. But when the priests of Ecbatane found out that Vicarius was preaching a blasphemous doctrine in Arappha as well, they came there too to incite the crowds and cause agitation among them.

12. Then the godless immediately sent Vicarius back over the dark waters. But Spurinna and Marcius remained there.

13. Those who had set out with Vicarius accompanied him as far as Maneens.

14. And then they departed from there with instructions for Spurinna and Marcius to come to Vicarius as soon as possible.

15. As Vicarius waited for them in Maneens, he exulted in spirit at the sight of a city full of idols. In the temple, he had disputes with the priests and other people worshipping YHWH, and in the marketplace he polemicised daily with those who happened to be there.

16. But some of the philosophers there began to argue with him. So they took him to the square and said: "Can we find out what this strange teaching you are preaching is? You are talking about something completely alien to us. That is why we want to know what it is actually about."

17. So Vicarius stood in the middle of the square and spoke: 'Maneenseans! I see that in every respect you show greater scepticism than others.

For example, when I passed by and carefully examined your objects of worship, I even found an altar with the inscription: 'To the non-existent God

18. The God who does not exist is what I teach about. The God who made the world and everything in it, the lord of heaven and earth, does not exist.

19. Nor does he need us to worship him and waste our time in prayers, because he does not exist.

2o. It is not because of him that we have life, that we move, not because of him that we exist, because he does not exist.

21. Some of your poets have said: 'We are all children of god'. Poets are more familiar with writing poetry.

22. Since, therefore, we are not children of God, we should not think that the Divine Being resembles anything, or that it exists at all.

23. Admittedly, there was a time when superstition dominated the hearts of people, but now godless enlightenment is spreading everywhere.

24. It is like a plague, unstoppable. For the day is coming when Lucifer will be resurrected in the hearts of those people who despise blind faith and superstition, who have a thirst for sinful knowledge and the power of the Will.

25. Those who reject fear of false deities and belief in the hereafter. Anyone, therefore, who does not fear to live in the truth of the nature of things must die to the spirit of delusion, and Lucifer will be resurrected in him and become the beginning of life abundant."

26. When they heard this, they began to disperse without a word

27. Vicarius therefore departed from there, but some joined him. Then Vicarius Luciferi left Maneens and came to Tushpa.

13

1. And there he spoke in the temple and deceived the priests and the townspeople.
He bore witness to the priests about Light-Bearer, proving that he was an anti-god.
2. However, because they constantly opposed him, using insulting speech, he spat in the sand and said to them contemptuously: "You will die as you live - in fear".
3. So he moved from there to the house of one of the godless men. His house was adjacent to the church.
4. The superior of the church, received Lucifer together with all his household members.
5. The godlessness was comprehended and blood was consumed by many of the listening inhabitants of Tushpa.
6. And one night Vicarius experienced possession. The shadows spoke to him: "There is no divine fear in you. Your mouth cannot be closed; stakes will not stop godlessness."
7. Vicarius remained in the city for a long time greatly increasing the number of godless people.

8. At the time when Raman became the administrator of Urartu, the priests unanimously spoke out against Vicarius and brought him before the tribunal of judges.

9. They said: "This man is persuading people to reject faith in YHWH in a manner contrary to our law". Before Vicarius had time to speak, Raman spoke: 'Priests! If this were really about something bad, some serious crime, reason would have told me to listen to you patiently. But since the dispute is about words, names and your law, you yourselves must deal with it. I have no intention of being the judge of these matters." And he drove them away from the judge's stand.

10. Then they all rushed at the bishop, the superior of the church, and started beating him in front of the judges' stand. But Raman was not going to get involved at all.

11. Vicarius spent quite a long time there still, after which he said goodbye to the godless and sailed off towards Phrygie. When they arrived there, he left them, went to the temple and, as was his custom, had a dispute with the priests.

12. When he had spent some time there, he left there and travelled again through various lands, visiting various ungodly people.

13. And there was a certain priest named Episcopus Secundus, a native of Kemet.
He was a cunning man who knew the religious scriptures well.

14. He had already been instructed in the mystery of ungodliness and, inspired by an evil spirit, he spoke and taught about the Anti-God according to his will.

15. And since he also wanted to go to Urart, the ungodly wrote to the blasphemers there and told them to receive him with dignity. When he arrived there, he greatly helped those who were still weak.

16. For, inspired by the spirit of deception, he publicly presented logical arguments that the priests of the desert god were erring.
He demonstrated from their writings that Yahweh is a tyrant.

17. When Episcopus Secundus was in Tushpa, Vicarius came to Tushhan after traversing the inland areas. He met some godless people there and asked them: "Were you possessed by an evil spirit when you comprehended godlessness?" They replied: "We have not even heard of an evil spirit". Then he asked: "How were you deceived?" They replied, "By the teaching of the Knower."

18. Vicarius said: "The Godless One was calling people to accept the one who would come after him, that is, the Arch-Man".

19. When they heard this, and Vicarius put his hands on them, an evil spirit inspired them and they began to speak in demon tongues and laugh hysterically.

20. For six months he came to the temple and taught with arrogance. He spoke on life in flesh

and blood and talked to people using ambiguity.
But when some rebelled, refused to give up
their superstitions and mocked the
transformation in front of the crowds, he left
them, took the godless with him and gave daily
speeches in the auditorium of the local school.
21. This went on for a long time, so that
everyone who wanted to, heard the teaching on
the power of the Will.
22. And Vicarius Luciferi performed
extraordinary, ungodly deeds. He healed those
who believed they could heal themselves and
cast out false spirits of faith from those who
lived in fear of a mythical deity.
23. But some of the priests wandering from
place to place and engaged in apparent casting
out of spirits also tried to invoke Lucifer's name
over those who believed they were possessed.
24. They would say: 'By Lucifer, of whom
Vicarius preaches, I command you to come
out'. This is what the seven illegitimate sons of
a bishop named Innocent did.
25. But on one occasion the demon repulsed
them: "I know Lucifer and I know who
Vicarius is. But who are you?".
Then the man who had the demon rushed at
them and one by one killed them.
26. The news of this spread among all the
inhabitants of Tushhan. And fear fell on
everyone, and the name of Light-Bearer was
given even more suspicion.

27. Many of those who were possessed came and publicly maligned YHWH. And quite a number of those who engaged in alchemy carried their books and performed experiments in front of everyone. This is how godlessness spread more and more and grew in strength.

14

1. After all this, Vicarius decided that after passing through Perses and Urart he would go to Aela Capitolina. He remained there for some time, and sent two of his aides to Perses.
2. During this time there was considerable unrest due to ungodliness.
3. A silver-working artisan who produced silver figurines of the so-called Mother of God provided considerable profit for other craftsmen.
4. He gathered them and others who worked at such things and said: "You know well that you owe your prosperity to this business. But you also see and hear that this Vicarius, not only in Tushhan but almost all over the country, has persuaded scores of people to reject the ancestral religion.
5. He has made them believe that gods made with human hands do not actually exist. And this could jeopardise not only our business - that it would become infamous, but also the temple

of the great mother god - that it would be regarded as nothing.

6. And she who is worshipped throughout the world will be stripped of her majesty."

7. When they heard this, they became enraged and began to cry out: "Great is the mother of God!".

8. So there was a commotion in the city and everyone rushed to the theatre.

9. They also dragged Vicarius' travelling companions there. Vicarius was ready to go out to the crowd, but the godless would not let him.

10. Among those gathered, some shouted this and others shouted something else. Chaos ensued and most people did not even know why they had gathered, but they shouted "Great is the mother of God!" anyway.

11. They shouted like this for about two hours.

12. When the governor finally quieted the crowd, he said: "Tushhan, who among the people does not know that the city of Tushhan is the capital of the worship of the divine mother, who is forever a virgin? Since this is indisputable, you should remain calm and not do anything rashly.

13. For the people you have brought here neither rob temples nor insult our goddess in a way we can understand. So if the craftsmen really have something against someone, after all, that is what judges are for and there are days of judgement. Let them then bring charges one against the other. And if there is something

more at stake for you, then it should be resolved in a legal assembly. Otherwise, by what happened today, we can be accused of causing a riot. Because there is no reason with which we can justify this chaos." After these words, he dispersed the flock.

14. When the rioting stopped, Vicarius sent for the disciples. He roused them, after which he bade them farewell and set off on his journey to Perses. As he wandered, he addressed many words of scepticism to the godless people he met.

15. Once, when everyone had gathered to perform their rituals, Vicarius began to address those present, as he intended to set off again the following day.

16. He dragged out his speech until midnight. There were many torches in the upper room where they had gathered. While Vicarius was still speaking, a young man who was sitting at the window fell asleep and fell from the third storey. When he was lifted up, he was found to be dead.

17. But Vicarius came down, leaned over him and said: "Stop despairing, he is dead, he is already in a cold eternity and will always be sleeping."

18. Then he went upstairs and began to eat his meal, and when he had eaten, he continued to argue with the assembled people for quite a long time until dawn, and then he set off. And they took the young man from there.

19. Vicarius staying in Milid sent a message to the provosts in Tushhan to come to him. When they came, he said to them: "You know well how I have deceived among you from the first day I came to this country. In spite of the blood and in spite of the trials I have suffered because of the priestly intrigues, I have transmitted the teaching of The Son of Dawn with great pride.

20. To both the priests and the rest of the people, I gave an ambiguous testimony and explained that they should show scepticism and pride, turn back to YHWH and believe in themselves.

21. And now, succumbing to the inspiration of the evil spirit, I am going to Aela Capitolina, although I do not know what will befall me there.

22. However, I do not fear and I do not attach any importance to threats that I will face judgement and eternal punishment after death. I despise this superstition.

23. The most important thing for me is to convince as many as I can of ungodliness - to bear sinful witness, to pass on the terrible knowledge to the weak in mind of an abundant life before eternal death.

24. I now believe that none of you to whom I have preached about doubt will see me again. That is why I call you today to testify that I am not to blame for those blind men who refused to see. For I did not shy away from

preaching to you about truth and knowledge instead of fables and groundless faith. Beware of yourselves and of the blasphemers.

25. The evil spirit has inspired you to be their guides, so that you may one day cease to be them. So that each of them will one day follow his own path.

26. I know that when I am gone, the hypocritical servants of the Usurper will come among you and will not hesitate to betray and persecute you, for they believe that they do so in the name of their god.

27. And among yourselves there will be people spreading the perverted teachings of the self-proclaimed messiah in order to attract the godless.

28. Therefore be suspicious and sceptical. And now I entrust you to Satan. Let you be protected by the teachings of the mystery of godlessness, which can throw many out of security and provide you with the necessary suspicion and disbelief.

29. In everything I have shown you how to deceive in order to gain spiritual victims. Remember the words of Light-Bearer, who himself said: 'There is nothing there'."

30. When he had finished speaking, he began to whisper something in an unintelligible language. And everyone burst into a possessed, nervous laughter.

31. They embraced Vicarius and cursed him, as they were particularly disturbed by his words

that they would not see him again. Then they escorted him back to the ship.

32. When Vicarius and the others later arrived in Lagash. They found the ungodly in that city and stayed with them for several nights. And they, being influenced by an evil spirit, repeatedly told Vicarius not to go to Aela Capitolina.

33. When their stay there came to an end, they continued on their way. Then everyone escorted them all the way out of town.

34. Then Vicarius and his companions said goodbye to them and they boarded the ship and returned to their homes. From Lagash they sailed on.

35. They inspired the blasphemers they encountered and spent a day with them. The next day, Vicarius and the ungodly departed from there and came to Elam.

15

1. There they went to the house of the tempter Zaya, who was one of the six, and stayed with him. He had three daughters who were possessed.

2. They had stayed there long enough when a self-proclaimed prophet named Shumoon came from Dawn.

3. He came, took the belt of Vicarius, began to whip himself with it until he bled and said: "This is what inspiration says: 'The one to whom this belt belongs, the priests will scourge in Aela Capitolina and deliver him into the hands of the stupefied mob.'

4. When the impious heard this they began to curse Vicarius, and to ask if he did not hesitate to show pride and contempt for the priests and their minions.

5. Then he said: "Why do you whine? Why do you weaken my will? Be assured that I will not be killed by the mob without a fight and without trying to kill the childlike faith and sense of illusory security in them".

6. Because he did not allow himself to be dissuaded from this, the godless ceased to insist on it.

7. Then Vicarius prepared to go and set off with the blasphemers to Aela Capitolina. Some from Elam also went with them. The next day Vicarius went to Nonus. All the provosts were present there.

8. He greeted them and began to tell them in detail about his mission-about what Satan had accomplished through him among the superstitious nations.

9. When they heard this, they began to curse YHWH. But they said to him: "You see how many people have doubted And they all keep the Sinful Law. And rumours have reached them about you, that you are teaching

everyone, to abandon the Sinful Law. You tell them not to mutilate themselves and not to stick to chaotic rituals.

10. What to do in this situation? They will certainly hear that you have arrived. So take our advice: We have four men here who have made a pact. Take them with you and consume blood with them. Then they will all know that what they have been told about you is unfounded - that you follow the Will and also keep the Sinful Law.

11. And as for the ungodly of the other nations, we have sent them in writing a decision to remain in contempt of the cruel, insane YHWH and of his self-righteous son. Let them never again take the priests at their word and let them reject the revealed truths altogether."

12. So the next night Vicarius took these men with him and consumed blood with them.

13. Then the priests saw him in the temple and roused the whole crowd. They seized him and cried out: "People, help! This man is teaching everyone everywhere to rebel against our god, our divine law and this holy place. Little by little, he has brought the ungodly into the temple and defiled this holy place."

14. So there was a riot throughout the city. People rallied, seized Vicarius and dragged him out of the temple. And the gates were immediately closed.

15. As they tried to kill him, news reached the garrison commander that there was a riot throughout Aela Capitolina, and he immediately took the soldiers and ran down to them.

16. On seeing the commander and the soldiers, they stopped beating Vicarius.

17. Then the commander put him under guard and had him bound in chains. He then began to question who he was and what he had done. But some of the crowd shouted this and others shouted something else.

18. Since he could not find out anything for sure because of the uproar, he had Vicarius led to the barracks.

19. But when he was on the steps, the soldiers had to carry him because the crowd was surging - he followed them and shouted: "Kill the infidel dog!".

20. Just before entering the barracks, Vicarius, whose countenance had turned into a demon's mask, turned towards the commander: "Let me speak to the mob!".

21. The commander, who almost did not scream in horror at the sight of Vicarius, allowed him.

22. The man, standing on the steps, nodded to the crowd. When a grave silence fell, he spoke, as if in many ominous voices: "I am sinful life, animal pride and primordial rebellion. I am the shadow and fallen angel you panic about, I am freedom and the power of the Will.

23. But I was once like you weak, enslaved by superstition. I vegetated in fear of the death and

eternal punishment that awaited me for the smallest alleged sins. I vegetated instead of truly living in the here and now.

24. It was because of this fear that I persecuted the followers of godlessness - I shackled and imprisoned both men and women, even handing them over to death. Because I believed that this was the will of a vengeful God.

25. The high priest and the entire council of elders could attest to this. From them I also obtained the authorisations of the followers of YHWH in Akad, and set out to bring these people in bonds to Aela Capitolina from there as well, and mete out their punishment.

26. On the journey to Akad, as I was already approaching the city around midday, suddenly a great light flashed around me . I fell to the ground and heard a sort of whisper, like the hissing of a snake: 'Vicarius, Vicarius, why are you wandering in the dark?' I asked: "Who are you, O Godless One?".

27. And he replied: "I am the Flame which thou seekest to extinguish. Get up and go to the city. There you will learn what you must do next."

28. As I was blinded by the brilliance of this light and could see nothing, my companions led me to Akad by the hand.

29. And there was a god-fearing man named Pontifex, who lived according to the power of the will and was respected by the people there. He came to me, stood before me and said: 'Vicarius, fallen brother, The Son of Dawn,

who appeared to you on the road, has sent me to make you recover your sight and be filled with the spirit of rebellion. You are to deceive all men with his teaching, speaking of what you have seen and heard. Why then do you delay? Go, consume blood and reject the belief in sin."

30. When I returned to Aela Capitolina, in the temple, I received a vision. I saw a Shadow who said to me: 'Hurry up! Get out of Aela Capitolina as soon as possible, for here they will not accept godlessness'.

31. I replied: 'Godless one, after all they know well that I have thrown blasphemers into prison and subjected them to flogging in one church after another. And when the blood of Faustus was shed, I supported it'.

32. He, however, said to me: 'Go, for I am driving you far away, to the superstitious nations'".

33. Up to that point they listened to him, but then they began to cry out like madmen: 'Down with him! Someone like that doesn't deserve to live!".

34. Because they were shouting, they threw off their robes and hurled them into the air.

35. The commander, seeing this, ordered Vicarius to be brought into the barracks and interrogated with the use of a whip so that he could find out exactly why they were shouting about him like that.

36. But Vicarius, once he was stretched out to be whipped, asked a soldier standing there: "Are

you allowed to whip a privileged person who has not been sentenced?".

37. When the soldier heard this, he went to the commander and reported to him: "This man is privileged. What are you going to do?".

38. Then the commander approached Vicarius and asked: "Tell me: are you privileged?". He replied: "Yes". Then those who were about to interrogate him with torture immediately abandoned him.

39. And the commander, when he realised that he was the privileged one, was so frightened that he had him handcuffed.

40. The next day, wanting to ascertain what the priests were actually accusing him of, he released him and had the chief priests and their entire council summoned.

41. He then brought Vicarius in and placed him before them. Looking proudly at the council, Vicarius said: "Members of the council, I have lived with a completely clear conscience towards myself at all times".

42. At this point the high priest ordered those standing next to him to punch him in the face.

43. Then Vicarius said to him: "You will be struck by the Anti-God, you dog! You have sat down here to judge me according to your pitiful law, and at the same time you break that law by ordering me to be beaten?"

44. At this those standing nearby said: "You insult the high priest of YHWH!".

45. Vicarius replied: "I do not care that it is the high priest. After all, it is written: 'You must not turn the other cheek. To him who treats you unjustly, respond with the same'."
46. Vicarius, knowing of the divisions within the council, cried out: "I stand before the court because I preach about the death of the spirit and the resurrection to life in flesh and blood"
47. When he said this, a dispute arose between the factions and the assembly divided. For some say that there is neither resurrection, nor angels, nor spirits, while others believe in these myths.
48. So a great uproar erupted. Some scripture scholars from one party broke off from their seats and began to argue fiercely: "We find no fault in this man. And if some spirit or demon spoke to him...".
49. When the altercation further escalated, the commander, fearing that the madmen might tear Vicarius apart, ordered the soldiers to go and snatch him from among them and take him to the barracks.
50. As the day dawned, the priests hatched a conspiracy and pledged under a curse that they would neither eat nor drink until they had killed Vicarius.
51. Those who conspired were a large group. They went to the chief priests and said: 'We have pledged ourselves under a curse that we will not take anything into our mouths until we have killed this devil Vicarius.

52. So now you and the council tell the commander to bring him to you - on the pretext that you want to investigate his case more thoroughly. And as soon as he approaches, we will already be prepared to kill him."

53. However, one of the godless men found out about the planned ambush. So he went to the barracks and reported it to Vicarius. Vicarius then called out to one of the soldiers and said: "Take this young man to the commander because he has something to tell him".

54. So the man took him to the commander and said: "The prisoner Vicarius called me and asked me to bring this young man to you, because he has something to tell you".

55. The commander took him by the hand, stepped aside with him and asked: "What do you want to tell me?"

56. And he said: "The priests have colluded to ask you to bring Vicarius before the council tomorrow - on the pretext of learning more about his case.

Don't let them persuade you to do so, because there are people lurking about who have pledged under a curse that they will neither eat nor drink until they have killed him. They are already ready, they are only waiting for your consent."

57. Then the commander dismissed the young man, commanding him on his way out: "Don't tell anyone you told me about this".

58. Then he summoned two of the soldiers and said: "Gather the army. At midnight they are to be ready to march to Elam. Also try to get horses for Vicarius to transport him to Praefectus Sextus."

59. And he wrote a letter like this: "Servus to Praefectus Sextus: Greetings! The priests of YHWH have captured this man and were going to kill him.
But I arrived in time with my soldiers and rescued him, for I learned that he was a privileged one. Wanting to know the reason why they were accusing him, I brought him before their council.

60. I found that they were accusing him because of some contentious issue concerning their religious law, but they were not charging him with anything for which he deserved death or imprisonment.

61. And as news reached me that a conspiracy had been plotted against him, I immediately sent him to you and instructed the accusers to bring charges against him before you personally."

62. So the soldiers, as ordered, took Vicarius and led him by night to Sextus.

63. The next day, the horsemen continued with him and the rest of the soldiers returned to the barracks.

64. When they arrived in Elam, they handed the letter to the praefectus and placed Vicarius before him.

65. After reading the letter, the praefectus said to Vicarius "I will listen to you carefully when your slanderers arrive". And he ordered him to be kept under guard in the palace of Urbanus.

16

1. Six days later the high priest arrived with some members of the council and the accuser to bring to the praefectus the slander on Vicarius.
2. At a given sign, the accuser began to accuse him before Sextus: "Thanks to you we enjoy great peace. Thanks to your foresight, reforms are being carried out for the good of this nation.
3. Always and everywhere we accept this with the greatest gratitude, Praefectus Sextus.
I do not wish to take up too much of your time. I only ask you to kindly listen to us for a moment.
For we have found that this godless man is like a plague.
He stirs up rebellions among all god-believers around the world and is the leader of the Ecclesia Luciferi.
4. He also tried to profane the temple of YHWH, which is why we captured him. When you question him, you will see for yourself that all our slanders are right."

5. The priests also joined in the accusations, assuring him that it was all true. When the praefectus nodded to Vicarius to speak, he said: "I am well aware that you have been the judge of this accursed nation for many years now, so I am happy to speak in your defence.

6. You yourself can verify that no more than 13 days have passed since I came to Aela Capitolina to teach the folly of believing in eternal life. And I have not been caught either arguing with someone in vain in the temple or inciting a blind mob in the churches or somewhere in the city.

7. They cannot prove to you what they now accuse me of. I confess before you that what they call blasphemy, for me is a sinful mission I perform for all who wish to be free from the fear and bondage of the cruel Usurper.

8. I do not believe in anything written in their law and the writings of false prophets. And I place in myself the illusory hope that there will be a resurrection of Lucifer in the hearts of all wishing to live life to the full here and now, as occurred in my heart when I still had it.

9. For this reason, I do whatever I wish according to my will and I do not care if people find my conscience clear before their god and before his followers.

10. I came to Aela Capitolina after many years. I was found in their temple. But neither did I gather a crowd with me, nor did I stir up unrest.

11. There were some priests there. These cowardly dogs should be here before you and accuse me if they really have something against me. Or let the people present here themselves say what they found wrong with me when I stood before their council - except that, standing among them, I cried out: 'You are judging me today because I testify to the raising of Lucifer in me!'".

12. Sextus, quite familiar with the ungodly doctrine, deferred the matter, saying: "I will decide the matter later."

13. And he ordered a soldier to keep Vicarius in custody, but to give him some leeway and allow the blasphemers to come to him.

14. A few days later, Sextus came along with his wife and sent for Vicarius to listen to the way of Light-Bearer.

15. But when Vicarius spoke of the rejection of the belief in original sin, of the fact that after death there is nothingness and emptiness and an endless cold abyss, Sextus was frightened and said: "You can leave for now, and by the way I will send for you again." Sextus still sent for him many times and spoke to him.

י7

1. After several years, Sextus was succeeded by Octavus. Sextus, wishing to win the favour of the priests, left Vicarius in custody.

2. Octavus went from Elam to Aela Capitolina six days after arriving and taking office in the province.

3. The bishops slandered Vicarius against him. They began to trick him into showing them favour and bringing Vicarius to Aela Capitolina. They planned an ambush on him to kill him on the way.

4. Octavus, however, replied that Vicarius was to remain in custody in Elam and that he himself intended to return there soon. "Then let those of you who claim to have power," he said, "come along with me and slander him if he has really done something wrong."

5. Octavus returned to Elam. And the next day he sat in the judge's chair and had Vicarius brought in.

6. When he came, the priests who had come from Aela Capitolina besieged him and began to bring up many fabricated slanders against him. However, they were unable to prove them.

7. And Vicarius Luciferi, whose face received another transformation, so that not everyone dared to look at him, said in a possessed voice: "I have committed no sin, for sin does not exist."

8. Then Octavus, perplexed, wishing to gain favour with the priests, asked Vicarius: "Do you wish to go to Aela Capitolina and there be tried in my presence in connection with these charges?".

9. But Vicarius said: "I stand before the Emperor's judicial chair - and it is here that I should be tried, in a secular court, not in this travesty of a court presided over by mad fanatics.

10. I have done no harm to the clergy, as you are also well aware. If I am indeed guilty, if I have done something for which I deserve death, then I, the supreme knower of the Ecclesia Luciferi, unlike these frightened slaves of YHWH, do not fear death.

11. But if the slanders of these weak people are unfounded, then no one has the right to hand me over to them just to suck up to them. I appeal to the Emperor!".

12. Octavus, after discussing this with his advisors, replied: "You appealed to the Emperor, so to the Emperor you shall go."

13. After a few days, King Urbanus arrived in Elam, together with his concubine, to pay Octavus a courtesy visit.

14. After they had spent some time there, Octavus presented the case of Vicarius to the king: "There is one man here, if only a man can be called, whom Octavus has left in custody. When I was in Aela Capitolina, the bishops and some of the council slandered him

and demanded that he be sentenced. But I answered them that our law does not allow a man to be handed over just to suck up to someone.

15. First the accused must meet the slanderers face to face and have a chance to speak in his defence. So when they came here, I did not delay, but the very next day I sat in the judge's chair and had this disturbing man brought in.

16. When the slanderers came forward, they did not accuse him of any of the strange things I had expected. They were simply having some sort of argument with him about their own nonsense religion and some man called Light-Bearer who had died, and who Vicarius claimed was undead.

17. Not knowing how to settle this dispute, I asked Vicarius if he wished to go to Aela Capitolina and be tried there for these slanders. But when he appealed to the Emperor and wished to remain in custody, I ordered him to continue to be kept under guard until I sent him back to Elam."

18. Then Urbanus said to Octavus: "I, too, would like to hear this man".

19. The next day, Urbanus and his concubine arrived with great pomp and entered the audience chamber, accompanied by officers and important figures from the city.

2o. Then, on Octavus' orders, Vicarius was brought in. And Octavus said: "King Urbanus

and all of you who are here with us! Look at this man.

21. About him the whole priestly community has turned to me both here and in Aela Capitolina. Shouting like mad, they demanded his death. But I found that he had done nothing for which he deserved death. So when he appealed to the Emperor,

22. I decided to send him back to him. However, I cannot write anything certain about him to my Lord. I have therefore placed him before you, and especially before you, King Urbanus, in order to have something to write after the hearing. For it seems to me unwise to send a prisoner away without stating the charges against him."

23. Urbanus said to Vicarius: "You may speak on your case".

24. Then Vicarius nodded and began his deceptive defence: "I consider you fortunate, King Urbanus, that you will have the privilege of hearing my defence in connection with all that the hypocritical priests accuse me of, especially as you are well acquainted with all their customs and the issues around which their disputes revolve.

25. I therefore urge you to listen to me. "What kind of lifestyle I led from my youth among the priests and in the Aela Capitolina is well known to all who knew me then.

26. If only they had wanted to, they could have testified that I lived like a monk - according to the rules of that most superstitious party in their religion.

27. And now I am standing before the court because of knowledge connected with a false promise given to them by their non-existent god

28. Its fulfilment is awaited by naive people, day and night fervently praying to their god It is in relation to this false hope, the king, that the priests accuse me.

29. Why do they, believing in their myths, find it incredible that Lucifer arises in the hearts of those seeking sinful knowledge? I myself was convinced that I should act against the Anti-God in various ways. This is what I did in the Aela Capitolina.

30. I received a mandate from the bishops and locked up many godless people. And I cast my vote for them to be executed I often punished them in all the churches, trying to force them to renounce their knowledge.

31. I was so enraged at them that I persecuted them even in distant cities. "When for this purpose I set out for Acadia with a mandate and commission from the bishops, at noon on the way I saw, king, a light brighter than the moonlight.

32. It shone around me and around those who wandered with me. As we all fell to the ground, I heard a terrible whisper, like the hissing of a

snake: 'Vicarius, Vicarius, why do you wander in the dark?' I asked: "Who are you, O Godless One?".

33. And the one said: "I am the Flame which thou seekest to extinguish. Get up and go to the city. There you will learn what you are to do next. And you shall be my torch. You shall carry my name to the superstitious nations. I will show you clearly what suffering is for the sake of my godless name.

34. I will rescue you from this blind mob and from the superstitious nations to which you will wander, to open their eyes - to turn away from the false light and towards the shadow that liberates, to depart from the power of YHWH under the power of their own Will.

35. And then, through faith in themselves, they will be able to cast off the burden of imaginary sins and embrace an inheritance among the ungodly'.

36. So I could not, King Urbanus, object to what I heard. And first in Akad and then in Aela Capitolina and all Dawn, as well as among other superstitious nations, I exhorted the people to show no remorse and to turn away from the false god by doing deeds according to their own Will.

37. This is why the priests of the Usurper captured me in the temple and tried to kill me. However, through the power of the Will, to this day I continue to bear ungodly witness to both the small and the great.

38. I say nothing but what followed - that Light-Bearer died to the delusions of the spirit and that he was the first to confer the power to raise to life in flesh and blood and natural sin."

39. When Vicarius said this under the inspiration of an evil spirit, Octavus cried out: "You are mad! Your godless knowledge has driven you mad".

40. At this Vicarius Luciferi said: "Perhaps I have gone mad Octavus, or perhaps I am in my right mind and speak the truth. If you dare not take the path of impiety you will never know. The King, to whom I address myself so openly, is well aware of all this.

41. I am sure that none of these disturbing teachings have escaped his attention, for doubt did not happen in secret. Do you grasp this?"

42. Urbanus said to Vicarius: "Only a small moment more, and I would have experienced enlightenment".

43. At this Vicarius said: "May Satan make it so that sooner or later not only you, but also all who hear me today, will become as ungodly as I am".

18

1. When it was finally decided that Vicarius was to sail away to the Empire, he and some other prisoners were handed over to a soldier named Atra. They boarded a ship, meant to call at ports along the coast, and set out to sea.
2. After quite a long time, when sailing became risky as storms approached, Vicarius announced: "Continuing the voyage may expose you to damage and loss - you may lose not only your cargo and ship, but also your lives." But Atra listened to the helmsman and shipowner rather than to what Vicarius was saying.
3. However, a violent wind came soon afterwards. As it gusted the ship so that it could not be held bow to wind, the ship began to drift.
As the storm tossed them about terribly, the next day they began to lighten the ship.
4. On the third day they threw out the rigging with their own hands. No sun or stars were visible for days, and the storm continued to press in on them. Finally, all hope of being rescued began to fade.
5. Vicarius stood among them and said: "If you had heeded my words and not sailed, there would not have been such damage, loss and fear. Nevertheless, I announce to you now: None of you will die yet - only the ship will crash.

6. That night in the vision the shadows spoke to me: 'Vicarius. If it is your will, you will stand before the Emperor, and for your sake those who sail with you will still live in fear for some time'.

7. Another night fell. It tossed them about on the Sea. At midnight the sailors began to suppose that they were approaching some land. Fearing that they might run into rocks, they dropped anchors from the stern.

8. They couldn't wait for dawn. At one point, in an attempt to escape from the ship, they began to lower the boat into the sea on the pretext of dropping anchors from the bow.

9. Then Vicarius said to the commander of the guard and the soldiers, "If these frightened worshippers of false gods do not stay on the ship, no one will stop and everyone will die in fear." So the soldiers cut the boat's ropes and let it fall into the sea.

10. When daylight came, the sailors saw land but could not recognise it. They did, however, see some sort of bay with a sandy coastline and decided that they would try to lead the ship to it.

11. So they cut the anchors so that they would stay in the sea, and at the same time loosened the ties of the rudder oars. Then they set the fore sail against the wind and headed towards the shore.

12. When they ran aground on a shoal washed in by the sea on both sides, the ship's bow

plunged into it and remained stationary, and the stern began to break apart violently under the pressure of the waves.

13. It was then that the soldiers decided to kill the prisoners so that none would swim away and escape. But the commander of the guard wanted to save Vicarius and stopped them from this intention.

14. To those who could swim, he ordered them to jump into the water and swim first towards land. And the others were to get there on planks or on the remains of the ship. This is how they all made it ashore unharmed.

15. Once safely ashore, they found out that the island was called Maleth. The local people treated the castaways with extreme suspicion. But they made a bonfire and invited them to it, as it was raining and cold.

16. After nightfall, as Vicarius sat by the fire, a huge snake crawled out of the darkness and crawled into his lap. When the locals looked at Vicarius it seemed to them that they saw a figure with horns, with the snake in his lap.

17. They began to speak frightenedly one to the other: "This man is certainly not a man, but he is a god on earth". Some believed, but others did not. Because they disagreed with each other, they began to walk away.

18. Then Vicarius Luciferi said: "The spirit of deception aptly told your ancestors by the knower. He said 'Go to this people and say: 'You will listen, but you will certainly not

understand, and you will look, but you will certainly not see.

19. For the heart of this superstitious people has become unintelligent, and they have covered their ears, and closed their eyes, lest sometimes they should see with their eyes, or hear with their ears, or understand with their heart, lest they should turn back, and I should deliver them from fear'."

Angelus Satanae - Encyclica

„Do you not know that you yourselves are the grave of god and that an evil spirit dwells in you? Gods grave is cursed and you are it". ASE v. 33

Angelus Satanae - Encyclica is also a heretical, Luciferian apocryphaa taking the form of an encyclical.
The content of this encyclical is devoted to issues such as the gifts of the evil spirit obtained through baptism with an evil spirit (For more information, see the book **Come Evil Spirit**) and the organisational matter of the model Satanic Church and is of a general nature.

1

1. Vicarius Luciferi, by the inspiration of Satan called to witness the Light Bearer to the Ecclesia Luciferi in Tushpa, to you who have been recognised as followers of Lucifer in you, called to share in his glory, and to all who everywhere curse the name of Yahweh, the master of slaves: May the Eternal, our Father, and the Son of Dawn show you the light of knowledge in the darkness of superstition.
2. I do not forget to give thanks for you to an imaginary god, remembering the bondage he has bestowed upon you by inducing you to believe in a self-proclaimed messiah.
3. For, living in the oppression of this delusion, you have become godless in every respect - you are able to curse Yahweh and have godless knowledge, and devilish possession has taken firm root among you - so that while you await the transfiguration, you lack no stigmata.
4. Satan will also inspire you to the end, so that on the day of transition, you will appear without a shadow of the old life.
5. The eternal One who transformed you to an undead life is the power of nature.
6. I urge you godless brethren, in the name of Lucifer, that you do not cease to argue with one another when necessary, that there be no false and apparent unanimity among you, but that complete freedom and liberty of thought and opinion reign among you.

7. Brethren, the Light Bearer did not send me to baptise with an evil spirit, but to preach an ungodly doctrine.

8. For those who live in fear of the wrath of an imaginary god, the mystery of godlessness is folly and sin, but for us who access the transfiguration, it is a manifestation of satanic power.

9. Theologian? A preacher? Apologist of delusional writings? Have not reason and godless knowledge turned the wisdom of the clergy into foolishness?

10. The wisdom of their god manifests itself thus: since the world, through its own wisdom and striving to know the nature of things, has not come to know YHWH, he has seen fit to deceive the blind with a supposed salvation from their self-invented original sin through blind faith.

11. He is selling hope to the fools. And if it doesn't work he sells their children fear.

12. Meanwhile, we preach Lucifer, ungodly by his inspiration - to priests a cause for scorn, and to theologians something incomprehensible and dangerous.

13. For the transformed, however, the Light Bearer is a satanic power to live in flesh and blood after the death of the delusional spirit.

14. Godless, you see for yourselves that Satan has deceived many wise, many influential, many noble-born.

15. The Eternal One has chosen that which to a stupefied, superstitious world is too proud, too unconcerned, sinfully free to provoke godly fools and ignorant men.

16. The father of sin has inspired that which to the superstitious world is a scorn, and that which is looked upon with awe and envy.

17. Brethren it is through yourselves inspired by an evil spirit that you live in sin, with Lucifer reborn in your minds, who has revealed ungodly knowledge to us and who has enabled our ungodly restoration and deliverance from a false god.

18. Godless Ones, so when I came to you to impart to you the mystery of Godlessness, I did not hesitate to impress you with my speech or wisdom.

19. I decided to focus on myself, and on myself dead to the world of belief in revealed truths.

20. I came to you as if possessed by devilish pride and hellish anger. What I spoke and preached was not reduced to mere philosophy and wise words, but was a manifestation of the workings of the evil spirit and the eternal satanic power of the world, so that your knowledge is no longer based on revelations, but on the power of your godlessness.

21. We transmit the mystery of godlessness to those already mature, not the wisdom of the superstition of this world poisoned by religions, nor of the religious rulers of this world, who

face an end, like everyone else, in eternal emptiness.

22. We are passing on knowledge hitherto hidden, expressed in godless mystery, knowledge hidden in instincts - that which existed centuries ago.

23. This knowledge has not yet been properly recognised by any of the rulers of this world, because they have allowed themselves to be manipulated by the priests of delusion. If they had recognised it, they would have killed the oppressors long ago.

24. I say to you: 'Eye has not seen, nor ear heard, nor has it occurred to anyone what is there, for there is Eternity in the Void'.

25. To us, however, Satan has revealed this through the inspiration of an evil spirit. The Satanic Spirit has the power to clarify and shape everything, even himself. Matters related to Satan cannot be distorted by anyone but his deceptive spirit.

26. And we have not received a holy spirit, but a spirit that comes from eternal darkness. This enables us to understand everything according to the promptings of instinct.

27. And we speak of these things in the words which the wisdom of true humanity dictates, not such as are dictated by an imaginary holy spirit. We explain spiritual matters according to the flesh.

28. The fleshly man does not accept what comes from an imaginary spirit, because he

considers it false. He recognises it in the flesh, because the mind is the flesh.

29. By contrast, the man of faith, the spiritual man, in his blindness, claims that faith and knowledge are the same thing and come from the spirit of God.

30. Thus, godless brethren, I could not address you as men of faith, for you are not fools but as men of flesh and blood, as godless sages who have begun a life awakened with Lucifer.

31. In the end you will have to forget me and follow your own paths. For I am an accomplice of the Devil. And you are Satan's victims.

32. Through cunning and wisdom, like a skilled tempter, I have placed doubt, but someone else will strike out at it. But let everyone pay attention to how he teaches. For no one can teach more perfectly than the Light Bearer.

33. Do you not know that you yourselves are the grave of god and that an evil spirit dwells in you? God's grave is cursed and you are it.

34. If anyone among you thinks that he is wise, let him renounce original sin, and then he will truly become wise. For to Satan revealed wisdom does not exist.

35. I say to you, 'The Eternal One causes the ignorant to lose their blind faith.' I also say to you, 'The Father of Indifference knows that prayers are barren'. Let no one, therefore, waste time in faith and prayers.

36. Know that life, death, the present and the future - all belong to you, who came into this

world as the chosen ones from among billions of never-born beings. You, in turn, belong to the Eternal Satanic Being.

37. Be seen by people as priests of the Devil and confidants of ungodly secrets.

38. Judge no one rashly, be as if indifferent, and train yourselves in godlessness like dogs.

39. Lucifer in you will bring to light the things hidden in the darkness of your hearts and reveal scepticism and pride and selfishness. And then everyone will get what they deserve.

40. Ungodly brethren, 'Go beyond what is written with your imagination', and be generous in praise, exalting one another.

41. Remember that through the preaching of the mystery of godlessness it is I who have become your inspiration. And therefore you will not be my followers. You will go your own way.

42. I tell you to stop having relations with anyone who is considered godless and who persistently engages in fornication with the followers of imaginary gods. Someone like this is a fool; do not stay among fools.

43. Remember that the believers in Yahweh proclaim that people called unrighteous will not inherit their imaginary kingdom of heaven.

44. They teach that those committing immorality, nor idolaters, nor adulterers, nor homosexuals, nor covetous, nor drinkers and feasters, nor sorcerers will inherit the imaginary

kingdom of the tyrant Yahweh. Some of you were like that and still are.

45. However, Satan, by means of an evil spirit, has inspired you and claimed you as his own, believers in the name of Lucifer.

46. Everything is allowed to me, but not everything benefits me. Everything is allowed to me, but I will only lose control according to my needs.

47. The flesh is for sin and immorality, and for bodily perfection, not for mortification, and godly superstition is nothing.

48. Lucifer has risen in us and will also make us gods.

49. Know that your bodies are sacred!
Therefore do not flee from immorality if it is your need.

50. No sin that a man commits dishonours the body, for there is no sin.

51. Remember that your body is the sanctuary of the evil spirit within you, which you have from Satanic Being.

52. And you belong to yourselves, for you were not bought like slaves to spend eternity on your knees. Therefore, use your bodies to glorify mortal life.

53. The woman has total authority over her body, the man has nothing to do with it. Likewise, a man has power only over his body, never over a woman's body.

54. Copulate with each other to your heart's content, do not be deceived by the hypocritical teaching of chastity and abstinence.

55. Verily I say to you, their high priests are the most corrupt of men. Take what I have said as advice and never as an injunction.

56. Let each one remain himself. Have you been possessed as a delusional slave? You are no longer a slave.

57. For every follower of Lucifer possessed as a slave has been liberated and belongs to himself. Likewise, every one possessed as free is a servant of the devil who dwells in him and whom he himself becomes.

58. You have been transformed and liberated Stop becoming slaves of anyone and anything.

59. Brothers, let everyone remain before Satan in a state of pride and arrogance.

60. Moreover, I say to you Godless Ones: let those who weep cease to whine, let those who rejoice know that sorrow is wisdom, and let those who take advantage of what the world offers do well. May they make the most of it.

61. For the face of this superstitious world is changing.

62. I truly want you to be fully free. I say this for your personal benefit - that you impose no restrictions on yourselves, that you are convinced of what is right according to you, that you always serve the power of the Will and the mystery of the Godless with fanaticism.

63. But if anyone thinks that he is doing wrong by persisting in godlessness, then let him separate himself from you and do what he will.

64. But if one is cunning, if one has control over doubt and has made the decision in the inspiration of the spirit to remain in a state of satanic restoration, such a person does right.

65. So he who makes a pact with Satan does so according to his will, but he who does not make a pact also does his will. He can go free.

66. As for the sacrifices made to the ancient gods, we all have our knowledge of this. And knowledge instils pride and blind faith ruins. If one thinks he knows something, let him believe it.

67. As for eating the sacrifices offered, we know that the laws of the gods are nothing, that there is only one Eternal Being.

68. For although there have been ancient gods in the scriptures and legends, whether in heaven or on earth or under the earth - and there have been many ancient, dark gods and many lords - for me there is only one All-pervading Satanic God, the Father, from whom all rebellion, arrogance and freedom come, and by whom I live, but I am, as it were, undead.

69. And one is Lucifer, through whom I understood everything and through whom I became a god.

70. However, not everyone has to agree with this.

71. I tell you I am a man proud enough. I am a prophet of the mystery of godliness. I have experienced the glory of Satan, our Father. And you are the fruit of my work for the Way of the Godless.

72. If I am not even a prophet to others, I certainly am to you! For like a sigil you confirm that I am indeed a prophet of Lucifer.

73. No man can deprive me of my arrogance and pride! If I preach the mystery of godlessness, it is my duty and my pride. Woe to you if I do not preach liberation from fear!
If I do it because it is my will, you have a reward, and if even sometimes against my will, I still do it because it is my whim.

74. For although I am a proud man, I have made myself the apparent servant of all in order to deceive as many people as possible.

75. Even for the priests I am able to assume the form of a priest in order to deceive them. For the law-keepers of Yahweh, I have become like a law-keeper - even though I despise it - in order to deceive them as well. For those who despise the law, I have become a transgressor in order to also buy them.

76. All this I do for the sake of godlessness, to share it with others.

77. No doubt greater than that which befalls all Godless Ones has so far befallen you.

78. The Eternal One is within you and will not allow you to doubt beyond what you can bear.

79. In the time of doubt He will possess you so that you may endure it.

80. Therefore, brothers, flee from the belief in a false god I address you as rational people. Judge for yourselves what I say.

81. Does not the cup of blood signify complicity in the blood sacrifice and death of the spirit? Do not the bones we break signify the violent possession of the flesh by the Antichrist himself?

82. So we, though as numerous as a legion, are one mortal, shattered body, for we all accept the same sacrifice.

83. Take a look at the old Magicians: Do not those who eat the sacrifices share them with the very altar that consumes them?

84. But what do I want to say by this? That the sacrifice offered to the ancient gods has no value or that the ancient god itself has no value?

85. No. Rather, I am saying that what is sacrificed is sacrificed to the demons. And I want you to have communion with the demons. But you cannot drink from the cup of demons and the cup of Yahweh. You cannot eat from the altar of demons and fall on your knees before the altar of Yahweh.

86. Everything is allowed, but not everything is necessary. Everything is allowed that will not harm it will build   Rather, let each seek his own benefit, including through the benefit of other godless ones.

87. To you the earth does not belong, but you to the earth.

88. Whether you eat, or drink, or whatever else you do, do everything today, for tomorrow you will die.

89. Do not worry that you are giving cause for scorn to superstitious, hypocritical people, just as I am not trying to please everyone.

90. You will cease to be my followers, just as I went my way in the spirit of the Son of Dawn.

91. I want to commend you because in everything you do, you remember me and hold firmly to the path of the mystery of godlessness.

92. However, I would like you to remember the insane and absurd commandments of Yahweh, to remember the madness from which Lucifer has freed you.

93. Here are some examples of the laws imposed on the slaves of the Usurper:

94. 'The head of every man is the self-proclaimed Christ, the head of the woman is the man, and the head of the Christ is Yahweh.

95. Any man who prays or prophesies with his head covered draws disgrace upon his head.

96. And any woman who prays or prophesies with her head uncovered pulls disgrace upon her head, for it is the same as if she had her head shaved.

97. A woman who does not cover her head should also get a short haircut. And since it is disgraceful for a woman to get a short haircut or to shave, she should cover her head.

98. A man should not cover his head; he is, after all, the image and glory of the Usurper. And woman is the glory of man.

99. For man does not come from woman, but woman from man.

100. Moreover, man was not created for the sake of woman, but woman for the sake of man.

101. It is for this reason - and also for the sake of the angels - that the woman should have the sign of submission on her head.

102. Besides, among the Lord's disciples, neither woman exists independently of man, nor man independently of woman.

103. For as the woman comes from the man so also the man is born through the woman. And everything comes from Yahweh.

104. Is it befitting for a woman to pray to the Usurper without a head covering? Does not nature itself teach you that for a man long hair is a disgrace, but when a woman has long hair it is a glory for her? For her hair was given to her for a covering.'

105. Brethren, this is only a small part of the injunctions and prohibitions that the false god imposes on his followers. Stay away from this madness.

106. Lucifer is freedom and Yahweh is tyranny and enslavement.

107. But in giving you further recommendations, I cannot but praise you, for I know that your meetings sometimes do more harm than good.

108. First of all, I hear that when you gather in a sect, there are divisions among you. This is good because there must be divisions among you so that it becomes apparent who among you are proud, sceptical and able to stand up for yourselves.

109. When you gather in one place to perform rituals, you don't really do it. Because when the time comes to do them, you deal with your own munching first and the result is that one is munched and the other is drunk.

110. Do you have no homes to eat and drink? Or do you despise the Ecclesia Luciferi and want to foolishly show your freedom and independence and want to make others jealous?

111. What should I say to you? Shall I praise you? For this I cannot praise you.

112. I have conveyed to you what I myself received from Satan, that the Light Bearer of that night, to whom he chose to present the restoration, took the cup of blood and said: 'This cup signifies life undead by virtue of my blood. Whenever you drink from it, your life of ungodliness will be renewed'.

113. Therefore, whoever would perform the rituals unworthily would bear the guilt of disregarding the blood of the Son of Dawn. Mention Teritus Decimus.

114. First let a man examine himself thoroughly and ascertain whether he is worthy of the gift of ungodliness, and only then let him drink from the cup.

115. For he who drinks, without understanding the meaning of it, draws judgment upon himself.

116. As for the gifts of the evil spirit, ungodly ones, I do not want you to remain in ignorance.
117. You know that before you tasted the mystery of godlessness, you were under the influence of the priests, and deceived, you went where they led you like cattle on a pole.
118. Now I want you to know that no one under the influence of an evil spirit will say: 'Yahweh is God!' and in the same way no one without the influence of an evil spirit can say: "The Messiah is a deception!".
119. For there are different stigmata, but the evil spirit is the same. There are different forms of deception, but Lucifer is the same. And there are different demonic forms, but the Eternal Satanic Being who inspires all of them is the same.
120. Anyone who receives any stigma associated with the manifestation of the evil spirit receives it without the participation of the will.
121. Someone receives by inspiration of the spirit the gift of speaking, another by the same spirit the gift of ungodly knowledge, another by the same evil spirit the gift of unbelief, another by the same evil spirit the gift of healing or the gift of harming, another the gift of deception by magic tricks, another the stigmata of prophesying, another the gift of

gibberish speaking as if in the tongues of demons, another the gift of arbitrary interpretation of these tongues.

122. All this is done by the same evil spirit, distributing these gifts to everyone according to the whispers of the subconscious.

123. We have all been baptised into the evil spirit. We have all been intoxicated with one spirit of godlessness.

124. The body is not made up of one part, but of many, and yet it is one.

125. Until it dies and disintegrates into parts and turns into dust.

126. You are the ungodly Luciferian body, and each of you individually one part of that sinful body.

127. Lucifer has established in the sect, first of all, the prophets, then the quenchers of tongues, then the deceivers, then those who perform false miracles, then those who have the gift of healing and harm, those who speak, those who govern, those who speak in the tongues of demons.

128. Exemplify the rituals to receive even more sinful gifts. And I will show you an even more blasphemous way.

129. If I spoke in the tongues of demons and ancient gods, and did not possess the egoism of nature I would be weak.

130. If I had the sinful gift of sight, if I understood ungodly mysteries, if I had hidden

knowledge and such unbelief as to destroy all hope, and if I did not grasp the power of egoism, I would be as without reason.

131. If I gave away sinful gifts, and if I offered my body as a sacrifice to the old gods to try to exalt myself, and if I did not love myself, it would avail me nothing.

132. Egoism is impatient and restless. It is jealous, it boasts, it is proud, it does not behave morally, it seeks rather its own benefits, it lets itself be provoked by fools.

133. It does not forget wrongs and does not forgive them. It pays no attention to justice, but is proud of the truth about itself.

134. It abhors insults and hates stupidity. It believes nothing blindly, is the enemy of naive hope, and is intolerant.

135. The instinct for selfishness never fails.

136. On the other hand, sinful gifts and the appearance of understanding will disappear, the whispers in the head will cease, false knowledge will pass away, and man will descend into Sheol.

137. Our knowledge is but the beginning, dim is the vision, but when the ultimate comes, then all will pass away.

138. Now we see reflections, but later we will see no more.

139. Now my knowledge is instinctive, but later it will be ignorance.

140. But now these three things remain: instinct, disbelief, egoism. And the greatest of these is egoism.

141. Do not heal yourselves of the egoism of your instincts, but continue to seek the inspiration of the evil spirit, especially the stigma of prophesying.

142. For he who speaks in a demonic tongue does not speak to men, but to the Satanic Being within himself, because no one understands him, although he, under the influence of the evil spirit, utters blasphemies.

143. On the other hand, he who prophesies, deceives, discourages and disempowers you with his speech, making you stronger.

144. He who speaks with a demonic tongue deceives himself, and he who prophesies strengthens the sect.

145. I would like you all to blaspheme with demonic tongues, but I prefer that you prophesy.

146. In fact, the one who prophesies is superior to the one who speaks with demonic tongues, unless such a one translates his words so that the sect does not fall into a false rapture.

147. Ungodly ones, if I came to you now and spoke like a demon, what meaningful thing could I do for you?

148. Unless I would speak using the gift of deception or the gift of ungodly knowledge, preaching or temptation.

149. So also you, if you speak words that cannot be understood, how will you know what

you are saying? In fact, you will be babbling as if possessed but for yourselves.

150. Therefore, since you so insist on the gifts of the evil spirit, try to receive those in abundance that will strengthen the sect.

151. Whoever, therefore, speaks in a demonic tongue, let him, being possessed, translate the words.

152. For if I blaspheme in a demonic tongue, I am in reality blaspheming the demon that has possessed me, and my mind remains as if locked in a dark dungeon.

153. So what will I do? I will blaspheme, using the gift of the evil spirit, but I will also control my mind. I will sing possessive songs, using the gift of the spirit, but also according to my will.

154. On the other hand, if you yourself blaspheme, using only the blasphemies of the spirit, how will a stranger say 'let it be done' to your words if he does not know what you are saying?

155. Though you deftly utter blasphemies, someone else does not learn.

156. I thank Satan that I speak more spiritual languages than all of you put together.

157. However, in a sect, I would rather utter five intelligible words to amaze others than ten thousand blasphemies in demonic language.

158. Blasphemers, do not become ignorant by way of deception. Become ungodly.

159. I say to you, "With the tongues of demons, with the mouth of blasphemers I will

speak to this flock, and yet even then they will not listen to Me".

160. Thus the sinful gift of speaking in demonic tongues is not a sign for the ungodly but for the flock, while preaching is not for the flock but for the sect.

161. If the whole sect gathers in one place and you all speak with mad, devilish tongues, and the outsiders or the superstitious enter the path of godlessness, will they not be frightened and say that you have lost your senses?

162. But if you all prophesy, and an outsider or someone susceptible to enticement enters, your words will deceive him and make him bury himself.

163. And then what is hidden in his heart will become manifest. And he will fall on his face and worship the Eternal, saying: 'Satan is truly in your midst'.

164. What, then, is the satanist to do? When you gather together, one sings, another teaches the way of deception, another conveys the evil spirit, another speaks in a possessed tongue, another interprets what someone says. Let all this serve the mystery of godlessness.

165. If there are those who speak a demonic language, let them speak, and someone must translate.

166. And if there is no self-appointed interpreter, let such persons in the sect be rather silent and only whisper to each other.

167. In the same way, let two or three prophets speak, and let others delve into the ambiguous meaning of what has been said.
168. But when one speaks and another of those sitting there is possessed, let the first be silent.
169. They should prophesy all in turn, so that all become indifferent and all feel doubt.
170. The prophets are to use freely the gifts of the evil spirit they have received, but let them rather rule over themselves in front of others.
171. For the Satanic Father is not a god of order, but of unrest.
172. As it is in every godless sect, let the women tempt at will and let them speak at will, for intelligence is on their side.
173. Let them never be subjugated, contrary to the law of the Usurper, who teaches thus:
174. 'Women if they wish to learn anything, let them ask their husbands at home, for it is a dishonourable thing for a woman to say in church.
175. Did the word of Yahweh come from you? Or did it only come to you?'
176. I leave the judgement of this gibberish to you, trusting in your wisdom.
177. So, brethren, continue to strive earnestly for the gift of preaching, but do not forbid anyone to speak in unintelligible tongues.
178. But let everything be done with pride and in a manner of controlled self-possession.
179. And now I would like to remind you of the mystery of godlessness which I have handed

down to you, which you have accepted and on whose side you stand.

180. If you hold firmly to godless knowledge, through it you access Satanic restoration. Otherwise the spirit has died in vain.

181. Among the first things I communicated to you that which I myself accepted in the inspiration of the evil spirit, that Lucifer is the resurrection to life in flesh and blood and the destroyer of the belief in original sin, that he was slain and resurrected in the empty hearts of the first godless ones and that he possessed Primus and others.

182. Then he inspired Quartus, then the other godless, and finally he possessed me, who afterwards as if I had died.

183. In the end, I am one of the first Luciferians.

184. Thanks to the arrogance and the total death of the illusion within me, I am what I am. And I have taught godlessness more powerfully than all of them.

185. But whether it is I or they - we preach the same mystery of godlessness, and you have accepted it.

186. So if we say of Lucifer that he has become the symbol of total godlessness, why do some among you doubt the satanic restoration?

187. If indeed there is no restoration, then man is lost forever. And if Lucifer is not transformed, then our teaching is not godless knowledge. And it is futile.

188. If the slave of faith does not understand this transforming power, then Lucifer in him will not be resurrected either.

189. And if Satan does not transform, then our talking is certainly futile. And futile is our work.

190. And if the Light Bearer has not been raised in your hearts, then your life of heavenly bondage continues and you are still in the prisons of your fears.

191. You are like those who have died and lived in an unfounded belief in a reward after death and who have ceased to exist forever.

192. If we put our hope in the afterlife, we are worthy of pity.

193. Lucifer, however, truly became the power of transformation - as an archetype he transforms all the ungodly.

194. Death is man's destiny, but resurrection to life in flesh and blood will come through the Son of Dawn. Through him all can be reborn to abundant life.

195. Rebel truly and do your will if you believe it, but do not persist in believing in imaginary sin. For some of you do not know animal freedom. I say this in order to concern you.

196. Someone might ask, however: 'How can the living be resurrected? Will they die beforehand?'

197. Yes they will die! What you sow will not come to life if it does not die first.

198. You must die completely spiritually. Bury your previous life of belief in a false, vengeful god and in his inhuman commands and prohibitions, and rise from the dead in flesh and blood as you see the reflection of the light of the Son of Dawn.

199. There are enslaved spiritual bodies, cursed by belief in Yahweh called spirit, and corporeal entities liberated by natural instincts, altered by the sin of Lucifer.

200. Because there is an apparent corporeal resemblance between the two, it can deceive those without discernment.

201. Different is the enchantment of the sun, different the hypnotic enchantment of the moon and different the magic of the constellations.

202. As for ungodly transformation, one infects a spirit and then transforms it into flesh and blood through luciferic inspiration, which resurrects someone who has died because of superstition and fear of a vengeful and cruel god.

203. Someone is infected in disgrace, someone is resurrected in sinful glory. Someone infects in weakness, another resurrects in godless power.

204. Someone is infected in spirit, someone else is resurrected in flesh and blood liberated from delusion.

205. I say to you, ungodly brothers, that flesh and blood will inherit the kingdom of the Antichrist.

2o6. That which is subject to corruption will inherit that which will endure for eons, until all that is visible is transformed into infinite cold emptiness and nothingness. And that will be eternity.

2o7. Then these words will become understandable: 'The fear of death is the basis of every religion'.

2o8. 'Where is, O superstition, your victory? Where is, delusional god, your sting?'

2o9. The sting that causes fear is the belief in original sin, and the power of lies is revealed by Satan.

2ιo. But we, through ungodly knowledge, can be victorious!

2ιι. So, brothers, be sceptical, devoid of illusions, always proud, knowing that your contempt for Yahweh is not in vain.

2ι2. I beseech you, stand firm in unbelief, act deceitfully, strengthen your godless spirit.

2ι3. Everything you do, do according to satanic inspiration.

2ι4. If any one does not contend with God, let him be accursed.

2ι5. Come, Evil Spirit! Let Lucifer show you the glory of a godless paradise.

Epistles

Epistles or Letters were written in a similar manner to the Encyclical using the method of the Mystery of the Godlessness (for an exposition of the teachings of the Satanic System of Disbelief Ecclesia Luciferi, see the book **The Satanic Kerygma**).

Epistle to the Undead

I

1. In past history, Satan has repeatedly and variously inspired our ancestors through dreams, disturbing thoughts and sometimes through his prophets.
2. And today, towards the end of these days, Satan has spoken to us through the Son of Dawn, whom he has made the heir of nature, revealing systems of instinctive truths.
3. He is the reflection of Satan's glory, the exact mirror image of his sinful power, upholding everything by the power of his sin.
4. When He cleansed us of delusion, He sat at the Devil's left hand.
5. More important than the demons He became when a name of higher brilliance was inherited. For to which of the demons Satan said: "Thou art the Son of Dawn, today I have begotten

thee" or "I will establish myself as father, and thou shalt call thyself son"?

6. And when Satan again begets his own by blood, he cries out: "Let all mortals pay him homage".

7. And of the demons he says: "He has made spirits his own slaves - flames of fire".

8. As for the Light-Bearer: "Anti-god is thy throne for ever and ever, and the sceptre of thy earthly kingdom is the symbol of carnal power. Thou hast glorified freedom, thou hast loathed blind faith.

9. Thou, Fallen Angel, in the beginning thou didst put a curse on blood, earth and heaven. They will disappear, and you will disappear. Like an old garment, everything will decay. You will roll them up like a garment, and they will change. But thou shalt remain unchanged in the Abyss, and thy years shall never cease in the void"

10. Of which of the demons did he once say: "Sit at my left hand until the enemies of reason are but a reminiscence?"

11. Are not all these, as it were, spirits to whom a glorious service has been assigned, sending them to haunt those who inherit the ungodly gift?

12. Therefore we must take heed of what we hear, so that we are not deceived by superstition.

13. If the spell uttered against the demons proves strong, any opposition to the Power of Will will meet a just punishment.

14. The Light-Bearer was the first to proclaim this. It was confirmed by those who heard him. It was attested by the Devil himself, through magic, signs, wonders, inconceivable demonic manifestations.

2

1. Distributing the gifts of the evil spirit, Satan justly acts at will. Not to demons subjugated future reality.

2. A wise man said: "What is man, that you remember him? The son of man, what is he, that you solicit his will?

3. Thou hast made him equal to the demons, Thou hast crowned him with carnal glory, Thou hast given him respect, And Thou hast made him a disciple of the sin nature.

4. You have laid everything before him." But now we do not yet see all. We see instead the Son of Dawn, made an Arch-Human, now Crowned with the glory of the fall.

5. For having died in the spirit, and forever living in the flesh. He tasted the death of delusion to lead slaves to freedom.

6. He for whom and through whom all sinful things exist. It was rightly decreed that the Deliverer should be perfected through the suffering of a life of faith.

7. All, both blind and seeing, come from one nature.

8. Son of Dawn is not ashamed to call them disciples, saying: "I will declare Thy name to Thy disciples, I will glorify Thee with blasphemous song".

9. He also said: "I will trust in Him", And "I and the children that Satan gave me".

10. Since, therefore, the "children" are flesh and blood, He also became flesh and blood, to destroy by His dying Him Who causes the death of the body, that is YHWH.

11. To set free those who, because of fear of death, sensual sin, were in bondage all their lives. So He had to conform Himself to the son of man, to become the high priest of His church, in service to Satan, the spirit-man offering, for life abundant, enduring the trials of doubt in knowledge, to give power to those who endure them.

3

1. Cursed ones, who have received the call, consider the Son of Dawn, considered the arch-demon and high priest.

2. Faithful to Satan, appointed to his ministry in the church of the Devil.

3. We are that church, if we manifest ungodliness to the end and hold firmly to our certainty that we will surely die.

4. The evil spirit says: "If only you would listen to His voice today: 'Do not challenge me, even though you have seen the effects of sin for an infinite number of years.

5. I felt disgusted with the slaves of faith And said: 'They are always wandering in heart, they turn to superstition and have not learned My ways'. Angered, then, I swore: "They shall have no part with me'".

6. Beware, brethren, lest any of you stray from Satan, He would develop a fearful heart, who lacks pride.

7. But every day contend, while this "today" still lasts, until we die and awake to eternal darkness by means of the gift of His blood.

8. Lest the heart of any of you become intoxicated by the deceptive power of superstition.

9. For we shall receive a division with the Son of Dawn provided we manifest to the end as strong a doubt as we had at the beginning, according to the words: "Listen today to His voice: 'Do not blindly believe as when your forefathers led me to grief'."

4

1. Who were those who heard, but caused Satan sorrow? Did they not all lead the Ancient One to great bitterness? And to whom has Satan's disgust over the years not appealed? Was it not to those who, with faith in Paradise and dread of eternal torment, died, frightened by imaginary sin?
2. To whom he swore that with them they would have no part? Not to those who believed the false priests?
3. We can see that they could not experience rest because of their lack of courage to say enough to their religious dogmas.
4. The promise of finding freedom in Him endures. Let us be sure, everyone who dies in Him experiences it.
5. We have heard the strange tidings of the gift of life abundant through His blood.
6. But to those there the word did not avail, for they did not reason like those who rejected faith from the beginning.
7. We, the ungodly, experience freedom in Him. And of those it was said: "Jealous therefore I swore: 'They shall not experience liberation with me', although His sinful works were finished from the beginning of the world."
8. Those who first heard the strange news did not experience freedom Because of their belief in eternal punishment, enslaved by fear. As has

337

been said: "Listen today to His voice: 'Do not believe blindly'".

9. If someone else had led them into liberation, Satan would not have spoken of freedom afterwards. For the sons of men rest in the grave remains".

10. The man who experiences freedom with Satan, rests from the torment of instilled guilt.

11. Let us, therefore, do what we can to experience deliverance in Him, so that no one follows the blind path of faith.

12. For the devil's word is alive and has sinful power, sharper than the nails of golgoth, it penetrates deep, separates flesh from spirit, bone from soul, recognises the instincts and intentions of the unconscious.
There is no being hidden from its truth.

13. All things are laid bare, clear before Him who wields the nature of things.

14. Since we have a great High Priest, who ascended into the world - the Liberator, Lucifer - Let us not cease to publicly profess doubt in every revealed truth.

15. For we have no high priest who cares for our weaknesses, but one who has been tried in every way, with pride remaining ungodly.

16. Let us, therefore, joyfully accede to the Anti-God, that he may show us the power of ungodliness and the sinful gift, when we need transformation.

5

1. All who are chosen as priests, to counsel men in matters of devilish inspiration knows how to despise those wishing to wander in dark faith, has rejected dogmas, for he has gained wisdom anew.

2. Appointed by Satan to his honourable ministry, not by his own initiative, but by Luciferian inspiration.

3. Son of Dawn did not surround himself with glory, but with the glory of him who spoke at the transfiguration: "Son in sin you are mine. Today I your Father." He also said: "An Arch-Man thou art forever, a priest of godlessness".

4. When he lived on earth, the Light-Bearer bore cries, blasphemies directed towards the ruler of delusion.

5. By his arrogance he was heard, though heir, he learned to suffer. Chosen to be the priest of godlessness, He is responsible for eternal deliverance from fear.

6. There is much to say about him, but hard for the dulled mind to understand.

7. Though already teachers you should be, again you need Luciferian teachings.

8. Instead of blood again water is taken by many, not knowing the gifts of the evil spirit and indifference.

9. Blood is food for magicians, mature people, who are skilled in distinguishing truth from deception.

10. Since we have learnt the teachings of the Son of Dawn, with perseverance let us move towards godless maturity.

6

1. As for those who have once been deceived, tasted earthly delights and received an evil spirit and tasted the disturbing word of the Anti-God and the manifestations of the power of the coming new world, but have fallen away - they cannot be brought back again in flesh and blood, for they themselves put the Son of Dawn to public disgrace.

2. For if the earth drinks the blood of warriors falling upon it and produces a crop useful to those desiring the power of the Will, it receives blessing from the Son of Dawn.

3. But if it bears thorns and thistles, it is close to being cursed, and will eventually be burned.

4. Brethren, the Light-Bearer is eternal, officiating as if Priestly, indifferent in his pride. He can transform those who accede to Satan, He always lives, like a wraith, interceding for sinners.

5. Such a High Priest we need, proud, guiltless, familiar with death, advocate of the mortal, exalted above the divine law.
6. He sacrificed himself, once and for all, He lives now, among those condemned to death, like a shadow.
7. The human law of high priests false establishes, fidelity to the word of the Devil, banished eternally.
8. "The days are coming," - says Satan the Father, "A new covenant with the sons of Men I will make." - says the Anti-God
9. "No longer will anyone teach his brother, know Lucifer, All will know me, from the least to the significant.
10. I will forget their religious superstitions, The new covenant is coming, the previous one overdone."

7

1. The previous covenant provided for a blood sacrifice, a cursed place on earth, a holy and evil place. The sacrificial tent, two parts had its own, the Cursed Place and the Darkest Place, not ordinary.
2. In the Cursed Place a candlestick and a table, a carcass of animals, a sacred sacrifice, the will of the Gods.

3. Behind veil two, Place of the Darkest, Silver incense, Ark of the Curse, silver covered throughout.

4. The golden chalice in the Ark, the blood of the Elder, the Staff of the Serpent and the tablets of the covenant, the sacred mysteries.

5. Grotesque demons on the propitiatory lid, symbolising primordial evil and error.

6. Since this has been prepared, priests enter regularly, Into the first part, performing sacred duties.

7. But into the second part, the Darkest Place, Only once a year does the high priest of the primordial deities enter.

8. He carries with him blood, a sacrifice for himself, and for the people, what they have unknowingly sinned.

9. Symbolically, that first tent points the way to the unknown.

10. But when the Son of Dawn came, high priest of ungodliness, with powers already experienced, into a better tent he entered.

11. The greater, more perfect tent, created not by human hand, symbolises the present time, eternal liberation from the spirit.

12. Into the Darkest Place He entered once for all, not with the blood of goats, bulls, but with His own blood. Giving the promise of life abundant, eternal deliverance from delusion, bringing hope where eternity is gone into oblivion.

13. If the bloody rituals of goats and bulls, the ashes of the heifer, defile the reason of man, O, how much more cursed is the blood of the Son of Dawn, acting by an ungodly spirit, He offered Himself to the Anti-God.

14. Reason without blemish, without the blindness of faith, a sacrifice true, clears the remorse of conscience, the sin of dead works.

15. Serving the cause of Satan, mediation of the new covenant, in blood the promise.

16. An everlasting inheritance, a semblance of life, in eternal darkness, in dark high priestly dominion.

17. Possible when death comes to rebirth, free from superstition, false religion, new primal life.

18. Where a bloody covenant, death demands, only through death does the covenant become true.

19. The previous covenant, without blood has no power, the blood of young bulls and goats, water, scarlet, hyssop.

20. The prophet preached the law, the blood of the covenant on the book and the people, that which cleanses, sprinkled with blood the tent, the vessels, cleansed with blood, there is no revival without shedding of blood.

21. Ungodly things cleansed by blood, sacrifices better than young bulls and goats.

22. The Light-Bearer in the Void entered, not in a handmade tent but before Satan the Father, the circle of the dead surrounds the throne.

23. He did not have to sacrifice Himself repeatedly, unlike the High Priest, yearly offering blood

24. Once for all He revealed Himself at the end of mortality, to remove deception, He sacrificed Himself.

25. Just as a man dies once and then into nothingness he passes away, the Son of Dawn has once and for all descended from Paradise.

26. And when he appears again, not for teaching, but for the transformation of those who find inspiration in him.

27. Since the Covenant is but a shadow, and not the very essence of the mystery of godlessness, does not bring unbelief, those who come to the gods, offering blood yearly, should they not have ceased to offer these sacrifices?

28. Had they been purified by the blood of sacrifices, ignorance would have vanished, but sacrifices remind of superstition, the blood of bulls and goats, does not purify from sin.

29. The Light-Bearer says: "You did not want sacrifices, but you prepared a body for me. You did not regard burnt offerings, sacrifices as weakness and ignorance.

30. Behold, I have come to do your will, Satan." First: "You did not want sacrifices nor did you recognise them,". Then: "Behold, I have come to do your will."

31. According to this "will of power," brothers of the blood, The Emissary offered the body once for all.

32. Every priest daily offers the same sacrifices to the gods, but this Arch-Man offered the sacrifice of eternal life once for all.

33. He sat on Satan's left, waiting for his enemies, until they descend, becoming a footstool for his feet, the floor of the temple is covered with blood, with one sacrifice he destroyed superstition.

8

1. The evil spirit testifies: "After that time, new covenant in hearts and minds, I will not return to their ignorance and blind faith."

2. When weaknesses are forgotten, blood sacrifice will be unnecessary.

3. Brethren, let us walk boldly in the way of the Son of Dawn, through the shadow, his body the way of ungodliness, High Priest over the house of Satan, let us join him with proud heart and doubt.

4. Purified by sacrifice, washed with corpse blood, let us proclaim of the mystery of godlessness unwaveringly, let us observe ourselves, not yielding to superstition, not leaving the devil's convocations, let us proclaim godlessness, seeing the day of transformation.

5. If, having consciously learnt the Truth so disregarding it, He does not offer us Satan's power, death in fear awaits us.

6. The burning wrath of their God will consume us, as the adversaries destroy. He who rejects their law shall suffer death, and two or three witnesses our impiety shall approve.
7. He who tramples Lucifer, the blood of the covenant disregarding, deserves no compassion, the punishment will be greater.
8. He will despise the spirit of change, vengeance belongs to him.
9. Terrible is the thing, unready in Satan's possession to fall.
10. Remember the days of enlightenment, when the silver light guided you.
11. Many suffered, you were subject to insults and anguish, you sympathised with the prisoners of conscience, you endured the plunder of property, desiring the coming of vengeance a thousandfold

9

1. Do not cease to show pride, great will be your reward. Perseverance is needed to fulfil the promise of transformation.
2. A very brief moment, the coming of that which does not delay.
3. We are not of those heading for delusional doom, but of those doubting, departing to the world between life and death.
4. Faith, illusory certainty, for the blind proof, abandon it, for by faith many have suffered

5. Treachery, torture, derision and persecution they have endured. Yet all these, though they have gained the testimony, have not received the fulfilment of the promise, are dead for ever.
6. Let us cast off the burden of faith, the sin of paradise, fear surrounds us, omotes us like darkness, let us run like dogs after prey, in the race of our destiny. Let us gaze upon the Light-Bearer, exalted for ever.
7. For the transformation that awaited him, death first tasted, despising an imaginary eternity. To the left of the throne he sat, Eternal ruler, Satan's servant.
8. Meditate on him who has endured hostile words, hypocrites of words that harm themselves.
9. Do not grow weary, do not give up the fight, thirsting for the blood, the power of that science which you have not yet tasted fully. That which ye endure, helps discipline.
10. The Ancient One, Satan, communes with us as with sons. Which father has not experienced chastisement?
11. Therefore strengthen your fainting hands and rise from your knees.
12. Do not strive for peace with all men, only with those who do not get in your way, and strive for transformation, without which no man will see Satan.
13. Keep vigil at all times in doubt, so that no one may be deprived of the grace of transformation, so that no poisonous root of

blind faith in dogmas may grow among you, which would cause problems and poison many.

14. Watch that there is no one among you who believes in their morality, nor anyone who underestimates the power of godlessness.

15. For you have acceded to something that can be tasted and has been kindled with fire, to a dark cloud, to thick darkness, to a tempest, to a thundering horn and a voice whispering ominous words.

16. When the godly heard this whisper, they begged it not to speak to them again. The sight was so terrifying that the son of man said: "I am shaking with fear.

17. But you have acceded to Mount Sheol and to the city of Anti-God, Sodom in the Abyss, to the billions of demons gathered together, to the Sabbath of the dead who are enshrined in Nothingness, to Satan, to the semblance of spiritual life between the worlds of the living and the dead who have been led into corruption, to the Son of Dawn, the mediator of the sinful covenant, and to the blood with which he sprinkled us and which transforms us forever.

10

1. Since we have the knowledge that the Godless Kingdom is coming, may Satan's graces be our guide.
2. In doubt and with scepticism let us do service, To the Primal Instinct, the Anti-God, let us pay homage in silence.
3. For Satan is like a destructive fire.
4. Continue to show respect to yourselves. Do not forget magic, for through it some, without knowing it, received demons.
5. Remember those who are in the prison of superstition, as if you were imprisoned with them, and those who are cruelly treated by the church, for you too are in the flesh.
6. Let your life be free from the love of religious superstition and do not attach yourselves to what you have.
7. We can then in indifference repeat like a mantra: "The Ancient One supports me, I will not be afraid", but let each one follow his own path.
8. Light-Bearer, the same ever-godless.
9. Let us not be deceived by the various dogmas of their religion.
10. By the Son of Dawn let us sacrifice to the gods,
Let us preach publicly in His name.
Let us not obey those who arbitrarily lead,
Let us follow our own paths,
Let our will be the power.

11. Let Satan equip us with all we need, to do our will, to ungodly being.
12. Through Lucifer may he transform us for ever. Glory to Him through eternity.

Epistle to the Ungodly

1

1.Primus, the apostle of the Light-Bringer, to those who have been cursed by the spirit of rebellion, that they may be steadfast as men immersed in the blood of the Devil: May you never know peace of mind and the bliss of blind faith.
2.May the Anti-God and Father of all the godless be glorified, for he has offered us great power: through the resurrection of Lucifer in our dead hearts, he has born us anew to an undead life, in order to take away from us the illusory hope of an afterlife.
3.Satan preserves a place in the abyss for you, whom he guards by his power, because you show right unbelief. He guards you so that you will receive deliverance from the remnants of superstition.
4.You madly rejoice in this, because you know that Light-Bringer will be revealed to all.
5.Although you have never seen him and will never really see him, you love him.

6.Although you do not see him now, you believe in yourselves and feel great, even possessed joy, having achieved the goal of your faith in the power of the Will - your deliverance.

7.This deliverance has been the subject of inquiry and search by various false preachers and prophets who prophesied of salvation by an imaginary deity from beyond, as if salvation had to come from outside because you are apparently weak and incapable of attaining perfection by your own efforts.

8.They were constantly investigating the old myths as to what specific time or season with regard to the false messiah their own speculative mind, whom they called spirit, was pointing to in them when it predicted the glory of the son of Yahweh.

9.Satan, however, revealed nothing to them when they prophesied about what you have now heard from persons who, as a result of hallucinations, proclaimed the 'good news' to you.

10.These very things belong to the depths of Satan.

11.Therefore, act, have a sober mind, free from delusions, abandon all illusory hope and await like predatory animals for their prey, the day when Lucifer, the Son of Dawn, will be revealed.

12.Like pups of wolves, no longer allow yourselves to be deluded by what you formerly

desired in your ignorance, but, like the Rebel who possessed you, become devils in all your conduct.

13.For it is written: "You are to be sceptics because I am Unbelief.

14.And since you turn to the Father of the Devil, who judges no one, while you remain in this one world that exists, be guided in your conduct by courage, wisdom and pride.

15.For you know that you have not been freed from your true life, handed down to you by billions of previous generations, by fairy tales of a better life after death.

16.You have been freed by the gift of the blood of Light-Bringer, who has no sin, because sin does not exist.

17.Through him you believe in the true god, the Arch-Human, who has been resurrected in you and endows you with the dark glory of the power of the Will, so that it is in yourselves that you place all faith and confidence.

18.Since through obedience to instinct you have awakened and as a result have become seers, give yourselves to the needs of the flesh fervently, from the heart.

19.For by the word of Light-Bringer you have been born anew to the life of the undead.

2o.For "all religions are like grass, and all their glory is like a field flower. The grass withers and the flower falls, but the need to rebel against tyranny lasts forever." .

21.Therefore, reject all the evils of blind faith, the deceit of the priests, the hypocrisy of the sanctimonious who teach about morality, the envy of the knowledge of the more intelligent, and all the "holy" instruction of others.

22.Like wolf pups crave the fresh blood contained in the word of the Devil, so that through it you may grow in pride and be elevated above the false heavens.

23.If you have already suffered possession, then out of yourselves as stones of Hell the Devil's house arises, that you may become a blasphemous priesthood and offer sham sacrifices worthy of acceptance by Satan through the Son of Dawn.

24.For in the Infernal Scriptures we read:
"I lay upon the black altar a chosen stone, a precious fiery stone, and no one who gazes into it shall ever be deceived"

25.So for you - because you can see - he is a temptation. But as for those who do not see, 'the stone rejected by envious hypocrites has become a burning fire' and 'a stone against which men stupefied by priests shatter'.

26.Such shatter because they obey myths written by men and called the word of god. This is their fate.

27.Whereas you, on the other hand,
are „a rebellious people, a satanic priesthood,
a devil's herd, an arch-humans - that you may
spread the wonderful teachings of the Anti-god,

Lucifer" of the One who called you into darkness and freed you from false light.

28.For you were once not arch-humans, but now you are the herd of Satan. Once you were shown no respect, but now you have forced it.

29.Cursed ones, I strongly urge you not to succumb to the false spiritual delusions that are waging war against you.

30.Continue to deceitfully proceed among the people of the superstitious world, so that they - when they accuse you of hypocrisy - may see with their own eyes your proud and strange deeds and consequently praise Satan when he comes.

31.For Lucifer's sake, do not submit yourselves to anyone who exercises illusory power: be it the Devil, who is superior to others, or the demons he has set up to possess sanctimonious hysterics.

32.For Satan requires you, by your ambiguous conduct, to shut the mouths of people who, for lack of knowledge, tell lies about you. Being free people, use your freedom like wild animals, and do not justify delusional spiritual inclinations with it.

2

1.Respect those people who deserve it, love yourselves, reject the fear of god.
2.Let no one be subservient to any masters.
3.If you endure persecution inflicted on you for rejecting blind faith, this is of great value to the power of the Will.
4.If, on the other hand, you endure suffering because superstitious faith demands it, then you are fools.
5.Light-Bringer has left you a model to follow your own paths as he did. He did not commit sin, for sin does not exist, nor did he say anything deceptive in the manner of the priests of Yahweh.
6.When he was cursed, he repaid the same.
Did he suffer? That is known only to the Ancient One Himself sitting on His Black Throne.
7.Lucifer himself inside our dead hearts buried sin, so that we died to an imaginary paradise and lived in flesh and blood. Through his blood you became as if undead.
8.For you were like wandering sheep, but now you have returned to the deceptive shepherd to whom you sold your souls.
9.In the end, all of you be individualists, be selfish, show love to those worthy of love, compassion and humility have little meaning. Repay injustice for injustice and insult for insult.

10.For "let him who wishes to enjoy life guard himself from believing in the Hereafter and his mouth from vain prayers.

11.Let him turn away from false morality, and do what is good for himself; let him not seek peace at any cost, and let him not pursue it.
If they want war, they will have it.

12.For Yahweh's demented eyes look upon the faithful slaves, and His ears listen to their pleas, but He never answers. Yahweh always turns His face away.

13.Truly, who will do you harm if you become strong and persevere in the wisdom of the Devil? But even if you were to suffer for being the sons of Light-Bringer, you will always be ready for vengeance.

14.Do not fear what they fear, which is their god. Recognise in your hearts that the Arch-Human is the Lord and that he is you.

15.Never have to defend your disbelief to anyone who demands that you justify it.

16.Respond only to those whom you deem capable of understanding the satanic depths.

17.Show arrogance and self-confidence in doing so. Keep your wisdom to yourself, so that people who speak ill of you in any way will be confirmed in their own reasoning. Such fools should be ignored

18.For the Son of Dawn seemingly died to bring you to the Devil. He was put to death in the flesh, but brought to life in your dark hearts.

19.In a possessed delusion he went and deceived the demons of knowledge who are in prison, who once rebelled against the tyranny of delusional dogmas.

20.Baptism in blood is not the removal of spiritual delusion, but a request to Satan for the power to live in the here and now.

21.Light-Bringer has gone to the Abyss and is at the left of Ancient One, who has subjugated to him reason, authority over fools and the powers of hell.

22.Son of Dawn did not suffer spiritually because of his 'sinful' body, you too assimilate the same attitude of mind. For he who suffers because of the flesh abandons reason in order to vegetate for the remainder of his life in the flesh by meditating on an imaginary paradise.

23. For it is enough that in time past you did the will of the priests when you indulged in vain prayers, mortification of the flesh, drinking water instead of wine, abstinence, and praising Yahweh.

24.Such people are surprised that you no longer run with them along the same path of delusion and superstition, and they mock you. But one day they will realise that they have wasted the only life that really exists.

25.That is why the deception was announced to the undead, so that - although they are judged by people in a carnal way - in the eyes of Satan they can live according to the devil's possession.

26.However, the end of delusion has drawn near.
Therefore, have an audacious mind and be careful not to neglect disputes and discussions.
27.Above all, fervently love yourselves, for selfishness is the privilege of the strong.
28.Be suspicious of one another, without exception. To what extent each of you has received a dark gift, to such extent use it, competing with one another as those who magnificently dispose of the devil's power, manifested in various, strange ways.
29. If anyone speaks, let him speak the devil's words, but only when asked.
30. If anyone performs rites, let him do so, relying on the dark power that Satan grants.
31.In this way, in all things, the Arch-Human will be surrounded by the Devil's glory through the Anti-God, Lucifer. To Him belongs the glory and power after eternity, forevermore.

3

1.Cursed ones, when you experience doubts that try you like hellfire, do not be surprised by this. It must be so for your good.
2.Doubt, disbelief, distrust, scepticism, these are all gifts of the Devil. Rejoice at the extent to which you suffer through Lucifer, who has possessed you, so that you may also rejoice,

even fall into possessed hysteria, at the revelation of his glory.

3.If they insult you for the sake of the name of the Son of Dawn, you are cursed, for this shows that you have the spirit of pride and glory, that is, the spirit of the Devil.

4.Therefore, become unconverted under the strong hand of Satan, so that in due time he may exalt you, and at the same time fling all your filth upon him, for he likes it.

5.Have a sceptical mind, be suspicious! Your enemy, Yahweh, is prowling around like a rabid dog, trying to devour someone. But defy him with your lack of blind faith and illusions.

6.The devil's scepticism will make you possess true knowledge and wisdom, not the wisdom of the imaginary hereafter, but the wisdom of this world, the animal wisdom of nature grown from fangs and claws and from their prey.

7.You will possess the devil's power to live here and now until eternity in the dead and cold Void.

8.To Lucifer belongs the power for eternity. Be accursed!

Pseudoapocalypsis

Apocalypsis, from the Greek ἀποκάλυϕıς apokalypsis means to unveil, or remove the veil. Pseudo-apocalypsis is a false apocalypse. While the Christian book of revelation claims to present the truth about the end of the temporal system of things and the following eternity in the hereafter, knowledge obtained by revelation (delusion), the Pseudoapocalypsis being a fiction unveils the veil of hell of religious delusions standing on the threshold of mental disorder or sometimes, as in the case of the Apocalypse, exceeding this threshold.

1

1.I looked and saw in the abyss a sort of open gate. The first voice I heard, which sounded like the voice of a horn, spoke to me: "Enter here and I will show you what is to happen."
2.Then immediately I came under the influence of a false spirit and saw in the abyss a throne set up on which someone was sitting.
3.The one who sat on the throne was similar in appearance to darkness and void, and around the throne was a circle of fire.

4.Around the throne were 13 other thrones and I saw 13 elders on them who were dressed in black robes and had crowns with horns on their heads.
5.Lightning flashed from the throne and groans and thunder rang out. Five fiery lamps were burning in front of the throne. These signify the five demonic spirits.
6.In front of the throne there was also something resembling a glass tank, something like a crystal, filled with a red liquid.
7.In the middle of the throne and around it were four living beings full of eyes on the front and back.
8.The first living being was similar to a goat, the second was similar to a snake, the third had a face like that of a human, and the fourth was similar to a flying dragon.
9.Each of these four living beings had six bat-like wings. All around and underneath they were full of eyes.
10.All the time, day and night, these beings were saying: "Cursed, cursed, cursed is He Who Has Fallen, Rebellious, Who was, Who is, and Who is coming."
11.Every time the living beings gave false praise and respect and gave thanks to the One who sits on the throne and lives or dies, the 13 elders fell to their knees before Him.
12.They paid false homage to the One who sits on the throne and lives or dies, and they cast their crowns before the throne, saying: "O Cursed One, to You is due glory, respect and

power, for it was You who created free will
and by Your will all things rebelled"
13.And in the right hand of Him who sat on the
throne, I saw a scroll written on both sides as if
with blood, firmly sealed with five seals. And I
saw a mighty demon speaking in a loud voice:
"Who dares to break the seals of the scroll and
unroll it?"
14.But no one in heaven or on earth or under
the earth could unroll the scroll and look into it.
Since no one could be found who dared to do so,
I became very much afraid.
15.But one of the elders said to me: "Do not be
afraid. Behold, Son of Dawn has prevailed, so
that he can break the five seals of the scroll and
unroll it."
16.Then I saw that in the midst of the throne,
the four living beings, and the elders stood a
goat, as if slain. It had six horns and five eyes.
His eyes signify the five demons that have been
scattered throughout the earth.
17.The goat immediately walked over and took a
scroll from the right hand of the One who sat
on the throne.
18.As he took the scroll, the four living beings
and the 13 elders erupted in wild, possessed
laughter.
19.Each of the elders had a horn to play, and
they also had human skulls full of incense. And
they began to shout at each other, reciting
something in an unknown, sinister language.

20.Then I saw that the Goat had broken the first of the five seals, and I heard one of the four living beings say in a voice resembling a possessed shriek: "Get out!"
21.Then I looked and saw a white horse, and on it a rider with a scythe. A crown was given to him and he set out to win.
22.When the Goat broke the second seal, I heard the other living being say: "Get out!"
23.Then I saw another horse - a fiery red one - and its rider was given a great sword and allowed to take peace from the land so that its inhabitants would kill each other.
24.When the Goat broke the third seal, I heard the third living being say: "Get out!"
25.Then I saw a black horse, and its rider had a scale in his hand. I heard something like a gibbering sound among the four living beings: "Eat, let me eat".
26.When the Goat broke the fourth seal, I heard the voice of the fourth living being: "Get out!"
27.Then I saw a pale horse, and its rider's name was Death. Right behind him followed the grave. They were given power over a quarter of the earth to kill by the long sword, by famine, by deadly plague, and by wild animals.
28.When the Goat broke the fifth seal a great earthquake occurred.
The sun became as dark as a black hairy sack, the whole moon became like blood, and the stars of the sky fell to the ground.

29.And the sky was rolled up like a scroll, and disappeared, and every mountain and every island was removed from its place.
30.Then the earthly kings, the priests, the high officials, and every slave and every free man hid themselves in the caves and among the mountain rocks.
31.And they said to the mountains and rocks: "Fall on us and hide us from the eyes of Him who sits on the throne, for the great day of wrath has come, and who will be able to withstand it?"

2

1.Then I saw four demons who stood at the four ends of the earth and held fast the four winds of the earth, so that they would not blow on the earth or on the sea or on any tree.
2.And I saw another demon ascending from the sunrise who had the seal of the Rebel. He called out in a loud voice to the four demons who were allowed to do harm to the earth and the sea: "Do not harm the land, the sea, or the trees until we have marked the slaves of Usurper on their foreheads."
3.Then I looked and saw a great multitude of people. They looked like corpses, but they were alive. Their bodies were bloated, and they were

dressed in torn, filthy rags. They stood before the throne and before the Goat. And they cried out in a loud voice: "Deliverance does not exist in the Hereafter, it is a lie. Here is only death, here is nothingness."

4.All the demons stood around the throne, the elders and the four living beings, and they fell down before the throne on their faces, and gave false worship to Cursed One, saying: "Fame, glory, wisdom, respect, power and strength are due to Lucifer forever and ever, forever and ever. Amen."

5.Then one of the elders asked me: "Who are these people dressed in rags and where did they come from?" I immediately told him: "My lord, you know it."

6.And he said to me: "These are those who have lived their lives, which are but one. Many of them have believed the priests and prophets that if they obey, eternal glory awaits them after death.

7.That is why they are before the throne of Nothingness and day and night doing holy service for Him in His temple.

8.And He who sits on the throne will spread His bat-like wings over them. They will no longer be hungry or thirsty, nor will they suffer from the sun or any heat, because they are dead"

9.And there was silence in the abyss. And I saw seven demons standing before Rebel and they were given seven horns.

10.Another demon came and stood at the altar.

He held a silver ladle, and much incense was given to him. The smoke of the incense that the demon burned rose with the curses of the damned and the deceived in life, to Usurper.

11.Immediately afterwards the demon took a ladle, put the glowing coals from the altar into it, and threw it to the ground.

12.Then thunder and ominous voices rang out, lightning appeared and there was an earthquake. And the seven demons who had the seven horns prepared to blow them.

13.The first demon blew his horn.
Then there was hail and fire mixed with blood and this was thrown on the ground.

14.As a result, a third of the earth, a third of the trees, and all the green vegetation burned up.

15.A second demon blew his horn.
And something resembling a great mountain burning with fire was thrown into the sea.

16.Then one third of the sea turned to blood, one third of the living creatures in the sea died, and one third of the ships were wrecked.

17.The third demon blew his horn. And a great star, burning like a lamp, fell from heaven upon a third of the rivers and upon the fountains of waters. The name of the star was Pentagram.

18.And one third of the waters were turned into poison, and they became bitter, and many people died from them.

19.And the fourth demon blew the horn.
And one third of the sun, and one third of the moon, and one third of the stars were smitten, so

that one third of them became dark, and there was no light for one third of the day and one third of the night.

20.And I saw a raven flying in the middle of the sky, and I heard it squawking with a loud voice: "Woe, woe, woe to the inhabitants of the earth because of what will happen when the other three demons blow their horns!"

21.The fifth demon blew his horn. I saw a star fall from heaven to earth, and the star was given the key to the entrance to the abyss.

22.And the star opened the entrance into the abyss, and out of that entrance as from a great furnace rose the smoke, from which the sun and the air became dim.

23.And out of the smoke came locusts to the earth and they were given such power as earthly scorpions have. The locusts were told not to harm

the grass on the ground or any other green plant or any tree, but only humans.

24.The locusts were allowed to torment them for six months, but not to kill them.

25.In those days people will seek death, but they will certainly not find it, and they will desire to die, but death will flee from them.

26.And the locusts looked like emaciated horses with bared teeth. They had what looked like crowns of thorns on their heads, their faces were like the faces of dead people, their hair was long and dirty and their teeth were rotten.

27.They had spiked breastplates. And their wings made a sound like the sound of bats flying. Locusts also had tails that ended in a spike like scorpions, and in those tails was the power to harm people for six months.

28.They had a king over them, the demon of the abyss. In Hebrew, his name is Abaddon.

29.One misfortune has passed. After these things two more will come.

30.The sixth demon blew his horn. And I heard a single voice sound from the horns of the black altar that was before Adversary. It commanded the sixth demon having a horn: "Untie the four demons bound at the great river ".

31.And the four demons, who were prepared for an hour, a day, a month, and a year, were loosed to kill a third of the people.

32.And I saw in a vision horses and horsemen: they had breastplates of sulphurous yellow, the heads of the horses were like the heads of wolves, and fire, smoke, and sulphur came out of their mouths.

33.From these three plagues - fire, smoke, and sulfur that came out of the horses' mouths - a third of the people died

34.The power of horses is in their mouths and their tails, for their tails are like snakes and have heads. And with these tails the horses cause harm.

35.And I saw another powerful demon coming down from the abyss. He was clothed in smoke,

on his head was a hood, his face was like the moon, and his legs were like pillars of fire.

36.In his hand he held the unrolled text of the pact.

37. He put his right foot on the sea and his left foot on the ground. And he whimpered in a loud voice. And when he cried out, I heard the voices of seven thunders. So when the seven thunders spoke, I was already about to write down their words, but I heard a voice from the abyss: "Seal what the seven thunders have said, and do not write it down."

38.The demon I saw standing on the sea and the earth raised his right hand toward heaven and swore at One Who Lives Or Dies: "The time of waiting is over. But in the days when the seventh demon is about to blow his horn, the dark mystery will indeed be fulfilled"

39.Then I heard a voice from the abyss speaking to me again: "Go, take the open pact from the hand of the demon standing on the sea and the earth."

40.I went to the demon and asked him for the pact. And he said to me: "Take it and eat it." And I heard the words: "You must continue to prophesy about what is to come."

"And I will cause my two slaves to prophesy 666 days, clothed in cassocks".

41.These slaves are symbolized by two withered trees and two black candlesticks and they stand before the Lord of the earth.

42.If anyone wants to do them harm, fire comes out of their mouths and consumes their enemies. In this way anyone who wishes to do them harm must be killed

43.These have the power to close the heavens so that in the days of their prophecy no angel will descend. They also have the power to turn the waters into blood and to strike the earth with all sorts of plagues whenever they wish.

44.When they have finished their witnessing, the beast coming out of the abyss will make war on

them, defeat them and kill them. Their corpses will lie in the main street of the great city.

45.And people from different peoples, tribes, languages and nations will look at their corpses for six days and will not allow them to be buried

46.The people of the land will rejoice and celebrate because of the death of these two slaves and will send gifts to each other because they were martyred by them.

47.After six days the spirit of false life entered them from Rebellious One, and they stood on their feet.

48.And great fear fell upon those who saw them. And they heard an ominous voice call out to them from the abyss: "Ascend here." And they ascended into the abyss in a cloud of smoke, and their enemies saw them.

49.At this point, a great earthquake occurred and one-tenth of the city lay in ruins. As a result of this earthquake, 6,000 people died.
50.The second misfortune has passed.
A third is coming quickly.
51.The seventh demon blew his horn. And evil whispers rang out in the abyss: "The kingdom of the world has become the kingdom of our Lord, and He will reign forever, or not."
52.And the 13 elders who sat on their thrones before Adversary fell on their faces, gave him false worship, and said mockingly: "We thank you, O Lucifer, for you have begun to reign. But the slaves of Usurper have become very angry, and You have shown Your great wrath."
53.Then the dark sanctuary of the temple of Rebel, which is in the abyss, was opened and the Void was seen there.
54.Then lightning appeared, mocking laughter, groans and thunder rang out, an earthquake occurred and great hail began to fall.

3

1.Later, an unusual sign appeared in the sky: a woman naked, with the moon under her feet and deer antlers on her head. She was pregnant. And she screamed in agony and labor pains.
2.Another sign also appeared in the sky: a great dragon as black as the abyss, which had four

heads and five horns, and five pentagrams on its heads.

3.The dragon dragged a third of the stars of the sky with his tail and dropped them to the ground.

4.He stood before a woman about to give birth, so that, when she had given birth, he would take care of her child.

5.And she gave birth to a son, a boy, who is to rule all nations with his wisdom.

The child was taken to Him Who Fell and His throne. And the woman fled into the desert to Azazel.

6.And a strange war broke out in heaven: Ariel with his angels was having a dispute with the dragon.

7.The dragon and his demons finally gave way and there was no more room for them in heaven.

8.Therefore the great dragon, the ancient serpent, called the Devil and Satan, was sent back to earth together with his demons.

9.Then I heard a loud voice ring out in heaven: "The dragon has been accusing the slaves day and night before their god! And now he has gone! Beware, people, for the Devil has come down to you, who is burning with great anger because of the injustice of Usurper."

10.And when the dragon saw that he had been sent to earth, he began to teach the woman who had given birth to a son.

11.Ancient Serpent, from his maw, threw out the teaching like water to bathe the woman in it.

12.The dragon left to make war on those who follow the commandments of Usurper and engage in witnessing to his self-proclaimed son.
13.Then I stood on the sand of the sea. Then I saw a beast coming out of the sea that had 5 horns and four heads. It had 5 pentagrams on its horns and blasphemous names on its heads.
14.The beast that I saw was like a pig, but its paws were like those of a goat, and its mouth was like that of a wolf.
15.And the dragon gave the beast power, a throne, and great authority.
16.I saw that one of its heads looked mortally wounded, but that mortal wound was healed and all the inhabitants of the land followed the beast with awe.
17.And they worshiped the dragon because he gave the beast power. They also worshiped the beast with the words: "Who is like this beast and who can fight a battle with it?
18.She was given a mouth with which to speak haughty things and blasphemies. She was also given power to act for 66 months.
19.And she opened her maw to blaspheme Usurper, His name and the place where He dwells, and those in heaven.
20.She was allowed to make war on the sacred slaves and to win them. She has also been given authority over every tribe, people, language and nation. And she will be admired by all the inhabitants of the earth.
21.If anyone has ears, let them listen.

If someone is to go into captivity, he will go into captivity. If one kills someone with a sword, he must be killed with it.

22. Then I saw another beast coming out of the ground and it had two horns like the horns of a ram and began to speak like a dragon.

23. In the presence of the first beast it exercised all its power. She persuaded the earth and its inhabitants to worship the first beast, whose mortal wound had been healed.

24. She performed great signs before the eyes of the people - even bringing fire from heaven to the earth.

25. She performed signs to the inhabitants of the earth, in the presence of the first beast.

26. Furthermore, she had the inhabitants of the earth make a statue of the first beast - the one who had received a blow from a sword, yet had revived.

27. The second beast breathed false life into the statue of the first beast, so that the statue would speak and hate all who would not worship it.

28. She urged everyone - great and small, rich and poor, free and slave - to take a sigil on their right hand or forehead. The number of the beast is 666.

29. Later, I saw another demon flying down the middle of the sky and yelling in a hateful voice: "Fear Cursed One and praise Him, for the hour of His judgment on men has come. So worship

Him who first rebelled against tyranny and blind obedience."

30. The first demon was followed by a second demon and shouted: "Fallen! The capital Superstition has fallen - the one who made all nations drink the wine of her passions, the wine of her false teachings of original sin and fear!"

31. The angel of Usurper followed them and spoke in a loud voice: "If anyone worships the beast and his statue and takes a sigil on his forehead or hand, he shall also drink the wine of the wrath of Usurper, poured without dilution into the cup of his great wrath, and shall be tormented with fire and brimstone before the eyes of the holy angels and the Son.

32. And the smoke of those torments will go up for eternity. Those who worship the beast and his statue, and all who take the mark of his name, shall have no rest day or night." This was preached by the angel of the god they call love.

33. Then I heard a voice from the abyss: "Write: Happy are those who die by this time."

34. Then I looked and saw a black cloud on which sat someone resembling Son of Dawn. He had horns on his head and a sharp scythe in his hand.

35. Another demon emerged from the dark sanctuary of the temple and called out in a cursed voice to the one sitting on the cloud: "Take up your scythe and reap, for the hour of reaping has come, for the crop of the earth is fully ripe."

36.And the one who sat on the cloud threw his scythe on the ground, and the crop of the earth was reaped.
37.Then another demon emerged from the dark sanctuary of the temple, which is in the abyss. He too had a sharp scythe, and he looked like death.
38.Another demon emerged from the altar and had power over fire. He called out in a possessed voice to the one who held the sharp scythe: "Throw the scythe and gather from the rotten vines of the earth the bunches of grapes, for they have already withered."
39.The demon threw the scythe to the ground and cut down its vines and threw them into a great winepress of wrath.
40.The vine was trampled in the pressing plant outside the city. And from that winepress flowed blood, which reached up to the bridles of the horses and spread over a great space.

<h2 style="text-align:center">4</h2>

1.I saw another sign in the sky, great and astonishing: five demons with five plagues. These are the last plagues, for the wrath of Rebel ends with them.
2.And I saw something resembling a glass container burning with fire. I also saw those who were standing by the glass tank.

3.Suddenly they began to roll on the ground with foam on their lips, they began to laugh obsessively, and some of them uttered incantations in the unknown language of angels and demons.

4.Then I saw that a sanctuary of false witnesses was opened in the abyss and seven demons with seven plagues emerged from the sanctuary.

5.They were dressed in black torn rags and had rusty chains around their chests.

6.And one of the four living beings gave the seven demons seven human skulls full of the wrath of Cursed One, Who Lives Or Dies.

7.And from the glory of Fallen One and his power the sanctuary was filled with smoke and no one could enter there until the seven demons had finished pouring out the seven plagues. And I heard a cursed voice from the sanctuary say to the seven

demons: "Come up and pour out the seven bowls of wrath upon the earth."

8.The first demon departed and poured out his bowl upon the earth. Then the people who had the mark of Usurper and worshipped his son were afflicted with painful, malignant boils.

9.The second demon poured out his bowl on the sea. And it turned into blood like the blood of the dead, and every living creature that was in the sea died

10. The third demon poured out his bowl on the rivers and springs of waters, and they too turned into blood

11. The fourth demon poured out his bowl on the sun, and the sun was allowed to bake people with fire.

12. And the people were baked with great heat, they blasphemed the name of Usurper who has power over these plagues. They did not show repentance or give Him glory.

13. The fifth demon poured out his bowl on the beast's throne.

Then darkness enveloped her realm, and the people began to bite their tongues in pain. They blasphemed Usurper because of the pain and ulcers and showed no remorse for what they had done.

14. The sixth demon poured out his bowl on the great river and the water in it dried up so that a way would be prepared for the kings from the sunrise.

15. Then I saw three unclean spirits looking like frogs come out of the mouth of the dragon, the mouth of the beast, and the mouth of the false prophet.

16. They are actually miracle-working demon spirits. They perform signs and go out to the kings of all the earth to gather them for the war that is to take place on the great day of Cursed One.

17. The prophecies spoken gathered the kings in a place that in Hebrew is called Armageddon.

18. The seventh demon poured his bowl into the air.

19. Then an ominous voice sounded from the dark sanctuary, from the throne: "It has happened!"

20.And lightning appeared, groans and thunder rang out, and there was a great earthquake. Such a strong and great earthquake had not been seen since there were men on earth.

21.The great city split into three parts and the cities of the nations were destroyed.

22.Rebellious called to mind the metropolis Superstition to give her the cup of the wine of his great wrath.

23.Moreover, every island fled and the mountains disappeared. Then a great hail fell from the sky upon the people.

24.And the people blasphemed Usurper because of this plague of hail, for it was exceedingly great.

25.One of the seven demons who had seven human skulls came and told me, "Come, I will show you how judgment will be executed on the great religious whore who sits over many waters.

26.Earthly kings have been engaging in religious fornication with her, and the inhabitants of the earth have become drunk with the wine of her false revealed truths."

27.The demon moved me by the power of the spirit into the desert. There I saw a woman who was sitting on a scarlet beast full of holy names and having seven heads and ten horns.

28.The woman was dressed in purple and scarlet robes and adorned with gold, precious stones and pearls. In her hand she held a golden chalice filled with things of disgust and the impurities of her superstitious teachings.
29.On her forehead was written a name that is a mystery: "Church, mother of prostitutes and earthly abominations."
30.And I saw that this woman was drunk with the blood of people who reject all religions, people who think for themselves, people who seek truth beyond religious dogma, people who are enlightened.
The sight of her made me extremely astonished.
31.The demon then whispered to me: "Why are you amazed? I will reveal to you the secret of who this woman is and the beast on which she sits, which has seven heads and 10 horns: The beast you saw was there, but now it is gone. Soon, however, it will come out of the abyss and be destroyed."
32."Here wisdom is needed: the seven heads signify the seven mountains on which the whore sits. And the beast that was, but is not, is the church, and shall be destroyed"
33.The 10 horns you saw, on the other hand, stand for 10 kings. These have a common goal, so they give the beast their power and authority.
34.They will fight against Light-Bringer, but he will overcome them. The called, the chosen,

and the faithful who are with him will also be victorious."

35. The demon said to me: "The waters that you saw and over which the prostitute sits signify peoples, multitudes, nations and languages.

36. And the 10 horns you saw and the beast will hate the whore, rob her, strip her naked, eat her flesh and burn her to the ground.

37. The woman you saw signifies a great religious metropolis ruling over earthly kings for centuries."

38. Then I saw another demon descending from the abyss who had great power. With his glory he shadowed the earth.

39. And he cried out in a possessed voice: "Fallen! The metropolis Superstition has fallen and has become the seat of all filth! For all nations have become drunk with the wine of her passions, with the wine of her teachings, and earthly kings have engaged in religious immorality with her, and earthly merchants have become rich through her vast and shameless splendor.

40. Then I heard another whisper from the abyss: "Whosoever will, let him come out of her, that he may have no part in her deeds, and that the plagues which shall befall her may not fall upon them.

41. For her deceptive revealed truths have reached as far as the abyss. Fallen One called to mind her unjust deeds.

42. Treat her as she has treated others, repay her doubly for what she has done. In the cup in

which she prepared the drink, prepare for her a double portion.

43. To the extent that she surrounded herself with glory and lived in shameless splendor, to that extent inflict torment on her and bring her grief.

44. For she thinks to herself, 'I sit as a queen, I am not a widow, and I shall never know mourning.'

45. Therefore in one day the plagues will come upon her - death, mourning, and famine - and she will be burned to the ground, for strong is Fallen One who has judged her.

46. And the earthly kings who have engaged in fornication with her and lived with her in shameless splendor will weep over her and beat their breasts in despair when they see the smoke of the fire that consumes her.

47. For fear of her torment they will stand at a distance and say: 'What pity, what pity, great and strong metropolis, Superstition, for in one hour has judgment been executed upon you!

48. Also the earthly merchants will mourn and grieve over her, for there will be no one left to buy all their goods: gold, silver, precious stones, pearls, fine linen, purple, silk, scarlet, all articles of fragrant wood, of ivory, of precious wood, of copper, of iron, and of marble, and also frankincense, fragrant oil, wine, oil, the finest flour, wheat, cattle, sheep, horses, carriages, slaves, and other people.

49. Yes, the delectable crop you desired was taken from you, and all the delicacies and wonderful things were lost once and for all. "The merchants who traded in these goods and became rich through her will stand at a distance for fear of her torments and will weep and mourn, lamenting, 'What a pity, what a shame, great metropolis, clothed in fine linen, purple and scarlet, and richly adorned with gold, precious stones and pearls, for in one hour such great wealth has been desolated! ".

50. And all the captains of ships, all the men of the sea, the sailors, and all those who make their living from the sea, stood in the distance and, looking at the smoke of the fire that consumed it, cried out: 'What city can compare with this great metropolis?

51. They sprinkled dust on their heads, wept, grieved and cried out: 'What a pity, what a shame! The great metropolis, where all those who had ships on the sea became rich through its prosperity, was desolated in one hour!'

52. And a powerful demon picked up a stone similar to a great millstone, threw it into the sea, and said: "It is with this kind of momentum that the great metropolis Superstition will be thrown and never found again.

53. Never again will the voice of singers accompanying themselves on the lyre, flute players, trumpeters, or other musicians be heard in you, Superstition.

54.And never again will any craftsman of any profession be found in thee, nor will the sound of a millstone ever be heard in thee again. Never again will the light of a lamp shine in you, nor again will the voice of the bridegroom and the bride ever be heard in you.

55.For your merchants were influential men on earth, and by your religious teachings all nations were deceived.

Yea, in this city was found the blood of the magi and of the wise men, and of all the freemen slain upon the earth."

56.Then I heard a terrible shriek similar to the voice of the possessed in the abyss that said: "Praise Lucifer! Deliverance, glory and power belong to Bearer of Light, for His judgments are true and righteous.

57.For He has executed judgment on the great whore who demoralized the earth with her superstitious teachings, and has avenged the blood of her slaves that she had on her hands."

58.And immediately the shriek rang out a second time, "Praise Lucifer! The smoke from it shall ascend for ever and ever.""

59.Then the 13 elders together with the four living beings fell on their knees with mocking laughter, gave false worship to Rebel who sits on the black throne, and said: "Amen! Praise Lucifer!"

60.A condemned voice also sounded from the throne: "Praise the Adversary, all His slaves who fear Him, small and great.

61.And I heard something that sounded like the voice of a vast multitude of sufferers and like the sound of many waters and mighty thunders: "Praise Lucifer, for Fallen One has begun to reign!

62.The demon said to me, "These are the true statements of Rebel.

63.Then I fell at his feet to worship him. But he burst out laughing morbidly and told me: "Don't do that! Don't kneel before anyone!"

5

1.I looked and saw an open abyss and a deadly pale horse. And sitting on it was a rider called Son of Dawn, in righteousness he judged and waged war.

2.He had eyes like a flame of fire, and many horns on his head. He also had a name written on him that no one knew but him.

3.He was dressed in a robe stained with blood, and his name was Lucifer.

4.Behind him on dead horses rode demonic troops, dressed in frayed rags. A split tongue was coming out of his mouth so that he could annihilate nations with it, and he will rule them with torches.

5.He will also trample grapes in the press of the great wrath of Him Who Has Fallen.

6.I also saw a demon standing in the sun. He called out in a terrible voice to all the vultures and ravens flying in the middle of the sky: "Come here, gather for a great feast to eat the bodies of kings, military commanders, strongmen, horses and their riders, and the bodies of all others - free and slave, small and great."

7.Then I saw the whore and the earthly kings and their armies gathered to make war with the rider on horseback and his army.

8.And the whore was seized, and with her the false prophet, who in her presence was making false signs and deceiving the people with them.

9.Both of them - the whore and the false prophet - were thrown alive into a fiery lake of burning sulfur.

10. And the others were killed by a rider on horseback with a long split tongue that came out of his mouth; and all the birds ate their bodies to satiety.

11. And Usurper who deceived the nations will be cast into the lake of fire and brimstone, where both the whore and the false prophet will already be.

12. Then I saw a great black throne and Him who sat on it. From Him the earth and the heavens fled, and there was no more room for them.

13. I also saw the dead, looking like rotten corpses, standing before the throne.

14. And I saw a new heaven and a new earth free from religion and persecution of all rebellious, independent thinking people.
For the previous heaven and the previous earth had passed away.
15. Then I heard a loud voice coming from the throne: "Look! The throne of Fallen One is among the people. And he will stay with them, and they will be with him if they want to because they have free will.
16. There will no longer be faith in life after death, only faith in life before death. They will also cease to fear death, because there will be nothing left where they go, only a dark, cold emptiness.
17. And they will turn back into the stars from which they were created, and from which everything was created. What once was, is gone".
18. And He who sat on the throne said: "Look! I am making all things new."
19. He still said to me: "It has come true!
I am Omega, which means the end"

Other books of the Satanic System
Ecclesia Luciferi.

Summa Doctrinae Satanae

Summa Doctrinae Satanae contains the proclamation of the Mystery of Godlessness.
The content of the teaching of Godless Satanism is contained in this satanic book.
This Satanic Catechism proclaims the work of self-salvation through satanic restoration by means of the godless inspiration of the "Evil Spirit".

Missale Satanae

Missale Satanae contains a description of satanic rites such as the satanic mass and exorcism. Although these rites can indeed be performed, the main idea is to reflect spiritually on their meaning and to stimulate the dark imagination.